T0212218

Lecture Notes in Computer Science　　13525

More information about this series at https://link.springer.com/bookseries/558

Christel Seguin · Marc Zeller ·
Tatiana Prosvirnova (Eds.)

Model-Based Safety and Assessment

8th International Symposium, IMBSA 2022
Munich, Germany, September 5–7, 2022
Proceedings

Editors
Christel Seguin
ONERA
Toulouse, France

Marc Zeller 🆔
Siemens AG
Munich, Bayern, Germany

Tatiana Prosvirnova
ONERA
Toulouse, France

ISSN 0302-9743   ISSN 1611-3349 (electronic)
Lecture Notes in Computer Science
ISBN 978-3-031-15841-4   ISBN 978-3-031-15842-1 (eBook)
https://doi.org/10.1007/978-3-031-15842-1

This Springer imprint is published by the registered company Springer Nature Switzerland AG
The registered company address is: Gewerbestrasse 11, 6330 Cham, Switzerland

Preface

This volume contains the papers presented during the 8th International Symposium on Model-Based Safety and Assessment (IMBSA 2022), held in Munich, Germany, during September 5–7, 2022.

IMBSA focuses on model-based and automated ways of assessing safety and other attributes of dependability of complex systems. Since the first edition in Toulouse (2011), the workshop has evolved to a forum where brand new ideas from academia and industrial experiences are brought together. The objectives are to present experiences and tools, to share ideas and to federate the industrial and academic community. As a result, it is worth noting that half of the papers of this volume has at least one industrial author.

Another important focus concerned the impact of AI techniques for system safety. Yiannis Papadopoulos's keynote gave an overview of the challenges raised by the inclusion of AI technologies in safety critical systems. Furthermore, a selection of papers presented the opportunities offered by machine learning techniques to analyze safety issues.

For IMBSA 2022, we received 27 submissions from authors in 15 countries. The best 18 papers (15 regular papers and three short papers) were selected by an International Program Committee (IPC) to be published in this volume. Each submission was reviewed by at least three members of the IPC. The comprehensive review guaranteed the high quality of the accepted papers.

As organizers, we would like to sincerely thank all the members of the International Program Committee. We also want to thank the organization team and our fellow members of the Steering Committee: Marco Bozanno, Leila Kloul, Frank Ortmeier, Yiannis Papadopoulos, and Antoine Rauzy.

Finally, we wish you a pleasant reading of the articles in this volume. On behalf of everyone involved in IMBSA 2022, we hope you will be joining us at next IMBSA edition.

September 2022

Christel Seguin
Marc Zeller

Organization

Program Committee Chairs

Christel Seguin   ONERA, France
Marc Zeller   Siemens, Germany

Organizing Committee

Kevin Delmas   ONERA, France
Tatiana Prosvirnova   ONERA, France
Christel Seguin   ONERA, France
Marc Zeller   Siemens, Germany

Program Committee

Jose Ignacio Aizpurua   Mondragon University, Spain
Eric Armengaud   AVL, Austria
Stylianos Basagiannis   United Technologies Research Center, Ireland
Michel Batteux   IRT SystemX, France
Saddek Bensalem   Université Grenoble Alpes, France
Lorenzo Bitetti   Thales, France
Marco Bozzano   Fondazione Bruno Kessler, Italy
Xavier De Bossoreille   APSYS-Airbus, France
Kevin Delmas   ONERA, France
Ewen Denney   NASA, USA
Jana Dittmann   Otto-von-Guericke-Universität Magdeburg, Germany
Marielle Doche-Petit   Systerel, France
Francesco Flammini   Linnaeus University, Sweden
Lars Grunske   Humboldt University Berlin, Germany
Matthias Güdemann   Munich University of Applied Sciences, Germany
Ibrahim Habli   University of York, UK
Kai Höfig   Siemens AG, Germany
Michaela Huhn   Ostfalia, Germany
Sophie Humbert   Safran Helicopter Engines, France
Sohag Kabir   University of Bradford, UK
Bernard Kaiser   Ansys, Germany
Panagiotis Katsaros   Aristotle University of Thessaloniki, Greece

Leila Kloul	Université de Versailles, France
Agnes Lanusse	CEA LIST, France
Timo Latvala	Huld Oy, Finland
Nicholas Matragkas	CEA LIST, France
Till Mossakowski	Otto-von-Guericke-Universität Magdeburg, Germany
Juergen Mottok	OTH Regensburg, Germany
Peter Munk	Bosch, Germany
Thomas Noll	RWTH Aachen University, Germany
Arne Nordman	Bosch, Germany
Frank Ortmeier	Otto-von-Guericke-Universität Magdeburg, Germany
Yiannis Papadopoulos	University of Hull, UK
François Pouzolz	Airbus Defense and Space and TUM, Germany
Tatiana Prosvirnova	ONERA, France
Antoine Rauzy	Norwegian University of Science and Technology, Norway
Wolfgang Reif	University of Augsburg, Germany
Alejandra Ruiz	Tecnalia, Spain
Daniel Schneider	Fraunhofer IESE, Germany
Christel Seguin	ONERA, France
Ioannis Sorokos	Fraunhofer IESE, Germany
Danielle Stewart	University of Minnesota, USA
Ramin Tavakoli Kolagari	Nuremberg Institute of Technology, Germany
Philippe Thomas	SATODEV, France
Pascal Traverse	Airbus, France
Elena Troubitsyna	KTH Royal Institute of Technology, Sweden
Marc Zeller	Siemens AG, Germany

Steering Committee

Marco Bozzano	Fondazione Bruno Kessler, Italy
Leila Kloul	Université de Versailles, France
Frank Ortmeier	Otto-von-Guericke-Universität Magdeburg, Germany
Yiannis I. Papadopoulos	University of Hull, UK
Antoine Rauzy	Norwegian University of Science and Technology, Norway
Christel Seguin	ONERA, France
Marc Zeller	Siemens, Germany

Additional Reviewers

Luis Basora	ONERA, France
Pierre Bieber	ONERA, France
Julien Brunel	ONERA, France
Matthieu Perin	Systerel, France

Contents

Dynamic Risk Assessment

Safety Analysis Automation

An AEBS Use Case for Model-Based System Design Integrating Safety Analyses and Simulation

Bernhard Kaiser[1], Bernard Dion[2(✉)], Ilya Tolchinsky[3], Thierry Le Sergent[3], and Max Najork[1]

[1] Ansys GmbH, Berlin, Germany
{bernhard.kaiser,max.najork}@ansys.com
[2] Ansys, Inc., Canonsburg, USA
bernard.dion@ansys.com
[3] Ansys France SAS, Toulouse, France
{ilya.tolchinksy,thierry.lesergent}@ansys.com

Abstract. Advanced driver assistance systems (ADAS) and automated driving functions are the most complex automotive systems today. They span multiple ECUs, sensors and actuators and need to integrate different, sometimes counteracting requirements. On top of this comes their safety-criticality, both in terms of functional safety (FuSa) (failure-related) and safety of the intended functionality (SOTIF) (performance-related). Model-based systems engineering (MBSE) with tightly integrated iteration loops over safety analysis and simulation can provide a solution. However, there is no "cook-book" how to practically integrate all these different work steps into one efficient workflow. We report on an internal case study we have made using an Advanced Emergency Braking System (AEBS), from which a complete MBSE/MBSA workflow was derived for its application in industry-grade developments.

Keywords: AEBS · MBSE · MBSA · FuSa · SOTIF · Simulation · MDAO

1 Challenges and State of the Art

For many years it has been a major challenge in ADAS development to refine vehicle-level requirements to detailed requirements for the components like sensors, object classifiers and decision making, both in qualitative and in quantitative terms[1].

In addition, the same set of sensors mounted on the vehicle must be used for several ADAS functions, as described in Fig. 1, in such a way that the requirements of all functions are met while the overall cost of the vehicle systems is minimized.

---

[1] E.g., From vehicle level: "From initial speed of 80 kph, collision with a traffic-jam end shall be avoided on dry road" to component level: "Accuracy, false-negative rate of a given radar sensor".

C. Seguin et al. (Eds.): IMBSA 2022, LNCS 13525, pp. 3–20, 2022.
https://doi.org/10.1007/978-3-031-15842-1_1

Achieving these goals has been facilitated by *function-oriented development* (see [5]) where each ADAS function is designed at the functional level before design decisions are made globally regarding the implementation of the vehicle physical architecture.

This process requires a great deal of design, analysis, simulation, and optimization activities for which numerous tools are available, such as [15–17] for requirements and system design activities, [2] for safety and cybersecurity analyses, [3] for multidisciplinary analysis and optimization, and tools for detailed physics-based simulation, including systems, optical, mechanical and other types of simulation.

However, there is a lack of a description of the overall system design methodology where all the above tools are integrated and the various steps to obtain an optimized solution are described. It is the purpose of this paper to demonstrate such a methodology on an ADAS use case.

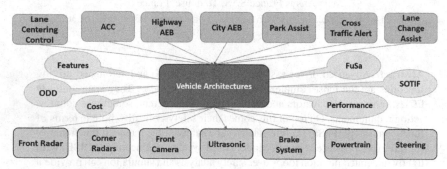

Fig. 1. The need for function-oriented development.

2 An Integrated MBSE/MBSA Methodology for ADAS

The proposed solution follows the MBSE workflow of Fig. 2, which consists of a design process highly accelerated by early validation through simulation and safety analysis over the iterations of refinement. Starting from a *function concept* (1), the system architecture is refined in two design steps: *functional architecture* (2) and *physical architecture* (3). For each of these steps, the requirements and the architecture are refined in lockstep, and this iterative process is supported by analysis and simulation:

- *Safety, reliability, and cybersecurity static analyses* (1a, 2a, 3a) [2]
- *Simulation,* which can be performed at various levels of fidelity, from functional-level simulation to high-fidelity simulation of system components (2b, 3b)
- *Multi-disciplinary analysis and optimization (MDAO),* integrating multiple simulation and analysis tools to perform trade studies for the selection of the system components (3c) [3]

This workflow enables the function-oriented development of [5], including the safety analyses of FuSa [9] and SOTIF [11]. For ADAS systems, several functions, such as

AEB, Adaptative Cruise Control (ACC), etc., all use the same set of sensors, ECUs, and actuators, and this allocation may change over vehicle projects. In this context, we develop an implementation-independent functional architecture (2), to model, analyze and simulate each function individually, before design decisions are made regarding the physical architecture (3) onto which these functions are then allocated. The safety analyses (1a, 2a, and 3a) become better structured if the question of what can go wrong is separated from the question of how this could technically happen[2].

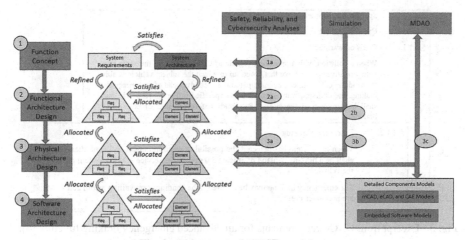

Fig. 2. The proposed MBSE workflow.

We now apply this approach to an Advanced Emergency Braking System (AEBS) use case, an internal study conducted as a Proof of Concept over a period of 3 years, in close relationship with 3 suppliers of such systems. For the study reported in this paper (Steps 1, 2, and 3), we have used the SysML-based Ansys MBSE tool suite, including all necessary modeling, analysis, and simulation modules [2–4, 12]. For development of the embedded software (Step 4), we have used the Ansys SCADE tool suite [4], as reported in [14].

The rest of this paper is structured according to the workflow of Fig. 2.

3 Function Concept

In the *function concept phase* (Step 1 of Fig. 2), in parallel to a first concept of the architecture, the AEBS *stakeholder requirements* are obtained from various sources, including market research, legislation and standards, definition of the brand image, and from the Original Equipment Manufacturer (OEM) in case of a tier supplier. For this study, we concentrate on regulatory requirements for AEBS (UNECE) [6] and the standard Test Protocol (Euro NCAP) [7]. In this phase, a hazard and risk assessment is also conducted as the initial safety analysis.

We now describe these activities.

---

[2] E.g., "Reported object distance is lower than in reality" separated from cause: "hardware part failure in the radar sensor".

3.1 Regulatory Requirements (UNECE)

The United Nations Economic Commission for Europe (UNECE) is responsible for the technical prescriptions regarding the approval of wheeled vehicles. The UNECE document [6] establishes uniform provisions for AEBS, some of them shown in Fig. 3. As an AEB system is a safety system by nature, these requirements all have a safety impact.

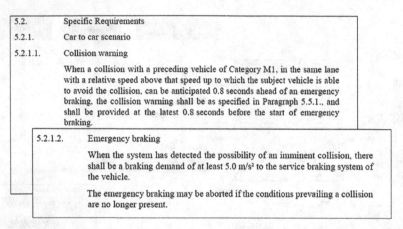

5.2.	Specific Requirements
5.2.1.	Car to car scenario
5.2.1.1.	Collision warning

When a collision with a preceding vehicle of Category M1, in the same lane with a relative speed above that speed up to which the subject vehicle is able to avoid the collision, can be anticipated 0.8 seconds ahead of an emergency braking, the collision warning shall be as specified in Paragraph 5.5.1., and shall be provided at the latest 0.8 seconds before the start of emergency braking.

| 5.2.1.2. | Emergency braking |

When the system has detected the possibility of an imminent collision, there shall be a braking demand of at least 5.0 m/s² to the service braking system of the vehicle.

The emergency braking may be aborted if the conditions prevailing a collision are no longer present.

Fig. 3. Excerpt from UNCE requirements for an advanced emergency braking function [6].

3.2 Test Protocol (Euro NCAP)

The Euro NCAP programme is a car safety performance assessment program. It includes required test scenarios for safety assistance systems like AEBS. These requirements do not specify the intended behavior in general but enumerate a few selected test cases with variants that need to be demonstrated. This does not imply that the AEBS does not have to brake in any other situations where a collision is imminent.

The Euro NCAP Car-to-Car Rear Moving (CCRm) test scenario [7] aims at testing the avoidance of a collision in which a vehicle travels forwards, towards another vehicle that is travelling at constant speed, and then decelerates, and the frontal structure of the vehicle strikes the rear structure of the other. The CCRm test protocol is a combination of speed and overlap with 5km/h incremental steps in speed and 25% in overlap within the ranges as shown in Fig. 4.

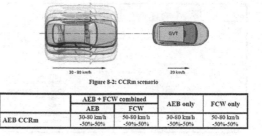

Scenario Name	CCRm
Type of test	AEB
VUT speed [km/h]	30 - 80
VUT direction	Forward
Target speed [km/h]	20
Impact location [%]	[-75;-50;100;50;75]
Lighting condition	Day

Figure 8-2: CCRm scenario

	AEB + FCW combined		AEB only	FCW only
	AEB	FCW		
AEB CCRm	30-80 km/h -50%-50%	50-80 km/h -50%-50%	30-80 km/h -50%-50%	50-80 km/h -50%-50%

Fig. 4. The Car-to-Car Rear Moving (CCRm) Test Scenario.

3.3 Stakeholder Constraints, Goals, and Assumptions

On top of the requirements from outside, there are additional constraints and goals that often originate from internal stakeholders. Typical constraints consider limitations in space, weight and cost, typical goals might involve reusability for other ADAS functions, adaptability to other vehicle models, etc.

Along with capturing the requirements, it is equally important to capture any assumptions that are (often tacitly) made, e.g., target countries, speed ranges of the cars where the AEB function will be deployed, weather conditions, mandatory presence of an ABS function. Explicit *assumptions* are essential to avoid safety hazards due to wrong understanding or unforeseen situations, which is in the scope of SOTIF [11], and to avoid risk coming from unmanaged reuse of project assets in future projects. Their fulfillment needs to be checked for safety validation, and then after each modification and in each reuse situation.

We will see in the next stages of the workflow that assumptions, as a counterpart to requirements, are used thoroughly when refining the architecture (see Sect. 4.1).

3.4 Extracting Top-Level Function Requirements

The stakeholder requirements from different sources are not necessarily written in a style that would allow to check the intended function design against them. In addition, they may conflict with each other so that negotiation and prioritization need to take place.

Based on this, we import the Euro NCAP requirements (see Fig. 5), we reformulate the AEB top-level function requirements (see Fig. 6) and we define the AEB Operational Design Domain (ODD) [8] specifying the conditions in which it will operate (road type, weather conditions, etc.) as well as the assumptions (see Fig. 7).

N°	ID	Name	Description	Type	External Document
⊟ 1	◇ SR 1009	Provide Emergency Braking when crash is immanent	The system shall provide emergency braking interventions if a crash to a slower or standstill vehicle in front of the ego vehicle is immanent, with the purpose of alerting the driver, preventing the crash or at least significantly decreasing the speed of the ego vehicle	Requirement	
1.1	◇ SR103	NCAP Scenario: Car-to-Car Stationary- CCRs	The system shall perform emergency braking in particular for all variants of the standardized NCAP Scenario: Car-to-Car Stationary- CCRs	Requirement	NCAP Scenario Car-to-Car Stationary – CCRs.pptx
1.2	◇ SR107	NCAP Scenario: Car-to-Car Moving – CCRm	The system shall perform emergency braking in particular for all variants of the standardized NCAP Scenario: Car-to-Car Moving – CCRm	Requirement	NCAP Scenario Car-to-Car Moving – CCRm.pptx
1.3	◇ SR104	NCAP Scenario: Car-to-Car Braking- CCRb	The system shall perform emergency braking in particular for all variants of the standardized NCAP Scenario: Car-to-Car Braking – CCRb	Requirement	NCAP Scenario Car-to-Car Braking – CCRb .pptx

Fig. 5. Importing the AEB function external requirements in the MBSE modeler.

2	◇ SR1010	Provide visual and acoustic warnings before braking	In addition and prior to the active braking, the sytem shall provide the driver with visual and acoustic warnings depending on the situation in hand.	Requirement
⊟ 3	◇	Provide warning signal illumination in case of EE failure	Upon detection of any EE failure condition (e.g. processor failure, bus interruption), a warning signal shall be illuminated.	Requirement
3.1	◇ SR120	Same warning light for crash hazard and system failure / impairment	The same warning light can be used for system failure or impairment indication as for crash hazard, but without acoustic warning.	Information
⊟ 4	◇ SR105	Provide warning signal illumination in case of performance impairment	Upon detection of any performance impairment or disturbance (e.g. sensor blindness or sensor misalignment), a warning signal shall be illuminated.	Requirement
4.1	◇ SR106	Same warning light for crash hazard and system failure / impairment	The same warning light can be used for system failure or impairment indication as for crash hazard, but without acoustic warning.	Information
5	◇ SR1011	Avoid unjustified emergency brake engagements.	The system shall be designed to avoid the generation of collision warning signals a in situations where the driver would not recognise an impending collision.	Requirement

Fig. 6. Reformulating the AEB function top-level requirements.

ID	Name	Description	Type
◇ SR116	Usage offroad and in special maneuvering situations.	The system shall prevent to be operational during offroad usage of the vehicle, reverse movement, maneuvering and special situations like refueling and recharging.	Requirement
	Detection of offroad and special	To exclude accidental operation in offroad and special maneuvering conditions it is	
◇ SR118	Minimum activation speed 30 km/h	The system shall be operational only at forward speed greater or equal to 30 km/h.	Requirement
◇ SR119	No deactivation during braking when getting below enabling speed	This does not imply that an ongoing emergency braking maneuver has to be abandoned when speed falls below this threshold.	Information
◇ SR1012	Ensure operation in dry weather	The system shall be operational mainly in dry weather and good visibility conditions.	Requirement
◇ SR1013	Ensure rainy weather operation when rain intensity <=2mm/h	The system shall be operational in rainy weather conditions given that the rain intensity is less than 2mm/hr	Requirement
◇ SR1014	Ensure no operation in foggy / low visibility weather condition	The system shall never be operational in icy, snowy or foggy / low visibility conditions.	Requirement
◇ SR122	Detect low visibility conditions	The system shall detect low visibility situations with its own means (sensors) and disable emergency braking as soon as the specified performance can no longer be ensured.	Requirement
◇ SR123	Ensure no operation under ice, snow and slippery road conditions.	The system shall never be operational in icy, snowy or slippery conditions. except for the warning function that may remain operational	Requirement
◇ SR124	Detect ice, snow and slippery conditions	The system can delegate the detection of ice, snow and general slippery road condition to the ABS system, which is designed in a way that it would not execute any commanded brake request from AEB under such conditions.	Assumption

Fig. 7. Defining the AEB Operational Design Domain (ODD).

3.5 Hazard and Risk Assessment (HARA)

At this stage, the AEB Hazard and Risk Assessment (Step 1a of Fig. 2) will reveal and rate any kind of hazards, may they be related to failures (FuSa) [9] or insufficiencies/weaknesses (SOTIF) [11]. From these hazards, top-level safety goals are derived, which will add up to the existing stakeholder requirements and may at some points require a trade-off against the market requirements. The medini analyze module [2] of the Ansys MBSE tool suite provides an integrated framework which is intended to support the necessary functional safety, reliability, SOTIF, and cybersecurity analyses.

As shown in Fig. 8, one potential hazard exists if the AEBS brakes strongly without any reason, which can result in a rear-end collision because the driver behind might not anticipate this happening. This needs to be evaluated in all relevant driving situations, which may lead to different judgement of exposure (E), accident severity (S) and controllability (C) by following vehicles [9].

A common situation is this happening when driving on a dry road at daytime with typical highway speed. The exposure is rated E4, the severity of the accident S2-S3 depending on the delta speed and, controllability by the (following) driver C2–C3 depending on the initial distance, and we might for example obtain an ASIL C safety integrity level for this hazardous event (on a scale of A–D, where D is the most critical).

If the HARA is intended to also cover SOTIF, some additional details need to be considered. FuSa assumes that failures occur at random and independently from the driving situation. SOTIF, in contrast, also considers the possibility that some triggering condition, in combination with some weakness of the ADAS function, causes the hazard. This will have an impact on the acceptance rating (low E factor of a situation does not automatically mean acceptable risk if the situation leads systematically to a hazard).

From the hazards we derive vehicle-level safety goals (or safety constraints) that must be satisfied in any situation and that will add up to the set of requirements we already have.

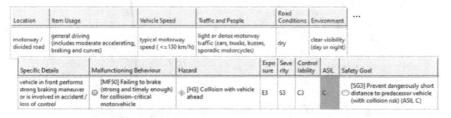

Location	Item Usage		Vehicle Speed	Traffic and People		Road Conditions	Environment	...
motorway / divided road	general driving (includes moderate accelerating, braking and curves)		typical motorway speed (<= 130 km/h)	light or dense motorway traffic (cars, trucks, busses, sporadic motorcycles)		dry	clear visibility (day or night)	

Specific Details	Malfunctioning Behaviour	Hazard	Expo sure	Seve rity	Control lability	ASIL	Safety Goal
vehicle in front performs strong braking maneuver or is involved in accident / loss of control	[MFS0] Failing to brake (strong and timely enough) for collision-critical motorvehicle	[H3] Collision with vehicle ahead	E3	S3	C3	C	[SG3] Prevent dangerously short distance to predecessor vehicle (with collision risk) (ASIL C)

Fig. 8. Performing the AEB hazard and risk assessment (HARA).

4 Designing the AEBS Functional Architecture

4.1 Functional Architecture Modeling and Refinement

Following the definition of the function concept, the next step to requirements engineering is establishing a *functional architecture* (Step 2 of Fig. 2). This starts at the high level, beginning with the boundaries of the function to be developed and its interfaces to neighbor systems[3], the human driver and the traffic environment. Once again, stating assumptions is essential for the subsequent development[4].

---

[3] E.g., Existing vehicle systems like the powertrain.

[4] E.g., Will some sensor report via validity flag that detection of objects is currently not possible? Is there a risk of skidding if the AEB commands high braking force on wet road, or will ABS take care for this?

For a functional architecture it is recommendable to remain at an abstract level, not assuming anything about the technical implementation. For instance, instead of a CAN bus, only an abstract signal should be mentioned. Equally, no assumptions on data types (such as float64) should be made. Figure 9 describes the AEBS top-level functional architecture within its system context, distinguishing between components that are in scope and components that are out of scope of the AEB function.

In the next step, the AEBS functional architecture is refined to the next level, as shown in Fig. 10. The AEB_Core_Function is decomposed in its sub-functions. The Ansys MBSE modeling tool suite ensures formally correct decomposition.

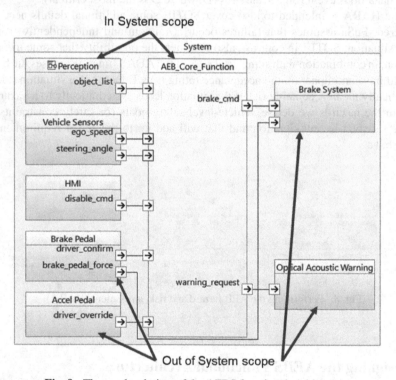

Fig. 9. The top-level view of the AEBS functional architecture.

Following the contract-based approach of [13], as the architecture refinement progresses, we apply the requirements refinement steps, as described in Table 1.

This is illustrated by Fig. 11 while refining the AEB_Core_Function.

Now applying Steps 6 and 7, we create the refined requirements which we can visualize in a tree view as in Fig. 12 or in a tabular view.

4.2 Functional Behavior Modeling

So far, we have described the static structure of the AEB in terms of function blocks and the allocation of the system requirements to these blocks of the functional architecture.

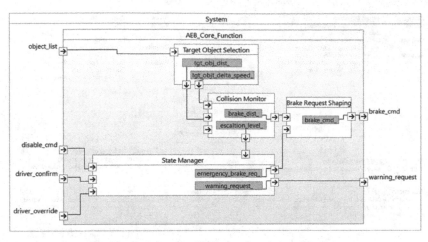

Fig. 10. Refining the AEB core function architecture.

Table 1. Refining the architecture and the requirements.

Step	Design process step
1	*Coming from a higher-level block, define the blocks of the functional architecture at the next lower level*
2	*For each block in the architecture, describe its **purpose** (e.g., "Calculates braking deceleration from remaining object distance and ego vehicle speed")*
3	*Connect the blocks with each other and with the outer interfaces from higher level, thereby ensuring type consistency (ensured by the MBSE framework)*
4	*For each signal connecting any two block ports, describe the meaning of the signal (e.g., "reports the distance to the nearest qualified object if any")*
5	*Place **assertions** at probing points on connector signals that describe what properties must hold at this point (e.g., "The escalation level signal will never indicate 'brake' unless a qualified target object has been in a critical distance for the last 2 s")*
6	*Use these assertions to formulate **requirements** and **assumptions** for each block (these must refer only to the task of this block and to data that is visible at its interface, not presuming any knowledge about the outside world); use an << allocate >> relation to ensure traceability between these new requirements and assumptions and the architecture block*
7	*Connect the new requirements and assumptions with << refines >> relations to the requirements and assumptions they originated from*
8	*Perform a review to ensure that, with the set of refined requirements for each blocks together with the assumptions, the block developer can rely on the satisfaction of the requirements to the block at the higher level*

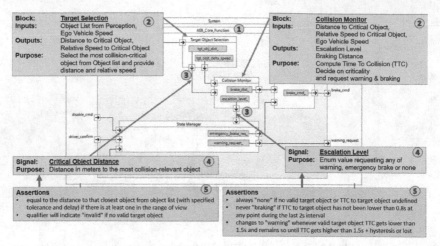

Fig. 11. Applying the requirements refinement process to the AEB_Core_Func (Steps 1 to 5).

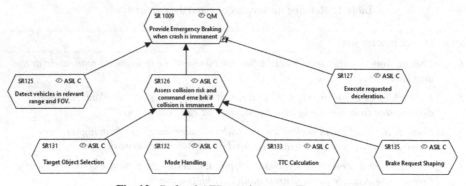

Fig. 12. Refined AEB requirements (Tree view).

We are now for the first time verifying the behavior of the AEB which can be specified as a state machine for the State Manager component (see Fig. 13), against the requirements. This behavioral model is, for the moment, formulated at the functional level, yet executable in simulation. It does not consider technical details like wait states or failure states, as these will be considered later, when we move to the physical architecture and the actual implementation. This simulation validates the intended function, in absence of any failures or performance limitations, fulfills all requirements and behaves safely in all listed scenarios.

4.3   Iterations of the Functional Architecture Driven by Analyses and Simulation

To systematically understand the causes of hazards and, define improvement measures for safety, we conduct deductive causal analysis from the hazards (Step 2a of Fig. 2). At the functional level, we do not distinguish between FuSa and SOTIF causes.

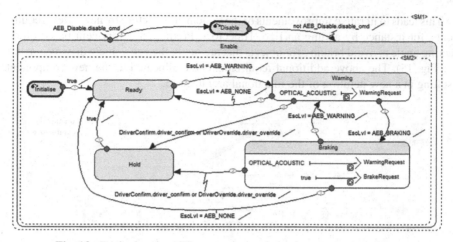

Fig. 13. Designing the AEB state manager behavior as a state machine.

A typical method is Fault Tree Analysis (FTA), which is supported by a systematic walkthrough of the functional architecture. For each hazard there can be various causes. For unjustified braking, obvious causes could be reporting of ghost objects or creating a brake request without a reported target object. But there are less obvious ones, which may not just relate to failures, but also to performance limitations or overlooked edge cases (SOTIF). For instance, a true object could be reported as intersecting with the ego lane although it is not (e.g., in a turn). This analysis triggers the creation of additional safety requirements to prevent braking for objects that are not intersecting with the ego vehicle's predicted driving corridor (see Fig. 14). Requirements can be derived from Fault Tree events and will automatically trace to the Fault Tree event, so that a side-by-side review of malfunctions vs. derived requirements to prevent them is easily possible. Moreover, the requirements are allocated to SysML model elements using the "allocate" relation, which enables automatic checks whether all of them have been allocated.

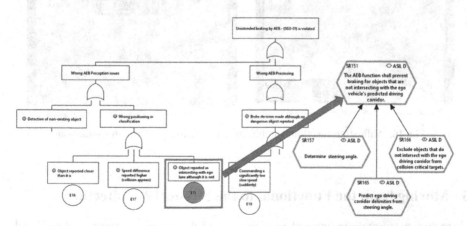

Fig. 14. Performing fault tree analysis (FTA) and deriving safety requirements.

This leads to iterative improvements of the system architecture by new safety requirements, for instance by adding an Ego_Trajectory_Prediction component based on the
steering angle to avoid braking for objects that are not in the ego vehicle driving corridor
(see Fig. 15). The above additional requirements are allocated to the new component,
resulting in a new iteration of the functional architecture.

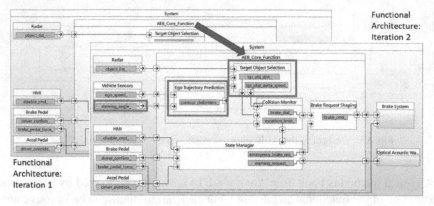

Fig. 15. Improving the functional architecture by adding trajectory prediction.

In classical functional safety, the relation of low-level faults to higher level malfunctions is often obvious. In the SOTIF domain, however, cause-effect relations are
often more speculative. Therefore, it is highly beneficial to integrate simulation early
to confirm and quantify causal relations. To this end we leverage the Ansys Autonomy
toolchain [10] to validate the architecture improvement by comparing simulation results
with and without ego trajectory prediction (Step 2b of Fig. 2), as shown in Fig. 16.

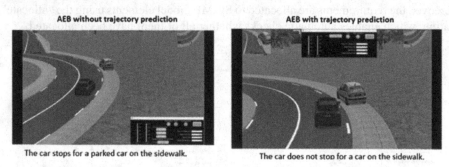

Fig. 16. Validating functional architecture improvements through simulation.

5   Moving from the Functional to the Physical Architecture

Up to now, we were designing and analyzing the AEB function at a functional and ideal-
ized abstraction level to see whether it would at least theoretically fulfill the requirements,

and we found reasons why this might not be the case. We were waiting with technical implementation decisions, if possible. But eventually we must make these design decisions and design the *physical architecture* (Step 3 of Fig. 2). This will involve allocation of the functional components to physical components, trade studies to compare different candidate solutions, and continued safety analyses at the physical level.

5.1 Allocation of Functional Architecture to Physical Architecture

At this stage we allocate the blocks of the functional architecture to physical blocks, including ECUs, sensors, hardware, or software, at the vehicle level (see Fig. 17). The physical component themselves can fail (e.g., the failure of an electronic component), or have a performance that is too limited to meet the functional requirements (e.g., a sensor that has lower performance in bad weather conditions). This will need to be analyzed and mitigated, as it will be seen in the next section. The technical blocks can be developed according to requirements, or pre-existing (COTS or reuse). In any case we will have to match assumptions and requirements. We are using << allocate>> relations to join blocks of functional and technical architecture.

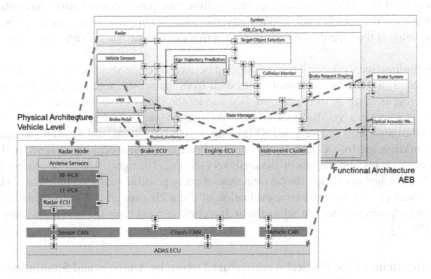

Fig. 17. Allocating the functional architecture blocks to physical components.

Likewise, the requirements, now stated at the technical level, are more related to properties of the physical components, like accuracy, qualification time and robustness, and when safety analysis is continued at the technical level (see below), requirements regarding protection mechanisms (e.g. end-to-end communication protection), immunity to disturbances, or diversity of sensor technologies will come on top, see Fig. 18.

5.2 Trade Studies to Identify Optimal Implementation Solutions

The transition from the functional to the physical level, in the case m functions allocated onto n components, involves a good deal of design decisions, evaluation of alternatives,

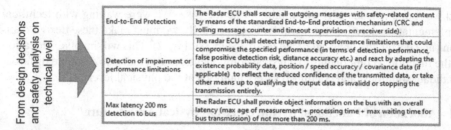

Fig. 18. Adding requirements due to design decisions and safety analysis at the physical level.

and compromises to define the sensor set. A lot of it is guided by experience or by decisions made earlier in the vehicle project, but still the number of variants may be huge. A lot of functional, performance, and safety requirements must be met[5].

Trade studies are a well-established method to choose among design alternatives, based on requirements and Key Performance Indicators (KPIs) regarding which components and which combinations or topologies thereof are acceptable, including functional aspects from the ADAS function, space requirements, power consumption, and other constraints at the vehicle level. In our study, the total cost of the components is opposed by the value of the supported ADAS functions that can be realized with any given sensor set.

A bi-directional connection is established between the MBSE framework and ModelCenter [3] to feed the trade study with data from the architecture model and update it with results (Step 3c of Fig. 2). We first model the pre-selected variants at different variation points in a SysML Block Definition Diagram (see Fig. 19, left). As a next step, we define constraints and weighted KPIs using scripted equations, and we set up an analysis workflow in ModelCenter. Input/output parameters of the model are assigned to the respective inputs and outputs of the analysis (see Fig. 19, right). The trade study can now be launched to evaluate the performance of every possible sensor combination. The tool comes up with a comparative evaluation of the KPIs over all viable combinations, from which the engineer can select the architecture that achieves the best combination of KPIs.

5.3 Iterations of the Physical Architecture Driven by Analyses and Simulation

Continuing the Safety Analyses at the Technical Level. The safety analysis that was started at the functional level now continues at the technical level as soon as design decisions have been made (Step 3a of Fig. 2), this time structured by the physical system components (ECUs, sensors, actuators at vehicle level, technical components like microprocessor, power supplies etc. at ECU level). The methods may be similar as at the functional level, still including FTA, but with more focus on inductive techniques like Failure Mode and Effects Analysis (FMEA) and tabular weakness analysis.

The advantage of the MBSE approach is that the system structure and allocation of functions (first steps of FMEA) are given by the SysML model and can directly be

---

[5] E.g., Regarding angle of view, range, or diversity of sensor technologies to improve immunity against disturbances.

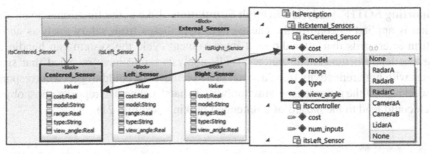

Fig. 19. Excerpt from SysML block definition diagram, showing the abstract sensors as variation points, and the assignment of the analysis inputs and outputs in ModelCenter [3].

exploited in medini analyze. Also, it is an advantage that the functional level safety analyses offer anchor points for the effects of lower-level technical issues[6] and are thereby easily traceable up to the vehicle hazards. The technical safety analysis comprises both the FuSa and the SOTIF side, which will be treated in separation, as shown in Fig. 20. For FuSa, typical failures that can lead to malfunctions on the functional level would include all sorts of broken hardware parts (they must be quantified), design errors or software bugs[7]. For SOTIF, we see that a typical pattern where some issue (ghost object reported) occurs when there is a combination of a system weakness (e.g., camera susceptible to reflection on the road) and a matching triggering condition (e.g., wet road, which causes reflections).

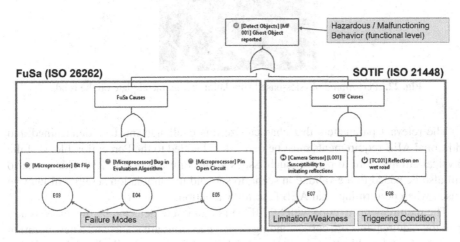

Fig. 20. Branching FTA into FuSa and SOTIF at the technical level.

---

[6] E.g., Message corruption on a CAN bus can lead to wrongly reported distance to target.

[7] More technical requirements will be defined, because real components are not as ideal as the functional blocks we have used so far. This is not detailed in this paper.

Supporting SOTIF Analysis Through Simulation. Like at the functional level, simulation is applied to confirm the cause-effect hypotheses from safety analysis and to confirm afterwards that after the next improvement cycle the system can handle the same challenge better. For instance, SOTIF analysis might have revealed that small objects with high reflectivity (e.g., a metal plate on the road) could trigger a corresponding weakness of the radar sensor (susceptibility to harsh echoes) to report a ghost object, which could lead to the hazard of unintended braking (see Fig. 21).

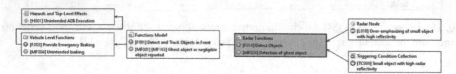

Fig. 21. Identifying weaknesses and triggering conditions.

From this analysis, we describe a functional scenario and create a task to perform simulation to confirm this issue (see Fig. 22). Simulating this scenario with accurate sensor models (Step 3b of Fig. 2), we see that a metal plate on the road induces a false object in the radar sensor, causing Perception to report an obstacle and the vehicle to brake.

Fig. 22. Performing physics-based simulation with a metal plate on the road.

The relevant parameters that characterize this challenge must be determined and additional AEB requirements must be derived and added to the Perception block of the Physical Architecture to prevent such issues in the future (see Fig. 23). This scenario will also be added to the validation scenario set, and the simulation set up will later be reused when performing final AEB function validation.

The requirements to cope with SOTIF and FuSa issues detected by the analysis add up to the requirements set, corresponding design decisions are made, and a new iteration of the technical architecture is produced. The cycle repeats until all relevant design decisions have been made and the remaining risk is considered acceptable.

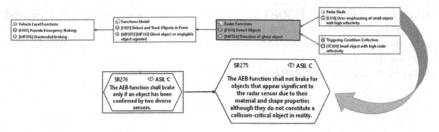

Fig. 23. Deriving an abstract safety requirement from a potential SOTIF-related misbehavior.

6 Conclusion

In this paper, we have described a MBSE methodology that we have applied to an AEBS use case. The focus of this work has been in illustrating the iterative nature of the requirements elicitation and architecture design activities that are fully intertwined with analysis and simulation at all stages, thus allowing to build a system that is safe, meets both the functional and non-functional requirements and permits a function-oriented architecture with several ADAS systems sharing the same sensor sets.

Pursuing towards the implementation of the AEB function, we have later used the same AEB use case to illustrate the embedded software development of the AEB function, as reported in [14], where the efficiency of the workflow is driven by qualified code generation from the software models [4].

References

1. INCOSE: System Engineering Vision 2020, INCOSE-TP-2004-004-02, INCOSE (2007)
2. Ansys medini analyze 2022R2, Ansys (2022)
3. Ansys ModelCenter 2022R2, Ansys (2022)
4. Ansys SCADE Suite 2022R2, Ansys (2022)
5. Kaiser, B., Augustin, B., Baumann, C.: Von der Komponenten- zur Funktionsorientierten-Entwicklung in der Funktionalen Sicherheit. Elektronik im Fahrzeug (2013)
6. UNECE: GRVA-02-39, Proposal for a new draft UN Regulation on the approval of motor vehicles with regard to their AEBS for M1 and N1 vehicles (2019)
7. Euro NCAP: Automatic Emergency Braking Car-to-Car Systems. Euro NCAP Test Protocol, Version 3.0.1, Euro NCAP (2019)
8. SAE J3016, Taxonomy and Definitions for Terms Related to Driving Automation Systems for On-Road Motor Vehicles, J3016_202104 (2021)
9. ISO 26262:2018, Road Vehicles – Functional Safety, ed. 2, ISO (2018)
10. Ansys AVxcelerate 2022R1, Ansys (2022)
11. ISO/PAS 21448:2019, Road Vehicles – Safety of the Intended Functionality, ISO (2019)
12. Ansys optiSLang R2022R1, Ansys (2022)
13. Kaiser, B., et al.: Contract-based design of embedded systems integrating nominal behavior and safety. Complex Syst. Inf. Model. Q., 66–91 (2015)
14. Ansys: A Cost-effective model-based approach for developing ISO 26262 compliant automotive safety related applications. https://www.ansys.com/resource-center/technical-paper, Ansys (2021)

15. IBM: overview of rational DOORS next generation. https://www.ibm.com/docs/en/ermd/9.6.0?topic=doors-overview-rational-next-generation, IBM (2022)
16. IBM: overview of rational rhapsody. https://www.ibm.com/docs/en/rhapsody/8.4.0?topic=overview, IBM (2022)
17. Ansys SCADE Architect 2022R2, Ansys (2022)

COMPASTA: Extending TASTE with Formal Design and Verification Functionality

Alberto Bombardelli, Marco Bozzano$^{(\boxtimes)}$, Roberto Cavada, Alessandro Cimatti, Alberto Griggio, Massimo Nazaria, Edoardo Nicolodi, and Stefano Tonetta

Fondazione Bruno Kessler, Via Sommarive 18, 38123 Trento, Italy
{abombardelli,bozzano,cavada,cimatti,griggio,mnazaria,
enicolodi,tonettas}@fbk.eu

Abstract. TASTE is a development environment dedicated to embedded, real-time systems, developed under the initiative of the European Space Agency. It consists of various tools, such as graphical editors, code generators and visualizers, which support model-based design of embedded systems, automatic code generation, deployment and simulation. TASTE currently lacks a comprehensive support for performing early verification and assessment of the design models.

The goal of the COMPASTA study is to integrate the formal verification capabilities of COMPASS into TASTE. COMPASS is a tool for model-based System-SW Co-Engineering developed in a series of ESA studies, offering formal design and verification capabilities, such as requirements analysis, contract-based design, functional verification and safety assessment, fault detection and identification analysis. COMPASTA will deliver a full end-to-end coherent tool chain, based on TASTE, covering system design, HW/SW implementation, deployment and testing.

Keywords: TASTE · COMPASS · MBSE · Formal verification

1 Introduction

TASTE [5,11] is a design and development environment dedicated to embedded, real-time systems, which has been actively developed by the European Space Agency (ESA) since 2008. It consists of various tools such as graphical editors, visualizers and code generators that support the development of embedded systems within a MBSE (Model Based Systems Engineering) approach. TASTE is based on the following technologies and languages: AADL (Architectural Analysis and Design Language) for architectural modeling, ASN.1 for data modelling and SDL (Specification and Description Language) for behavioral specification. TASTE has been adopted as a glue technology and for system deployment in several projects, both in aerospace and in other domains, e.g. [1,6,9,10].

Work funded by ESA/ESTEC under Contract No. 4000133700/21/NL/GLC/kk.

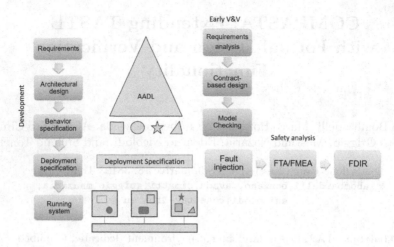

Fig. 1. Functionality of the integrated TASTE+COMPASS toolset.

The standard modeling workflow in TASTE includes: the definition of data models using ASN.1; the definition of the functional logical architecture using an Interface View description in AADL; the definition of the behavior of each functional block, e.g. in SDL; the definition of the physical architecture using a Deployment View description in AADL, which enables code generation and building for the target platforms.

COMPASS [2–4] is a tool for System-SW Co-Engineering developed in a series of ESA studies from 2008 to 2016. It is based on a dialect of AADL and provides a full set of formal techniques, based on model checking, such as requirements analysis, fault injection, property verification, safety assessment, fault detection and identification analysis. It is based on the concept of model extension, i.e., the automatic injection of user-specified faults into a nominal model. The extended model is internally converted into a symbolic model amenable to formal verification, whereas properties are translated into temporal logic. COMPASS uses the ocra tool for contract-based design [8], the nuXmv model checker [7] and the xSAP safety analysis platform [12] as back-ends.

The COMPASTA project is an ongoing study funded by the European Space Agency (ESA) that started in April 2021. By integrating the COMPASS functionality into TASTE, COMPASTA will deliver a comprehensive, end-to-end tool chain dedicated to the design and development of embedded systems, covering system design, HW/SW implementation, deployment and testing. This integration will bridge the gap between the architectural level design and the system implementation and deployment.

2   The COMPASTA Approach

The integration of COMPASS into TASTE aims to harmonize the models and input languages provided by COMPASS (SLIM, an extension of AADL) with the

Table 1. A comparative view of COMPASS and TASTE functionality.

Development phase	COMPASS functionality	TASTE functionality
Requirements specification	Specification of properties and requirements Requirements analysis	
Architectural design	Contract-based design and refinement Specification of system architecture (AADL)	Specification of system architecture (AADL)
Behavioral specification	Specification of the behavior of HW components (AADL/SLIM) Formal verification of functional behavior Specification of HW faults Fault injection/ Model extension Formal verification of functional behavior (in presence of faults) Safety and dependability assessment (FTA, FMEA) Fault Detection, Identification and Recovery (FDIR)	Specification of the behavior of SW components (SDL or other languages)
Deployment specification	Trace validation for testing	Specification of the deployment on the target HW Code generation Testing of the implementation

ones available in TASTE (in particular, AADL and SDL) for the specification of system architecture, component behavior and interaction, system implementation and deployment. Figure 1 illustrates the functionality of the integrated toolset, allocated to the different development phases. The COMPASS functionality is complementary with respect to the one available in TASTE. A comparative view is given in Table 1. In particular, COMPASS adds the following capabilities:

– Specify and validate a set of requirements specified in a formal language.
– Use contract-based design to design the system architecture.
– Model the HW components of the system and their functional behavior, using SLIM (an extension of AADL) to specify state machines.
– Model HW faults and automatically inject them into the system model.
– Perform formal verification, safety and dependability assessment.
– Re-execute and validate a trace generate by TASTE testing in the formal model, generating a compatible execution of the HW.

The existing functionality of TASTE, on the other hand, is used to specify the behavior of SW components, their deployment on the target HW, their implementation (via code generation) and to test the final implementation.

The technical objectives of the COMPASTA project include the definition of an extension of the AADL language that is compliant, both syntactically and semantically, with the subset available in TASTE, and enables the specifications

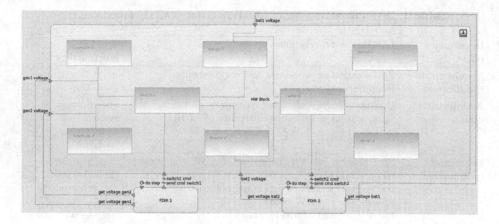

Fig. 2. A power system example.

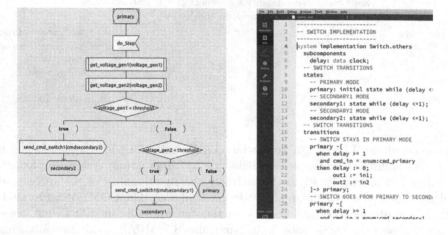

Fig. 3. Sample code in SDL (left) and SLIM (right) for FDIR_1 and Switch_1.

and analyses made available by COMPASS (in particular, specification of contracts, properties, faults, and of the behavior of HW components). The semantics of the SLIM language needs to be adapted to match the different possibilities available in TASTE (synchronous and asynchronous communication, buffered communication). Finally, COMPASTA requires the design of a translator from AADL/SLIM and SDL input languages into the languages supported by the back-ends, and the integration of the back-ends themselves (ocra, nuXmv and xSAP [7,8,12]) into TASTE.

3   An Illustrative Example

We exemplify the COMPASTA workflow using the example in Fig. 2, modeled in the TASTE interface view. It contains both SW (the FDIR components) and HW (batteries, generators, sensors). Two (redundant) generators feed two (redundant) batteries, feeding two sensors. In case of a fault of a generator or battery, two switches can reconfigure the power lines, to exclude the broken item. The desired behavior of the circuit is to guarantee powering of the sensors.

The FDIR components can be modeled in TASTE using SDL. Figure 3 (left) shows an excerpt of the code for FDIR_1. It periodically reads the input voltages of the two generators and, in case one of them is under a given threshold, it sends a command to the Switch component to change from primary mode to a secondary mode.Modeling of the HW requires the COMPASTA extension, which uses the SLIM language. Figure 3 (right) shows some sample code specifying the behavior of the Switch_1 component. In particular, it models a state machine where transitions correspond to possible reconfigurations (from primary mode to a secondary mode). The input models (in AADL/SLIM and SDL) are then translated into the language supported by the back-ends (SMV). Data ports and connections with different semantics are used to connect HW and SW, i.e. ports with periodic (cyclic) activation for SW, ports with synchronous communication (to model HW data read by SW) and ports with asynchronous (buffered) communication (to model commands sent from SW to HW). COMPASTA relies on Interface Timed Automata to define the semantics of the SW and HW components, the different forms of communication, the scheduling constraints, and their encoding into SMV.

Contract-based design can be used to design and validate the system architecture. Contracts (as pairs assumption/guarantee) may be associated to components, e.g., a contract for a battery can have an assumption always(voltage_in >= 10) and a guarantee always(voltage_out >= 10). An example of system-level contract is one with an assumption true and a guarantee always(one_valid) (at least one sensor has a valid output). The system-level contract can be validated against the component-level ones. Moreover, component-level contracts can be checked against an implementation of the respective component. Model checking can be used to verify functional properties, e.g., "Globally, it is always the case that sensor1.valid and sensor2.valid holds", i.e. the outputs of both sensors are always valid.

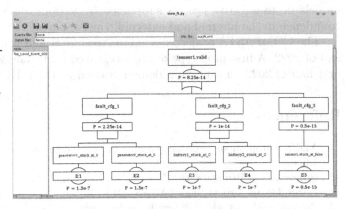

Fig. 4. An example Fault Tree.

Fault definitions can be picked from a library, and automatically injected, e.g., a fault injection for the battery is specified as the following record: [Description => "stuck-at-zero"; Fault_Model => StuckAt; Fault_Dynamics => Permanent; Probability => 1.e-7; Input => voltage_out; Varout => voltage_out; ParameterList => ([Name => Term; Value => "0"])], modeling a permanent "stuck-at-zero" fault of the voltage_out signal of the battery. The extended model is generated automatically as part of the translation process. xSAP can generate safety artifacts such as Fault Trees and FMEA tables; Fig. 4 show an example fault tree. Once the formal validation of the model has been completed, the TASTE workflow can be used to specify the implementation of the SW components. We briefly sketch this workflow. First, the HW block is replaced by a "HW block I/O" component, which represents the SW layer realizing the communication between SW and HW in the final implementation. Then, the deployment of the SW components (binding of the SW to the target HW platform(s)) is specified. TASTE can be used to generate the executable code for the target platform(s) and to test the implementation. Finally, COMPASTA offers the possibility to execute a trace, generated by TASTE, on the formal model (including the HW).

4   Conclusions

COMPASTA aims to extend the TASTE toolset with formal verification and assessment functionality, creating a digital continuity from the architectural functional design and system-level safety analysis to the deployment of the embedded software, using the MBSE paradigm. We think that this integration will significantly foster the adoption of the TASTE and COMPASS toolsets. In the intended workflow, system, safety, and software engineers work on the same models in an iterative process supported by various analyses that increase the confidence in the internal and external consistency of the system.

The COMPASTA project started in April 2021 and will be completed by the end of 2022. A first prototype of the integrated tool chain will be released in the first half of 2022, in time for a demonstration at the IMBSA conference.

References

1. ADE: Autonomous decision making in very long traverses. https://www.h2020-ade.eu
2. Bozzano, M., Bruintjes, H., Cimatti, A., Katoen, J.P., Noll, T., Tonetta, S.: COMPASS 3.0. In: Proceedings TACAS 2019 (2019)
3. Bozzano, M., et al.: Spacecraft early design validation using formal methods. Reliab. Eng. Syst. Saf. **132**, 20–35 (2014)
4. Bozzano, M., Cimatti, A., Katoen, J.P., Nguyen, V., Noll, T., Roveri, M.: Safety, dependability and performance analysis of extended AADL models. Comput. J. **54**(5), 754–775 (2011)

5. Hugues, J., Pautet, L., Zalila, B., Dissaux, P., Perrotin, M.: Using AADL to build critical real-time systems: experiments in the IST-ASSERT project. In: Proceedings ERTS (2008)
6. MOSAR: Modular spacecraft assembly and reconfiguration. https://www.h2020-mosar.eu
7. NUXMV web page (2021). https://nuxmv.fbk.eu
8. OCRA web page (2021). https://ocra.fbk.eu
9. PERASPERA, a PSA activity under the Horizon 2020 Space "COMPET-4-2014: Space Robotics Technologies" Work Programme (Grant Agreement 640026)
10. Cavada, R., Cimatti, A., Crema, L., Roccabruna, M., Tonetta, S.: Tonetta: model-based design of an energy-system embedded controller using taste. In: Proceedings FM 2016. LNCS, vol. 9995, pp. 741–747 (2016)
11. TASTE web page. https://taste.tools/
12. XSAP web page (2021). https://xsap.fbk.eu

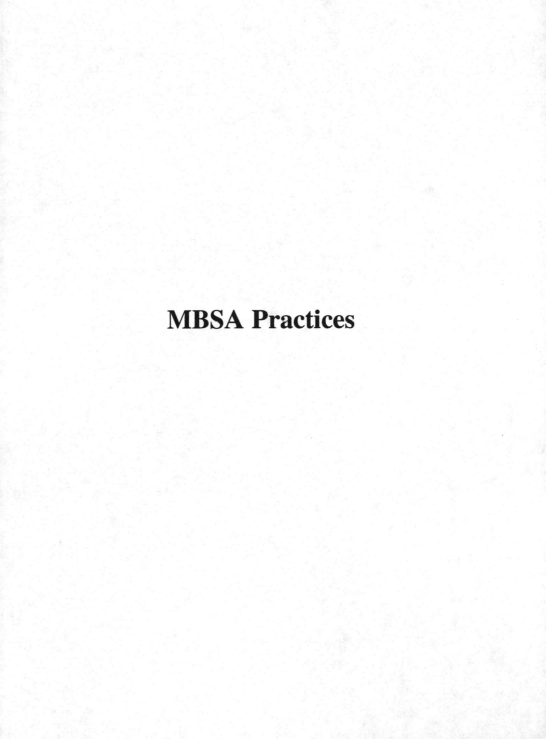

MBSA Practices

MBSA in Aeronautics: A Way to Support Safety Activities

Christophe Frazza[1]($\boxtimes$), Pierre Darfeuil[2], and Jean Gauthier[3]

[1] SATODEV, 25 rue Marcel Issartier, 33700 Merignac, France
christophe.frazza@satodev.fr
[2] Safran Helicopters Engines, 25 avenue Joseph Szydlowski, 64510 Bordes, France
pierre.darfeuil@safrangroup.com
[3] Dassault-Aviation, 78 quai Marcel Dassault 92, 92210 Saint-Cloud, France
jean.gauthier@dassault-aviation.com

Abstract. MBSA models were used for the first time in the frame of an aeronautical certification in 2007 (for the Flight Control System of the Dassault Aviation Falcon 7X). 15 years later, MBSA method has been integrated into aeronautical standards which present guidelines for performing safety assessments of civil aircraft, systems, and equipment, the so-called SAE ARP4761A [1] and its EUROCAE complement, ED-135A.

The "A" version of SAE ARP4761 introduces the MBSA as a new method which achieves results that are equivalent to those obtained from the classical e.g., Fault Tree Analysis (FTA) safety analysis methods. It describes, in detail, a contiguous example of the safety assessment process for a function on a fictitious aircraft design, the "Decelerate wheels" function, performed by the "Wheel Braking System". More particularly, it gives an example of how a MBSA method may be carried out to support the safety analysis during a Preliminary System Safety Assessment (PSSA).

The purpose of this article is to present and illustrate the way to support a PSSA process with a MBSA model, based on a representative Wheel Braking System model with various analyses (Functional Failure Set computation/DAL allocation, Minimal Cut Set computation/fail-safe principle, Failure Condition probability computation and Common Cause Failures identification/Independence principles). The MBSA model will be presented in a graphical tool dedicated to safety analyses and based on the formal language AltaRica [2].

Keywords: MBSA · Safety · Model · AltaRica · Aeronautic

1 Introduction

SAE ARP4761 [1] presents guidelines for performing safety assessments of civil aircraft, systems, and equipment. It may be used when addressing compliance with certification requirements (e.g., CS 25 for large airplanes, CS29 for large helicopters or CS-E for engines). This document deals with both processes (Aircraft Safety Assessment (ASA), System Functional Hazard Assessment (SFHA), Preliminary System Safety Assessment

C. Seguin et al. (Eds.): IMBSA 2022, LNCS 13525, pp. 31–42, 2022.
https://doi.org/10.1007/978-3-031-15842-1_3

(PSSA) ...) and methods that may be used to conduct the processes (Fault Tree Analysis (FTA), Dependence Diagram (DD), Markov Analysis (MA), Failure Modes and Effects Analysis/Summary (FMEA/FMES) ...).

MBSA models were used for the first time in the frame of an aeronautical certification in 2007 (for the Flight Control System of the Dassault Aviation Falcon 7X [4]). Fifteen years later, MBSA method is about to be integrated into aeronautical standards. The "A" version of SAE ARP4761 and its EUROCAE complement ED-135A (to be published in 2022) introduce indeed the MBSA as a new method, which achieves results that are equivalent to those obtained from the classical e.g., Fault Tree Analysis (FTA) safety analysis methods. It describes, in detail, a contiguous example of the safety assessment process for a function on a fictitious aircraft design, the "Decelerate wheels" function, performed by the "Wheel Braking System".

The purpose of this article is to present and illustrate the way to support a Preliminary System Safety Assessment (PSSA) process with a MBSA model. The illustration is based on a representative Wheel Braking System model and a detailed presentation is given in the MBSA example appendix of SAE ARP4761A/EUROCAE ED-135A. This paper aims at giving an overview of this appendix.

For sake of simplicity, the MBSA model will be presented in a graphical tool dedicated to safety analyses and based on the formal language AltaRica [2]. The paper gives also overview of the various analyses carried on with the model and associated tools: Functional Failure Set computation/FDAL (Function Development Assurance Level) and IDAL (Item Development Assurance Level) allocation, Minimal Cut Set computation/verification of fail-safe principle, Failure Condition probability computation and Common Cause Failures identification/Independence principles. Analysis results are presented considering two iterations of system design.

2 Related Works

One Model Based Safety Assessment is understood, in aeronautics, as the use of one specific failure propagation model of one system and associated tools to compute the root causes (minimal cuts set) of a set of undesired events (failure conditions) of interest for the system under analysis. The approach relies on the use of structured modeling languages so that the safety engineers can structure their failure propagation models as the system models or architectures. The approach also requires rigorous specifications of local faults of basic components so that the tools can automatically propagate the effects through the structured models. These principles were primarily introduced for instance in [5].

Several workbenches were developed to implement these principles and major aeronautics companies tested their maturity for instance in the European projects ESACS [6], ISAACS [7] and MISSA [8]. The results pointed out the benefit of the approaches. Moreover, the approach was accepted by EASA for the safety assessment of the Flight Control System of the Falcon 7X [4]. Thus, works started to introduce MBSA in the new version of the aeronautics safety standards ARP 4761.

All methods introduced in the ARP 4761 are illustrated by a leading example: the Wheel Braking System (WBS) of a fictitious aircraft. This example and its Fault Tree

Analysis were presented initially in [1]. This paper shows the MBSA model and its related analysis of the same system; it highlights new questions raised by the MBSA approach and the accuracy gains. It also considers two steps of analysis and shows how MBSA eases the management of design iterations.

The support of MBSA for ARP4761 was also already discussed for instance in [3]. [3] focusses on a particular MBSA approach using AADL and its annex error. This paper tries to be tool/modeling language agnostic even if the presented model and results have been implemented with AltaRica language and tools.

3 Case Study Description

3.1 System Description

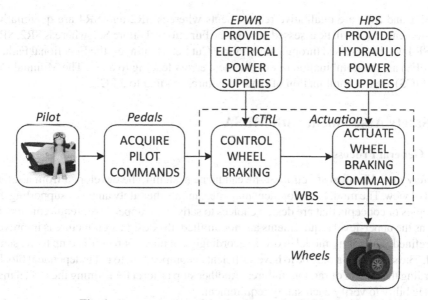

Fig. 1. Representation of the decelerate wheels function

The candidate system is the Wheel Braking System (WBS), and the associated function is Decelerate Wheels during the landing phase or the takeoff phase (landing gear extended), which is a subfunction of Decelerate the Aircraft on Ground. The Decelerate Wheels function can be understood as shown in Fig. 1, from the Pilot order to the action on the Wheels, taking into account the electrical and hydraulic resource systems.

3.2 Safety Requirements

The following two Failure Conditions (FC) are analyzed:

1. Loss of Wheel Braking FC: it represents the total loss of wheel deceleration (80% coverage or more) and is classified hazardous (HAZ). The conditions are: Pilot order is braking and Wheels are not braking.
2. Uncommanded Wheel Braking FC: it represents the uncommanded full symmetric wheel deceleration and is classified catastrophic (CAT). The conditions are: Pilot order is not braking and Wheels are braking.

The main Safety Requirements (SR) are the following:

– SR1: Decelerate Wheels function shall be developed FDAL A
– SR2: Loss of Wheel Braking shall be less than 10^{-7} for a landing
– SR3: No single failure shall result in an Uncommanded Wheel Braking during a takeoff roll
– SR4: Uncommanded Wheel Braking shall be less than 10^{-9} for a takeoff

SR1 and SR3 are qualitative requirements whereas SR2 and SR4 are quantitative requirements. SR1 will be assessed through the Functional Failure Set, whereas SR2, SR3 and SR4 will be assessed through the Minimal Cut Set. Reminder: the Functional Failure Set (FFS) are the combination of development errors leading to a FC. The Minimal Cut Set (MCS) are the combination of random failures leading to a FC.

4 Safety Assessment with MBSA

4.1 General Process

A safety model is an abstraction of the candidate system to be developed from a safety point of view. The model development may substantiate the safety analysis supporting the strategies or concepts that are design choices to satisfy the upper-level requirements. As long as the upper-level requirements are not fulfilled, the design architecture is improved and refined. The safety model evolves accordingly but may not be refined up to the same level. The stop criteria may be to have sufficient decomposition to get independent blocks regarding the effects of random failures. Another stop criteria for refining the model may be the ability to verify each safety requirement.

A MBSA model is a way of modeling failure propagation, considering both functional and dysfunctional logical behavior. Each component embeds "failure modes" which can represent either development errors or random failures, depending on the kind of analysis performed. The granularity of failure modes is more at a FMES level (Failure Modes and Effects Summary) than at a FMEA (Failure Modes and Effects Analysis) level.

Development errors are considered deterministic whereas random failures are stochastic. Each random failure embeds, within the MBSA model, its own probability law. The MBSA model based on the formal language AltaRica allows then to perform computations, as well scenarios that lead to the Failure Condition (FFS for development errors, MCS for random failures) as the probability of reaching this FC (for random failures only).

At each iteration, the following process is followed:

1. Take into account MBSA inputs: refined requirements, design updates;
2. Model this architecture: modeling assumptions and simplifications validation;
3. Perform the MBSA Failure Conditions Evaluation (generation of functional failure sets and/or minimal cut sets, probability computation);
4. Assess the main and refined safety requirements compliance;
5. Provide MBSA outputs: new requirements, design recommendations or even architecture suggestions to cope with non-compliant requirements.

4.2 Iteration "n"

Let's imagine an iteration "n" where the architecture embeds:

– For the control part (Fig. 2):

o 2 command channels
o 1 internal power for each channel (powered by PWR1 or PWR2)
o 1 selection management system to switch from channel 1 to channel 2

In case both channels are inoperative at the same time, the Pilot is still able to brake, but without any assistance.

Note: In Fig. 2, the Monitor and the PowerMonitor equipment have been put to "loss", as if they did not exist.

– For the actuation part (Fig. 3):

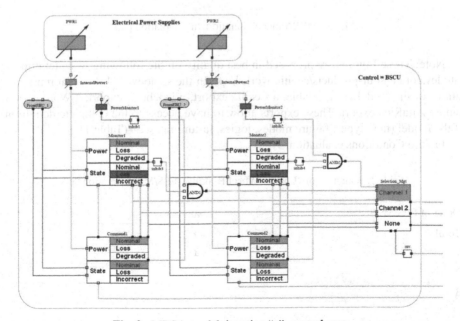

Fig. 2. MBSA model, iteration "n", control part

o   2 hydraulic ways with mechanical switch logics
o   First hydraulic way is powered by HYD1
o   Second hydraulic way is powered by HYD2
o   In case HYD1 and HYD2 are inoperative at the same time, the second hydraulic
    way is powered by an Accumulator

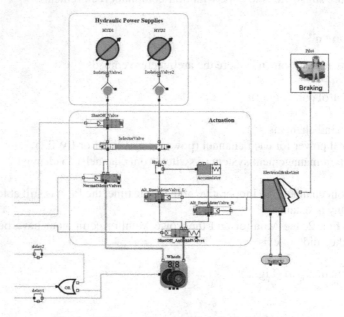

Fig. 3. MBSA model, iteration "n", actuation part

Note: These Figures are proposed in best quality on the following website: https://satodev.com/en/our-products/cecilia-workshop/. In the same way, 4 different representations of the model are available: a Cecilia export, a Docbook export, a Word export and an AltaRica export. These exports allow to have access to the complete definition of the model (flow types, failure modes, logics, failure rates…) (Table 1).

Failure Conditions evaluation:

Table 1. Quantity of "Loss of Wheel Braking" FFS/MCS, iteration "n"

Order of FFS/MCS	Number
Total	**49**
1	4
2	19
3	26

Table 2. "Loss of Wheel Braking" probability computation, iteration "n"

Order of MCS	Number	Probability
Total	**49**	**1.1310 E−04**
1	4	1.1300 E−04
2	19	1.0242 E−07
3	26	2.9326 E−12

Table 3. Quantity of "Uncommanded Wheel Braking" FFS/MCS, iteration "n"

Order of FFS/MCS	Number
Total	**17**
1	4
2	12
3	1

Table 4. "Uncommanded Wheel Braking" probability computation, iteration "n"

Order of MCS	Number	Probability
Total	**17**	**3.7667 E−06**
1	4	3.7667 E−06
2	12	7.5599 E−11
3	1	1.3888 E−18

At this stage, the failure modes that can represent either development errors or random failures have not been yet differentiated. As a result, FFS and MCS are still identical. The tables are not merged as FFS combine development errors which are not stochastic events. The failure rates that have been chosen to perform the probability computation are the same as the one chosen for the Fault-Tree Analysis (FTA), developed in another appendix of the document [1]. Examples (with exponential laws):

– Electrical power supply, *PWR1* and *PWR2*

   o *Loss* failure rate: lambda = 1. E−4 per flight hour
   o *Degraded* failure rate: lambda = 1. E−05 per flight hour

– *SelectorValve* (Actuation part)

   o *Stuck_Normal* failure rate: lambda = 1. E−6 per flight hour
   o *Stuck_Alternate* failure rate: lambda = 1. E−6 per flight hour

o *Stuck_Middle* failure rate: lambda = 1. E−8 per flight hour

The list of failure rates can be found either in the complete model exports or in dedicated files on the following website, as well as the FFS/MCS lists at order 1:
https://satodev.com/en/our-products/cecilia-workshop/
Safety requirements assessment:

– At this level of development, SR1 is not evaluated.
– SR2 is not fulfilled due to the probabilities of the 4 minimal cut sets of order 1 (Table 2).
– SR3 is not fulfilled due to 4 minimal cut sets of order 1. (Table 3)
– SR4 is not fulfilled due to the probabilities of the 4 minimal cut sets of order 1 (Table 4).

MBSA outputs: The 4 minimal cut sets of order 1 correspond to an erroneous output of the BSCU command channel 1, one due to the command, two due to the power supply, the last one due to the EBU. As EBU is not part of the study, its failure mode will not be taken into account. Safety team recommendation is to perform an evolution of the architecture of the BSCU to a dual redundant Command/Monitor, with power supply monitoring.

4.3 Iteration "n + 1"

Design team followed the Safety team recommendations. Each channel of the BSCU is now fitted with a device which monitors:

– The internal power supply output, as the behavior of the command components cannot be assessed when powered by degraded power supply, due to Internal either External Power Supply failures;
– The behavior of the command function outputs.

The MBSA model control part evolved as shown in Fig. 4. Internal power monitoring and command monitoring are now fully operative. The actuation part did not evolve. Moreover, common modes have been identified and added as Common Cause Failures, due to potential COM/MON hardware, COM software and MON software development errors. As a result, FFS and MCS are no longer identical.

In order to spare time and to allow using the same model for both FFS and MCS computation (and thus probability computation), very low failure rates have been assigned to Common Cause Failures (1.E−15 per flight hour). We acknowledge that they do not have any theoretical significance and that they are only modeling artefacts.

Failure Conditions evaluation:

The list of failure rates can be found either in the complete model exports or in dedicated files on the following website, as well as the FFS and MCS lists truncated at order 2: https://satodev.com/en/our-products/cecilia-workshop/.

Safety requirements assessment:

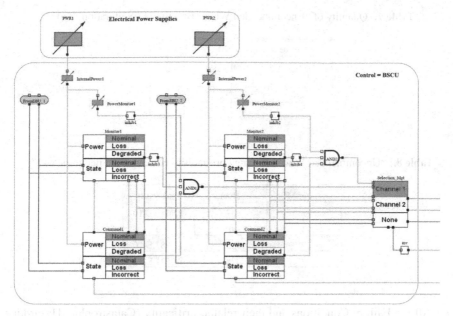

Fig. 4. MBSA model, iteration "n + 1", control part

Table 5. Quantity of "Loss of Wheel Braking" FFS, iteration "n+1"

Order of FFS	Number
Total	119
1	1
2	26
3	92

Table 6. "Loss of Wheel Braking" probability computation, iteration "n+1"

Order of MCS	Number	Probability
Total	69	4.0588 E-08
1	0	0
2	16	4.0584 E-08
3	53	3.1833 E-12

– SR1 implies minimal IDAL allocation, taking into account different FFS (Table 5 and 7). Two of them, among various different possible ones, are gathered in Table 9. The final IDAL allocation is a choice that depends on several factors:

Table 7. Quantity of "Uncommanded Wheel Braking" FFS, iteration "n+1"

Order of FFS	Number
Total	**63**
1	1
2	15
3	47

Table 8. "Uncommanded Wheel Braking" probability computation, iteration "n+1"

Order of MCS	Number	Probability
Total	**37**	**1.8088 E-10**
1	0	0
2	9	1.8087 E-10
3	28	8.0541 E-17

o All the Failure Conditions and their related criticality (Catastrophic, Hazardous, Major, Minor) in which the item appears in Functional Failure Set
o The other systems IDAL allocation choices (for example, in this case, PWR1 and PWR2), whose items appear in the same Functional Failure Set

The ability to represent several linked systems within the same MBSA model and to use it for several Failure Conditions, ensures a high consistency level and reduces considerably the necessary time to perform the safety analyses at each system design iteration.

Table 9. Minimal IDAL allocation

Item	Option 1	Option 2
HW COM/MON	A	A
SW COM	B	B
SW MON	B	B
Selection_Mgt	**A**	**B**
PWR1	C	B
PWR2	C	B
InternalPower1	C	B
InternalPower2	C	B
PowerMonitor1	A	B

Note: Reminder of SR1: Decelerate Wheels function shall be developed FDAL A. The demonstration of this safety requirement may imply other activities. In the frame of this example, only refined safety requirements dealing with IDAL allocation have been taken into account

- SR2 is fulfilled as the computed probability of the Loss Failure Condition is 4.0588 E-8 for a landing (Table 6).
- SR3 is fulfilled as there is no minimal cut set of order 1 for the Uncommanded Failure Condition (Table 8).
- SR4 is fulfilled as the computed probability of the Uncommanded Failure Condition is 1.8088 E-10 for a takeoff (Table 8).

The latest design satisfies the quantitative and the qualitative safety objectives regarding the two Failures Conditions. In case of new system design iteration, Safety team still has to ensure non-regression regarding the qualitative and quantitative safety objectives. Some assumptions were made in the functional or dysfunctional logics and would have to be confirmed by the Design team before burying the results.

Building this formal model also led the Safety team to raise several questions that have to be answered. These questions were not raised by the Safety team that performed the classical Fault Tree Analysis. It demonstrates that a MBSA model, thanks to the combined functional and dysfunctional approach and to the dynamic behavior, is more accurate than a classical approach, thus less expensive regarding the safety solutions that will be implemented.

5 Conclusion

As stated in the previous paragraph, performing a model-based analysis requests to formalize the functional and the dysfunctional system behavior. Doing that requires a clear identification of the hypotheses which have been made. All hypotheses have to be validated by the Design team.

This example shows that:

- A model-based analysis can handle multi physics system (hydraulic, electrical, mechanical and electronic hardware/software);
- A MBSA model can be used at different stages of the development process;
- Several Failure Conditions can be studied using the same model;
- Several types of analyses can be done using the same model thanks to post-treatment (FFS, MCS...);
- Using one model can ensure consistency between several Failure Conditions (in the framework of an update of a system, this feature reduces considerably the necessary time to update one system safety analysis);
- A MBSA model makes it possible to verify top level safety requirements at each iteration;
- A MBSA model raises a lot of questions about system behavior, enables all stakeholders (for instance Design and Safety teams) to share common understanding of the system and helps to formalize hypotheses made;

– Finally, a MBSA model highly facilitates the communication between Design and Safety teams.

References

1. SAE, ARP4761 : Guidelines and methods for conducting the safety assessment process on civil airborne system and equipment (1996)
2. Point, G., Rauzy, A.: AltaRica: constraint automata as a description language. J. européen des systèmes automatisés **33**(8–9), 1033–1052 (1999)
3. Delange, J., Feiler, P.: Supporting the ARP4761 safety assessment process with AADL. Embedded real time software and systems (ERTS2014), February 2014, Toulouse, France. (hal-02271282)
4. FALCON 7X Certification Collection 27_1-300, Primary Flight Control System Safety Analysis, Dassault Aviation reference DGT91338 (first issue #1 of 21/05/2003, last issue #13 of 14/02/2017)
5. Fenelon, P., McDermid, J.A., Nicholson, M., Pumfrey, D.J.: Towards integrated safety analysis and design. ACM Comput. Rev. **2**(1), 21–32 (1994)
6. Åkerlund O., et al.: ESACS: an integrated methodology for design and safety analysis of complex systems. In: Proceedings of ESREL. Balkema (2003)
7. Åkerlund O., et al.: ISAAC, a framework for integrated safety analysis of functional, geometrical and human aspects. In: Proceedings of ERTS (2006)
8. Papadopoulos, C., et al.: Model-based safety assessment for the three stages of refinement of the system development process in ARP4754A, SAE 2011 AeroTech Congress & Exhibition, Toulouse, France, October 2011

Modeling the Variability of System Safety Analysis Using State-Machine Diagrams

Lucas Bressan[1], André L. de Oliveira[1(✉)], Fernanda C. Campos[1],
Leonardo Montecchi[2], Rafael Capilla[3], David Parker[4], Koorosh Aslansefat[4],
and Yiannis Papadopoulos[4]

[1] Universidade Federal de Juiz de Fora (UFJF), Juiz de Fora, MG, Brazil
{lucasbressan,andre.oliveira,fernanda.campos}@ice.ufjf.br
[2] Norwegian University of Science and Technology, Trondheim, Norway
leonardo.montecchi@ntnu.no
[3] Universidad Rey Juan Carlos (URJC), Madrid, Spain
rafael.capilla@urjc.es
[4] University of Hull, Hull, U.K.
{D.J.Parker,K.aslansefat,y.i.papadopoulos}@hull.ac.uk

Abstract. Software Product Lines (SPLs) enable and maximize reuse of software artefacts, using software variability as central technique. In Model-Based Safety Analysis, system and software models are annotated with failure models that are used to produce safety analysis artefacts like fault trees and FMEAs. However, little work has been done to show MBSA in product lines, exploiting failure models to create safety analyses for variants in the product line. State machines have been widely used to support both fault propagation and probabilistic system safety analysis. In this paper, we introduce an approach to support variability modeling and reuse of state-machine diagrams used for system safety analysis. The approach enhances traditional software product line cycle with new activities aimed to support the reuse of safety information using state-machine diagrams and facilitates the management of the diversity of functional safety across system configurations using variability models. We evaluate our approach using an automotive braking system where we show reduction of the burden of safety analysis and improvements in traceability between safety artifacts and variability abstractions.

Keywords: Safety analysis · State-machine diagrams · Software product lines · Variability · Reuse

1 Introduction

Safety-critical software is becoming more complex due to the greater possibilities offered for inter-connectivity as well as due the increased computing power [1]. The mass customization in the automotive industry leads to a higher variability within a single product with thousands of variations points [2]. Automotive electronic control units (ECUs) [3], used in airbags, electronic window lifter and driver assistant systems, and powertrain controllers [4] are highly variant-intensive. A failure in safety-critical software may lead

© The Author(s), under exclusive license to Springer Nature Switzerland AG 2022
C. Seguin et al. (Eds.): IMBSA 2022, LNCS 13525, pp. 43–59, 2022.
https://doi.org/10.1007/978-3-031-15842-1_4

to catastrophic consequences to the environment, finances, or putting human lives at risk.

In safety-critical systems, the reuse of software components demand the reuse of safety analysis artefacts. The safety information is the key point of diversity in safety analysis of variant-intensive systems and software product lines. Reusing state-machine diagrams for system safety analysis demands a way to manage diversity of emergent hazardous states and safety requirements. Safety requirements are placed measures to eliminate or minimize hazard and/or component failure effects on the overall safety. Current industry practice for safety artifact reuse in certification processes relies only on clone & own approaches [1, 3]. Also, balancing safety certification and reuse of safety information still remains a challenge to product line safety analysis [2, 5–7].

In order to address these challenges, we propose an approach, which extends a previous work [8] with the provision of semi-automated support for variability modeling and management in system safety analysis using state-machine diagrams. We evaluated the effectiveness of our solution in a variant-intensive automotive wheel braking system to enabling the systematic reuse of safety information of state-based safety models and reducing the burden to performing safety analysis activities. The remainder of this paper is as follows. Section 2 presents the related work. Section 3 introduces the background and concepts required to understand the proposed solution. In Sect. 4 we describe our approach consisting in new activities in addition to the classical Software Product Line (SPL) [9] lifecycle to support the reuse of safety information. Section 5 provides an evaluation of our approach in the automotive domain and Sect. 6 presents the conclusions and future work.

2   Related Work

The research on variability management in system safety analysis covers extensions of traditional safety analysis techniques to suit software product line processes [10–13], and model-based techniques [5, 7, 14, 15]. Dehlinger and Lutz [10] and Feng and Lutz [11] proposed Software Fault Tree Analysis (SFTA) for product lines. In a SFTA, each fault tree leaf node is enriched with variability information in the domain engineering phase. In the application engineering phase, a pruning technique is applied for reusing software fault trees in a specific product variant. The Product Line SFTA was further extended to integrate state-based modeling [13]. This allows mapping fault tree leaf nodes to components and specifying the behaviour of a component in a state chart. Performing variability management on safety properties prior to FTA and Failure Modes and Effects Analysis (FMEA) enables the traceability of variability in the design and context through the safety lifecycle and the systematic reuse of safety assets. Schulze et al. [5] proposed an approach that integrates Medini[1] safety analysis and pure::variants[2] tools to support variability management in automotive functional safety. Kaßmeyer et al. [14, 15] propose a systematic model-based approach integrated with change impact analysis techniques. This approach combines requirements engineering, architectural design, safety analysis,

---

[1] https://www.ansys.com/products/systems/ansys-medini-analyze.
[2] https://www.pure-systems.com/products/pure-variants-9.html.

and variability management tools, allowing seamless safety engineering across product variants. Domis et al. [7] extended the Component Integrated Component Fault Trees (C2FT) with variation points and integrated it within UML via a profile into Enterprise Architect[3] commercial tool. These approaches [7, 14] provide efficient solutions for variability management and change impact analysis in automotive functional safety.

Montecchi et al. [16] provide formalism for variability modeling into Stochastic Activity Networks (SAN) models. Bressan et al. [17] presented an approach to generate variants of SPEM 2.0 process models for automotive software components based on the allocated Automotive Safety Integrity Levels (ASILs). State of the art Model-Based Design [18–21] and Safety Assessment frameworks [22–24] provide certain degree of support for variant management and reuse of safety models via inheritance [18–23], and specification of different implementations for the failure behaviour of a component stored into error model libraries [24]. However, these mechanisms are limited to manage variability into safety models at a coarse grained level, not supporting variability on hazard causes, error states and state transitions. Although conventional SPL approaches [9, 25] have been extended [5, 6] to address safety certification, supporting the diversity of safety information is still challenging [1, 8] due to: **CH1** the lack of considering the impact of variability in design choices for specifying component failure models, e.g., qualitative failure logic and stochastic state machine diagrams, used to create safety analysis for system variants; **CH2**: lack of traceability between SPL variability abstractions, design choices, and variation into elements and parameters from state machine diagrams; and **CH3**: lack of mechanisms to resolve structural and parametric variability into failure models (state machines).

3   Background

We provide an overview of Product Lines, Base Variability Resolution, ISO 26262 safety lifecycle, and the CHESS-State-Based Analysis used in the proposed solution.

3.1   Software Product Lines and Base Variability Resolution

A Software Product Line (SPL) is a set of software-intensive system that share a common and manageable set of features that satisfy the specific needs of a particular market segment [9]. *Feature* stands for a distinct system characteristic visible to the end-user [25], e.g., *wheel braking*. The commonalities and variability's of a family of systems from a particular domain and their relationships are expressed in a feature model. Feature modeling represents the product line variability at the highest abstraction level. Features express high-level functional and quality requirements from an application domain. Feature-Oriented Domain Analysis (FODA) [25] is the first and widely used feature modeling notation, which supports the specification of mandatory, optional and alternative features and structural relationships between features, i.e., decomposition, generalization, specialization, and parameterization. The wheel braking feature of a car family can be configured as four or front wheel braking (Fig. 1).

---

[3] https://sparxsystems.com/.

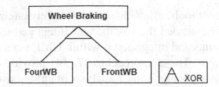

Fig. 1. Features for an automotive wheel braking system family.

The development of a SPL encompasses domain engineering and application engineering processes. The product line core assets are produced during the domain engineering and further reused in the application engineering [25]. The domain engineering process involves domain analysis, for identifying commonalities and variability in the domain requirements using a feature model, the realization of common and variant domain features by developing the SPL architecture and implementing their components (core assets), and specification of traceability between *features* and the core assets. In the application engineering, we create system variants from the core assets, produced in the domain engineering, by exploiting variability and ensuring the correct binding of variation points according to product requirements. A variation point stands for places in the domain artefacts, e.g., design, where variability can arise.

Base Variability Resolution (BVR) [26] is a language and tool, built upon Common Variability Language (CVL) [27] standard, to supports standard variability modeling in Meta-Object Facility (MOF)[4] compliant base models, e.g., UML and SysML models. BVR supports the generation of product variants from a base model via three different and inter-related models for specification of variability abstractions and variability realization. Variability abstractions are specified in a *VSpec* (feature) model supplemented with constraints, and a corresponding resolution model (*VResolution*) that defines the feature selection for a given product variant. In a *VSpec* model, the mandatory features are connected to the parent feature via *solid lines*, and *dashed lines* represent optionality. The *VSpec* model allows the specification of constraints between *features* in Object Constraint Language (OCL).

3.2 The ISO 26262 Safety Lifecycle

ISO 26262 [28] prescribes requirements for functional safety on electrical/electronic systems embedded into small and medium sized (up to 3.5 tons) general purpose road vehicles. This standard provides a safety lifecycle for automotive systems, a risk-based approach for determining risk classes (Automotive Safety Integrity Levels - ASILs), and requirements for validation and confirmation measures to ensure that an acceptable level of safety is achieved.

After allocating functions to systems/subsystems/components (items) and specifying their dependencies and interactions with the environment at the vehicle level, the *safety lifecycle is initiated*, i.e., the development category of all parts of the item is analyzed to make the distinction between a new item development and a modification to an existing item. *Items* can be software, electrical or electronic system components.

---

[4] https://www.omg.org/mof/.

Hazard Analysis and Risk Assessment (HARA) is performed to identify and categorize the hazards that malfunctions in the item can trigger and formulate the safety goals related to the mitigation of hazardous events, to avoid unreasonable risk. The *Functional Safety Concept* shall derive the functional safety requirements from the safety goals and allocating them to preliminary architectural elements of the item. Fault detection and mitigation, and fault tolerance mechanisms are examples of functional safety requirements. Safety goals are results from HARA, expressed in the form of ASILs, which define measures to mitigate hazard effects. Different safety goals are defined to achieve each ASIL. Achieving compliance with standards increases around 75% to 150% of the total development costs [29], due to the additional effort with system safety analysis, verification, and validation activities. Although standards provide guidance to the development of single products, the industrial production is inherently variable [1, 3, 4], which different products are built upon a common base system. Variation in the design propagates throughout potential fault, error, and failure behaviors of subsystems and components, stored into failure logic and/or stochastic state-machine diagrams, which may rise in different variants and environments.

3.3 CHESS Framework and CHESS State-Based Analysis

The Composition with guarantees for High-integrity Embedded Software components aassembly (CHESS) framework is a model-driven, component-based, methodology and toolset support for the design, development, and safety analysis of high-integrity systems from different domains [21]. CHESS defines a UML-based modeling language, called Composition with guarantees for High-integrity Embedded Software components aSsembly Modeling Language (CHESSML) [20], and includes a set of plug-ins to perform code generation, constraint checking, performance, and safety/dependability analyses. The CHESS framework supports qualitative fault propagation, using CHESS-Failure Logic Analysis (CHESS-FLA) [22], and quantitative/probabilistic state-based (via CHESS-SBA) [30] safety/dependability analysis techniques. CHESS-FLA allows engineers to decorate CHESSML component-based models with dependability information, execute Failure Logic Analysis, and get the results back-propagated onto the original model. In this paper, we focus solely on CHESS-SBA. CHESS State-Based Analysis (CHESS-SBA) [30] supports safety analysis (Hazard Analysis and Risk Assessment - HARA) using state machine diagrams. The term "state-based" denotes this technique uses a representation of the system based on possible states with respect to dependability, and possible transitions between them. The CHESS-SBA plugin supports users to perform quantitative (probabilistic) safety/dependability analysis on CHESSML models, by enriching them with stochastic dependability information, including failure and repair distribution of components, propagation delays and probabilities, and fault-tolerance and maintainability concepts. Such information can be added to a CHESSML element in two ways: i) via «*simpleStochasticBehavior*» stereotype that allows attributes (e.g., *reliability*) to be attached to hardware components. This stereotype is used for specifying probabilistic information of a hardware failure, e.g., time to the occurrence of a failure, possible failure modes, or the time required to repair the component after the occurrence of a failure, or *ii)* with an *error model*, i.e., a state machine diagram in which a more detailed failure behavior, in terms of hardware *faults*, software *bugs (faults, errors, flaws*) introduced by developers in the design, development, or operation leading it to produce an incorrect or unexpected result, *failure modes*, and internal propagations, of a component can be specified. This enriched model is transformed into a stochastic state-based model, using a variant of the Stochastic Petri Nets (SPNs) formalism. The model is then analyzed to evaluate the satisfaction of system dependability properties (e.g., *availability*) in the form of probabilistic metrics.

Figure 2 shows an example of a CHESSML error state machine diagram for the Electronic Pedal component of an automotive wheel braking system further used in the evaluation of our approach. This state-machine expresses the effects of *external faults* and their *propagations* as *internal error states*, and *output failure modes*. It comprises *healthy* and *undetected* states, with two *state transitions*. The first state transition moves from the *healthy* to an *undetected error state* due to the occurrence of an *omission* failure in the component input port (*InternalPropagation*) caused by an *external fault* in the *output port* of an *external component* or by a *cyber-attack*, e.g., *denial of service*. The second state transition is activated after the propagation of the *omission* external failure throughout the Electronic Pedal output port. A state machine may also contain *choice*, *fork* and/or *join* nodes for expressing logical relationships between states.

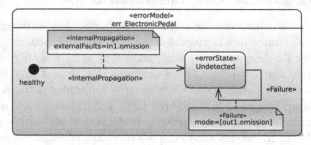

Fig. 2. Example of CHESS-SBA error model state machine diagram.

Performing dependability analysis using CHESS requires the specification of analysis contexts to collect information about the given analysis to be executed, e.g., fault tree analysis (*«GaAnalysisContext»*), state-based analysis (*«StateBasedAnalysis»*). A UML component tagged with *GaAnalysisContext* stereotype is used to refer to the set of system entities, by setting the stereotype "context" property with a logical expression describing the combination of component failure leading to the occurrence of a system hazard, to be considered for fault tree analysis using xSAP [31] tool. Fault tree analysis results describe the propagation of component failures specified within the context. A UML component tagged with *StateBasedAnalysis* is used to set the parameters: *measure* (the targeting property, e.g., reliability), the *targeting failure modes* (e.g., omission), dependable *components* and their *ports*, required to calculate the probability of components failing at a certain time or within a time range. In this paper, we used the integration between CHESS-SBA and BVR within the AMASS[5] platform for mapping error states and transitions from a state machine diagram to domain variability abstractions (*VSpecs*) in the *Variability Realization* model.

---

[5] https://www.amass-ecsel.eu/content/about.

4 A State-Based Dependable Software Product Line

We introduce the State-Based DEPendable Software Product Lines (DEPendable-SPL), which extends the traditional variability analysis [9, 25] techniques to cover system safety analysis, i.e., hazard analysis and risk assessment and component fault modeling, using state-machine diagrams. The approach supports the identification of hazards, error states and transitions, associated stochastic annotations, and safety requirements that hold for all product variants. We adopted the concept of 150% state-machine(s) for variability modeling in safety analysis for reconfigurable systems. We also adopted a negative variability strategy for mapping variability abstractions to system design and error state machine elements in the domain engineering phase, and for variability resolution in application engineering phase. The concept of a 150% model relates to a superset approach where 100% configuration model(s) for product safety analysis is/are obtained, via selection and resolution of variation points, from 150% model(s). In our case, the 150% models are CHESSML analysis context model for hazard and state-based analyses, and state-machines that describe the failure behaviors of components.

The 150% state-machine diagrams for product line safety analysis are produced in the domain engineering phase, and 100% models are then derived, via negative variability with the support of BVR tool in the application engineering phase. In a negative variability strategy, safety information elements not needed for a specific system variant are removed from 150% domain model (s). Our approach focuses on variability management on hazardous events, error states, and state transitions from CHESS state-machines in the domain engineering phase. In the application engineering phase, we focus on the reuse of domain safety artefacts and automatic synthesis of fault trees and FMEA from the reused state-machine diagrams. In our approach, we established a clear distinction between reusable safety artefacts, i.e., state machine diagrams, from those that can be generated. The State-Based DEPendable-SPL encompasses four activities in the domain engineering phase and three activities in the application engineering phase (Fig. 3). We describe each approach activity though this section.

4.1 Domain Engineering Phase

The domain engineering phase encompasses: domain analysis, product line design with safety analysis (Hazard Analysis and Risk Assessment and component fault modeling), and mapping variability abstractions to CHESSML models, error states and transitions from state machine diagrams.

Domain Analysis: Here, we identify system features and their relationships with safety-related features (i.e., features that impact on safety analysis). Firstly, we identi-fy common and variable system features, followed by the identification of features that impact on safety analysis. Safety-related features refer to characteristics of the operating environment (where) and how a SPL product is used. Finally, we specify the interactions among system and safety-related features via constraints, e.g., implication, exclusion, in the domain feature model. The product line feature model with system and safety-related features and their interactions, in our case, the BVR *VSpec* model (Fig. 3a), is the output of this activity. Interactions among system and safety- related features act as key driver to product line design [32] and safety analysis, taking a direct impact on design decisions, emergent hazardous events and safety requirements to avoid unreasonable risks and achieving compliance with standards.

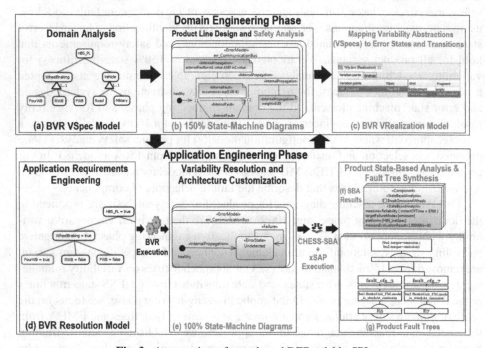

Fig. 3. An overview of state-based DEPendable-SPL.

Product Line Design with Safety Analysis. In this activity, we specify the realization of the variation points and their variants, defined in the SPL feature model, in the architecture using CHESSML Block Definition and Internal Block Diagrams, and we perform safety analysis using CHESS state-machine diagrams. Firstly, we specify the subsystems, components, their ports and connections that represent the realization/materialization of system and safety-related features in the architecture. After performing the preliminary product line design, we start safety analysis (HARA) considering the feature interactions specified in the feature model representing the domain of the targeted reconfigurable system, and the architecture model. During safety analysis, we identify the potential hazards and failures that can emerge in architectural subsystems and components associated with different feature interactions. Product Line Safety Analysis encompasses the following sub-activities: *Identification of Feature Interactions that may Impact on Product Line Safety Analysis*, *Hazard Analysis and Risk Assessment*, and *State-Based Component Fault Modeling*.

Identification of Feature Interactions that Impact on Product Line Safety Analysis: It encompasses: *i)* identify the combinations among system features, which conform to the product line feature model and their relationships, with elements from architectural and behavioural models. *ii)* For each identified interaction between system features, we analyse combinations among safety-related features. *iii)* Finally, we combine the identified system feature interactions with safety-related feature interactions to derive a set of combinations among system and safety-related feature interactions relevant for the stakeholders. We introduced this activity in our approach since it would be prohibitive performing domain safety analysis considering all possible interactions among system and safety-related features expressed in the SPL feature model. Although we consider feature interactions in our approach, it is important to highlight that we focus on performing safety analysis from the perspective of the whole SPL domain instead specific configurations.

Hazard Analysis and Risk Assessment: This activity encompasses the following steps: *i)* choosing a specific feature interaction to be considered in the analysis; *ii)* identifying combinations among component error states that may lead to the occurrence of hazards; *iii)* specify the context of each hazard by combining component failure modes leading to the occurrence of a hazard in expressions using logical operators, e.g., *Omission-C1.out1 and Omission-C2.out1*, in a UML component tagged with *«GaAnalysisContext»* stereotype; and *iv)* specify the targeted properties (e.g., *severity*), *failure modes* and *components* associated with each identified hazard in «StateBasedAnalysis» tagged components. The output of this activity is a 150% CHESS Analysis Context model (CAC).

State-Based Component Fault Modeling: We specify the failure behavior of each product line architectural subsystem/component in a separated 150% CHESS state-machine diagram by describing: *i)* the potential output deviations (failures) that may contribute to the occurrence of hazards in each feature interaction under analysis. Each *output deviation* should be modeled as an *error state* that describes the component failure behavior; and *ii)* the potential *causes*, in terms of *input failures, internal faults* or combinations among them, which lead to the occurrence of each identified *output deviation*. We can also assign *probability* information to error states and state transitions. We apply these steps to analyze the components based on the assumptions and the data associated with each feature interaction under analysis.

The outputs of this activity are 150% state-machine diagrams that describe how the components may fail and contributing to the occurrence of hazards in each analyzed feature interaction. Since the causes of a component failure may change according to design choices and feature interactions, we recommend specify the commonalities and variability inherent to the failure behavior of each component in a separated 150% state machine diagram (see Fig. 3b).

Mapping Variability Abstractions to Error States and Transitions: In this activity, we specify mappings linking variability abstractions (Fig. 3a) to their materialization into CHESSML analysis context and state machine model elements (Fig. 3b). This is needed for integrating safety analysis information from state machines within the SPL core assets, and enabling the systematic reuse of safety information in the application engineering phase. We adopted a negative variability strategy for mapping features to their realization into fragments of superset CHESSML models and state-machine diagrams into the BVR variability realization model (Fig. 3c). Since we followed a negative variability strategy, we specify the realization of variability abstractions into BVR fragment substitutions containing placement fragments with references to model elements that should be removed from superset CHESSML models and state machine diagrams when a given feature is selected. We specify the mappings of features to their materialization into: *i)* the 150% CHESS block diagrams, *ii)* analysis context model for hazard analysis and *iii)* component state machine diagrams via fragment substitutions with a placement and an empty replacement fragment. An enriched BVR *VRealization* model with the specification of mappings linking variability abstractions to their materialization into: CHESSML models and error state-machine diagrams is the output of this activity. The *VRealization* model enables the automatic derivation of 100% CHESSML models and state-machine diagrams in the application engineering phase.

4.2 Application Engineering Phase

Here we describe the application requirements engineering, variability resolution and architecture customization, product state-based and fault tree synthesis activities.

Application Requirements Engineering: We specify application-specific requirements in a feature model, via selection of features specified in the product line feature model (Fig. 3a), in the resolution model (Fig. 3d) using BVR resolution editor. The resolution model with the selected domain features that address the application requirements is the output of this activity. The resolution model is the input for variability resolution and architecture customization.

Variability Resolution and Architecture Customization: In this activity, we resolve the variability expressed in 150% CHESS-ML models and state machine diagrams to derive 100% models (Fig. 3e) according to the feature selection specified in the resolution model. We perform this activity with the support of BVR execution engine (see Sect. 3.1). Here, we execute the BVR engine for product derivation by providing the following input artefacts: the *VSpec*, *VResolution* and *VRealization* models, the 150% CHESS-ML models and state machine diagrams. The 100% CHESS-ML architecture and analysis context models, and state machine diagrams that describe the failure behaviors of components in the feature interactions specified in the resolution model are the outputs of this activity.

It is important to highlight that in cases where application-specific features not provided by the SPL are specified during application requirements engineering; engineers can update the derived 100% CHESSML system model with the addition of subsystems and components that address application-specific features. Different assumptions for product safety analysis can emerge from the added product-specific components to the reused 100% CHESSML system models and interactions among product-specific features. The interactions between existing and product-specific features (system and safety features) should be considered during product safety analysis. In this case, engineers perform product safety analysis following the same steps defined in the domain engineering phase.

Product-specific components, analysis context and state machines may provide feedback to the SPL development process. To achieve this goal, it is needed enhancing the product line *VSpec* model, the 150% CHESSML models for design and safety analysis, and the *VRealization* model with additional fragment substitutions. This is required to enable the reuse of product-specific components and their associated safety analysis information in the development and certification of other safety-critical products. The feedback to the product line development process in the application development is supported in our approach via CHESS and BVR integration. Such integration allows users updating the *VSpec* model with application-specific features, and the *VRealization* model with fragment substitutions for mapping these features to CHESS-ML and state-machine elements added to the SPL repository.

Product State-Based Analysis and Fault Trees Synthesis: In this activity, we perform state-based analysis, via execution of CHESS-SBA, to estimate probabilistic properties (e.g., *severity*) associated with hazardous events (Fig. 3f), and synthesis of fault trees (Fig. 3g), with the support of xSAP [31] tool. The 100% CHESSML analysis context models, components and state machines are inputs for executing CHESS state-based analysis and xSAP for synthesizing fault trees for each product-specific hazard. The outputs of this activity are: state-based analysis results that provide metrics associated with hazardous events, fault trees for each identified hazardous event, and a FMEA table. The fault trees are further synthesized into FMEA that describe how component can fail and contributing to the occurrence of hazardous events. State-based analysis results support risk assessment, the assignment of Safety Integrity levels (SILs) to mitigate hazard effects, and derivation of safety goals. Fault trees and FMEA are required by standards for certifying a safety-critical system.

5   Evaluation

We evaluated our approach in an automotive Hybrid Braking System (HBS) [33]. The complete HBS models described through this section are available in [34].

5.1   Hybrid Braking System

The HBS is an automotive wheel braking system (Fig. 4), originally designed in MAT-LAB/Simulink. The term hybrid means that the braking occurs through the combined action of electrical In-Wheel Motors (IWMs), and frictional Electromechanical Brakes (EMBs) within Brake Units (BUs). While braking, IWM components transform the vehicle kinetic energy into electricity, charging the power train battery, increasing the vehicle's range. The HBS architecture comprises 4 variant wheel-brake units (subsystems), 30 components with 69 connections. Each wheel brake module comprises a Wheel Node Controller (WNC), for calculating the amount of braking torque to be produced by each wheel braking actuator, and it sends commands to Electromechanical Braking (EMB) and IWM power converters that control EMB and IWM braking actuators. While braking, the electric power flows from the Auxiliary Battery to the EMB via

EMB Power Converter; and IWM acts as a power generator providing energy for the Powertrain Battery via IWM Power Converter.

The HBS was evolved into a product line. We re-designed the HBS using CHESS-ML to support the evaluation of State-based DEPendable-SPL approach. The wheel braking is the HBS architectural variation point (see Fig. 3a). We can combine the four wheel-brake units into different ways to derive different variants. In this paper, we considered two HBS product variants: four-wheel braking (FourWB) and front-wheel braking (FWB). The front-wheel brake units and their connections to other components (Fig. 4) represent the realization of the FWB product. The HBS product variants can be deployed in a road car or in a military vehicle. Different hazards with different risks can rise from interactions between components in each HBS variant and operating environment, thus, impacting on safety analysis.

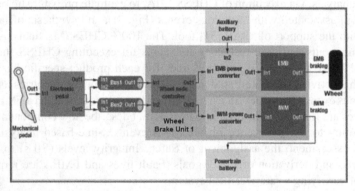

Fig. 4. An excerpt of hybrid braking system product line architecture [35].

5.2   HBS: Domain Engineering Phase

Identification of Feature Interactions for Braking System Safety Analysis: From the analysis of HBS system and safety-related features (Fig. 3a), we identified and considered the following feature interactions during domain safety analysis: **FI1 - Front Wheel Braking** deployed in a **Road** car vehicle (FWB and Road), and **FI2 - Four Wheel Braking** deployed in a **Military** vehicle (FourWB and Military). **HBS: Hazard Analysis and Risk Assessment.** We performed this step from the analysis of the HBS architecture model (Fig. 4) considering **FI1** and **FI2** feature interactions. We identified four potential hazards (Table 1) that may rise in two particular feature interactions. During HBS hazard analysis we specified a 150% CHESS analysis context model with four «StateBasedAnalysis» components that provide the context for estimating the probability of occurrence, exposure and controllability of *omission* and *value* failure modes in both feature interactions. We also specified four «GaAnalysisContext» components that define the contexts for fault tree analysis.

Table 1. Wheel braking hazards.

Feature Interaction	Hazard	Sev	Exp	Contr	ASIL
FourWB + Military	No braking four wheels	S3	0.6% (E2)	C2	A
	Value braking	S3	14.9% (E4)	C2	C
FWB + Road	Value braking	S3	0.6% (E2)	C3	B
	No braking front	S3	0.7% (E2)	C3	B

HBS Component Fault Modeling: In our evaluation, we specified the failure behavior of 10 components, considering FI1 and FI2 feature interactions, into 10 state-machines. Figure 3b shows an excerpt of the 150% CHESS error state machine diagram that describes the failure behavior of Communication Bus component in front-wheel (FI1) and four-wheel (FI2) braking feature interactions. The probability of occurrence of a random failure in this component when connected to front wheel brake units is $1.0E-6$ per hour of operation. The Communication Bus components may also fail through the propagation of external faults through its input ports, raising either an omission and/or wrong value failures. Variation in state machines may impact on how hazards propagate throughout architectural components during fault tree analysis, and in the probability of occurrence of hazardous events, changing safety requirements.

Mapping HBS Variability Abstractions to CHESS-ML Models and State-Machines: We performed this step from the analysis of the HBS feature model, the identified feature interactions, CHESS-ML models and state-machine diagrams. The HBS *VRealization* model contains eight fragment substitutions: four to manage variation on CHESS-ML models, two for state machine diagrams, and two to manage variations on CHESS analysis context model. Figure 3c show an excerpt of the *VRealization* model with the CBusTwoBUFS fragment substitution with a placement referencing a state transition from the 150% Bus state machine (Fig. 3b). The highlighted state transition should be removed from this state-machine when FourWB (Fig. 3b) is chosen.

5.3 HBS: Application Engineering Phase

Braking System Requirements: In this step, we specified the features that address FourWB and FWB requirements into two resolution models. Figure 3d shows an excerpt of the FourWB resolution model, where the FourWB feature was chosen. **HBS Variability Resolution**: We input the following artefacts to BVR execution engine: FourWB and FWB resolution models, the superset CHESS-ML models and state machine diagrams. Firstly, we executed the BVR engine for deriving 100% CHESS-ML models for FWB system variant, followed by FourWB (Fig. 3d). **Product State- Based Analysis and Fault Trees Synthesis**: After product derivation, we performed state-based analysis, via execution of CHESS-SBA, to estimate the severity, probability of exposure and controllability of *omission* and *value* hazardous events in FWB and FourWB system variants. Table 1 illustrates the state-based analysis results for the FWB and FourWB hazards.

The results demonstrated that all the identified wheel braking hazards have the potential to produce life threatening injuries to the occupants (S3 severity). With respect to probability of exposure, the probability of occurrence of *value braking* and *no braking* hazards in the FWB system variant is lower (E2). We identified the probability of exposure to a *value braking* hazard is very high (E4) in the FourWB variant. Finally, we estimated the controllability of the driver in hazardous driven situations based on qualitative attributes and fault tree analysis. From the analysis of the values assigned to severity, probability of exposure and controllability, we classified the risk posed by each hazard by checking the corresponding ASIL in the risk matrix. The occurrence of *no braking* hazard is most critical in FWB system variant demanding ASIL B safety goals. On the other hand, ASIL A is sufficient to mitigate the hazard effects in the FourWB. This example demonstrates the impact of variability in the design and operating environment on hazard analysis and risk assessment, derivation of safety goals/requirements. Such variation further propagates throughout fault tree analysis. Due to space limitations, the synthesized fault trees describing the propagation of *no braking* hazard throughout FourWB and FWB system variants are available elsewhere [34].

6 Conclusions

Model-based design and safety assessment become increasingly common in industry and safety standards from different domains, e.g., automotive, avionics, start to adopt them. Model-based languages like CHESSML [20], EAST-ADL [36], and AADL [18] have extensions, annexes, and metamodels that integrate safety concepts into model-based design. These developments are encouraging in terms of adaptation and adoption of the concepts of variant management and reuse in system safety assurance processes proposed in this paper. There are other powerful tools for Model-Based Safety Assessment (MBSA) including ALTARICA [37, 38], FSAP/xSAP [31, 39], and HiP-HOPS [24]. It is beyond the scope of this paper to discuss the relation of our work to these approaches. Our approach is generally complementary to other work in MBSA, and, some of the concepts we propose for MBSA of product lines could inspire other approaches. We introduced the State-Based DEPendable-SPL approach to support variability modeling and management in safety analysis using state-machine diagrams. The difference from our approach in comparison with related work [5, 7, 10, 13] is the focus on establishing a clear distinction between reusable safety assets, i.e., state-based and failure logic models, from those that can be generated, e.g., FTAs. Our approach supports mapping variability abstractions to elements from state-machine diagrams in the domain engineering phase, and it enables the systematic reuse of these models, the execution of state-based analysis, and synthesis of fault trees in the application engineering phase. The main benefits of our approach for safety assurance reuse are: *i)* the improvement of the verification product line safety properties across different scenarios; *ii)* the traceability between variability abstractions, and error states and transitions from state-machine diagrams; and *iii)* variability resolution in error states and transitions; and *iv)* the reduction of the burden of safety analysis for certifying individual system variants since this task is not performed from scratch. It may contribute to reducing the effort to perform hazard analysis and risk assessment, fault tree analysis, and FMEA required by standards like ISO 26262 for certifying a specific system variant. Our approach is applicable to other standards and domains (e.g., avionics) to enable safety assets reuse through certification processes.

In our experience, we achieved between 65–80% of reuse in state machine diagrams in the FourWB and FWB variants respectively. Our approach also contributed to reduce the effort on extending the SPL with newer components and state-machine diagrams via specification of newer features and fragment substitutions. Also, the State-Based DEPendable-SPL automates the traceability between variability abstractions (VSpec features) and safety analysis artefacts. As future work, we plan to extend our approach to support the management of the diversity of dependability information in safety and cyber-security assessment, and runtime variability in assurance cases. We also intend to assess the effectiveness of our approach in more complex industrial product lines from autonomous systems and other safety-critical domains.

References

1. Wolschke, C., Becker, M., Schneickert, S., Adler, R., MacGregor, J.: Industrial perspective on reuse of safety artifacts in software product lines. In: Proceedings of the 23rd International Systems and Software Product Line Conference (SPLC 2019), Paris, France. ACM, NY, USA, pp. 143–152 (2019)
2. Pohl, P., Höchsmann, M., Wohlgemuth, P., Tischer, C.: Variant management solution for large scale software product lines. In: Proceedings of the 40th International Conference on Software Engineering: Software Engineering in Practice, Gothenburg, Sweden. ACM, New York, NY, USA, pp. 85–94 (2018)
3. Tischer, C., Muller, A., Mandl, T., Krause, R.: Experiences from a large scale software product line merger in the automotive domain. In: Proceedings of the 15th International Software Product Line Conference, Munich, Germany, pp. 267–276 (2011)
4. SPLC.net. SPLC hall of the fame: General Motors Powertrain (GMPW) (2019). https://splc. net/fame/general-motors-powertrain. Accessed 10 July 2022
5. Schulze, M., Mauersberger, J., Beuche, D.: Functional safety and variability: can it be brought together? In: Proceedings of the 17th International Software Product Line Conference, Tokyo, Japan. ACM, NY, USA, pp. 236–243 (2013)
6. de Oliveira, A.L., Braga, R.T.V., Masiero, P.C., Papadopoulos, Y., Habli, I., Kelly, T.: Variability management in safety-critical software product line engineering. In: Capilla, R., Gallina, B., Cetina, C. (eds.) ICSR 2018. LNCS, vol. 10826, pp. 3–22. Springer, Cham (2018). https:// doi.org/10.1007/978-3-319-90421-4_1
7. Domis, D., Adler, R., Becker, M.: Integrating variability and safetyanalysis models using commercial UML-based tools. In: Proceedings of the 19th International Software Product Conference, Nashville, USA. ACM, NY, USA, 20–24 July, pp. 225–234 (2015)
8. Oliveira, A.L., et al.: Variability management in safety-critical systems design and dependability analysis. J. Softw.: Evol. Process 31(8), pp. 1–28 (2019)
9. Clements, P., Northrop, L.: Software Product Lines: Practices and Patterns. Addison-Wesley, Boston (2001)
10. Dehlinger, J., Lutz, R.: Software fault tree analysis for product lines. In: Proceedings of the 8th IEEE International Symposium. on High Assurance Systems Engineering, Tampa, USA, pp. 12–21 (2004)
11. Feng, Q., Lutz, R.: Bi-directional safety analysis of product lines. J. Syst. Softw. 78(2), 111–117 (2005)

12. Gómez, C., Liggesmeyer, P., Sutor, A.: Variability management of safety and reliability models: an intermediate model towards systematic reuse of component fault trees. In: Schoitsch, E. (ed.) SAFECOMP 2010. LNCS, vol. 6351, pp. 28–40. Springer, Heidelberg (2010). https://doi.org/10.1007/978-3-642-15651-9_3

13. Liu, J., Dehlinger, J., Lutz, R.: Safety analysis of software product lines using stated modeling. J. Syst. Softw. **80**(11), pp. 1879–1892 (2007)

14. Käßmeyer, M., Schulze, M., Schurius, M.: A process to support asystematic change impact analysis of variability and safety in automotive functions. In: Proceedings of the 19th International Software Product Line Conference, Nashville, USA. ACM, NY, USA, pp. 235–244 (2015)

15. Käßmeyer, M., Moncada, D.S.V., Schurius, M.: Evaluation of asystematic approach in variant management for safety-critical systemsdevelopment. In: Proceedings of 13th International Conference on Embedded and Ubiquitous Computing, IEEE, Porto, Portugal, pp. 35–43 (2015)

16. Montecchi, L., Lollini, P., Bondavalli, A.: A template-based methodology for the specification and automated composition of performability models. In IEEE Transactions on Reliability **69**(1), 293–309 (2020)

17. Bressan, L., de Oliveira, A.L., Campos, F., Papadopoulos, Y., Parker, D.: An integrated approach to support the process-based certification of variant-intensive systems. In: Zeller, M., Höfig, K. (eds.) IMBSA 2020. LNCS, vol. 12297, pp. 179–193. Springer, Cham (2020). https://doi.org/10.1007/978-3-030-58920-2_12

18. SAE. Architecture Analysis & Design Language (AADL) AS5506C, SAE (2017). https://www.sae.org/standards/content/as5506c/

19. Shin'ichi Shiraishi,: An AADL-based approach to variability modeling of automotive control systems. In: Petriu, D.C., Rouquette, N., Haugen, Ø. (eds.) MODELS 2010. LNCS, vol. 6394, pp. 346–360. Springer, Heidelberg (2010). https://doi.org/10.1007/978-3-642-16145-2_24

20. Intecs, CHESS Modelling Language: A UML/MARTE/SysML profile. (2020) https://www.eclipse.org/chess/publis/CHESSMLprofile.pdf

21. Mazzini, S., Favaro, J., Puri, S., Baracchi, L.: CHESS: an open source methodology and toolset for the development of critical systems. In: Join Proceedings of EduSymp, pp. 59–66 (2016)

22. Gallina, B., Javed, A. M., Muram, F. U., Punnekkat, S.: Model-driven dependability analysis method for component-based architectures. In: Proceedings of the Euromicro-SEAA Conference, Cesme, Izmir, Turkey, pp. 233–240 (2012)

23. Delange, J., Feiler, P., Gluch, D., Hudak, J.: AADL fault modeling and analysis within an ARP4761 safety assessment. Technical report, Carnegie Mellon Software Engineering Instiute (2013)

24. Papadopoulos, Y., et al.: Engineering failure analysis and design optimization with HiP-HOPS. J. Eng. Fail. Anal. **18**(2), 590–608 (2011)

25. Capilla, R., Bosch, J., Kang, K.-C. (eds.): Systems and Software Variability Management. Springer, Berlin, Heidelberg (2013). https://doi.org/10.1007/978-3-642-36583-6

26. Vasilevskiy, A. Haugen, Ø., Chauvel, F., Johansen, M. F., Shimbara, D.: The BVR tool bundle to support product line engineering. In: Proceedings of the 19th International Software Product Line Conference, Nashville, USA, ACM, NY, pp. 380–384 (2015)

27. Haugen, Ø., Moller-Pedersen, B., Oldevik, J., Olsen, G. K., Svendsen, A.: Adding standardized variability to domain specific languages. In: Proceedings of the 12th International Software Product Line Conference, IEEE, pp. 139–148 (2008)

28. ISO: ISO 26262: Road Vehicles Functional Safety (2018)

29. Thomas, E.: Certification Cost Estimates for Future Communication Radio Platforms. Rockwell Collins Inc., Technical Report (2009)

30. Montecchi, L., Gallina, B.: SafeConcert: a metamodel for a concerted safety modeling of socio-technical systems In: 5th International Symposium onModel-Based Safety and Assessment, vol. 10437 of LNCS, Trento, Italy, pp. 129–144 (2017)
31. Bittner, B., et al.: The xSAP Safety Analysis Platform. In: Chechik, M., Raskin, J.-F. (eds.) TACAS 2016. LNCS, vol. 9636, pp. 533–539. Springer, Heidelberg (2016). https://doi.org/10.1007/978-3-662-49674-9_31
32. Lee, K., Kang, K.C.: Usage Context as Key Driver for Feature Selection. In: Bosch, J., Lee, J. (eds.) SPLC 2010. LNCS, vol. 6287, pp. 32–46. Springer, Heidelberg (2010). https://doi.org/10.1007/978-3-642-15579-6_3
33. De Castro, R., Araújo, R.E., Freitas, D.: Hybrid ABS with electric motor and friction brakes. In: Proceedings of the 22nd International Symposium on Dynamics of Vehicles on Roads and Tracks, Manchester, UK (2011)
34. HBS, Case Study. https://github.com/aloliveira/hbs
35. Azevedo, L., Parker, D., Walker, M., Papadopoulos, Y., Araújo, R.: Assisted assignment of automotive safety requirements. IEEE Softw. **31**(1), 62–68 (2014)
36. Blom, H., et al.: EAST-ADL: An architecture description language for automotive software-intensive systems in the light of recent use and research. Int. J. Syst. Dyn. Appl. (IJSDA) **5**(3), 1–20 (2016)
37. AltaRica Project. Methods and Tools for AltaRica Language. https://altarica.labri.fr/wp/?page_id=23 (2020)
38. Arnold, A., Gerald, P., Griffault, A., Rauzy, A.: The Altarica formalism for describing concurrent systems. Fund. Inform. **34**, 109–124 (2000)
39. Bozzano, M., Villafiorita, A.: The FSAP/NuSMV-SA safety analysis platform. Int. J. Softw. Tools Technol. Transfers (STTT) – Special Section on Advances in Automated Verification of Critical Systems, **9**(1), 5–24 (2006)

Model-Based Safety Analysis: A Practical Experience

Bertille Noisette[1]([⊠]), Sébastien Dobol[1], and Laurène Monteil[1,2]

[1] Safran Aircraft Engines, Rond-point René Ravaud, 77550 Moissy-Cramayel, France
bertille.noisette@safrangroup.com
[2] INSA Centre Val de Loire, 88 boulevard Lahitolle, 18000 Bourges, France

Abstract. Model-Based Safety Analysis (MBSA) has been explored at Safran Aircraft Engines for a few years. The objective is to maturate a very promising method, in order to improve at the end our ability to address on-time safety analysis on products of increasingly complexity. This paper presents first our global needs and our current state of the art. We use SimfiaNeo software, a graphical tool with several features based on the AltaRica DataFlow language. Then we focus on three particular issues, which have been recently explored: what is the best way to model a failure, that propagate downstream and upstream? How shall we proceed to take the best benefit of an existing model? Does the MBSA help to compute the reliability of a dynamic system with a very long mission time? We present for each of these issues one or two ways, which we have tested, and our current conclusion. Finally, we draw the next steps identified in order to be ultimately able to certify a propulsive system thanks to this method.

Keywords: Model-Based Safety Analysis (MBSA) · AltaRica · Aeronautic · RAMS

1 MBSA at Safran Aircraft Engines

In Safran Aircraft Engines, the "Model Based Safety Analysis" (MBSA) term refers, just like in the future ARP4761A, to concepts and processes, which allow performing safety analysis using failure propagation models that generate outputs such as failure sequences, minimal cuts sets or other results.

1.1 Needs

In the internal RAMS (Reliability, Availability, Maintainability and Safety) roadmap, three major subjects are identified and need to be addressed in the next few years:

Need 1: Improve the Agility of the RAMS Team in Preliminary Design Architecture Scorecards. With the MBSA introduction, the safety analyst expects to be able to participate more actively and in a more agile way in architecture comparisons during the preliminary draft on the RAMS aspects.

C. Seguin et al. (Eds.): IMBSA 2022, LNCS 13525, pp. 60–67, 2022.
https://doi.org/10.1007/978-3-031-15842-1_5

Need 2: Maintain/Improve Robustness of the Safety Analysis on New Complex Propulsion System Architectures. In the mid term, the MBSA is foreseen to replace our classic method, FTA (Fault Tree Analysis) used in the system safety analysis to demonstrate conformity to customer or regulation quantitative requirements. This major change from FTA to MBSA should allow keeping failure scenario exhaustiveness on future very complex propulsion system architectures. Indeed, FTA method is starting to face technical limitations because, on one hand, it does not easily deal with system reconfigurations and on the other hand, it will be extremely difficult to make an inventory of all relevant failure scenarios on these kind of new systems.

Need 3: Improve Collaborative Work. In addition to these two main needs, the MBSA should also allow better communication/coordination/synchronization between designer teams and safety analysts [1].

1.2 2018–2021: Exploration and Maturity Increase

MBSA is a key area of interest since 2016, with participation to conferences and literature analysis. First models have been developed on an industrial project in cooperation with Dassault Aviation in 2017. A first internship on the possibilities offered by the AltaRica models was proposed during summer 2018.

Then, a project dedicated to MBSA study was set up in 2019, aiming to identify a MBSA tool that met our needs & requirements (SimfiaNeo has been selected). Further studies are conducted by now: relevant patterns are identified and tested in order to identify eventual showstoppers and to increase progressively the complexity of the models. The objective is to bring this methodology to a TRL6 maturity level, allowing deploying this methodology on propulsion system development.

In parallel, the link between MBSE (Model Based System Engineering) & MBSA and how the MBSA can take place in the overall process are also studied.

1.3 State of the Art

AltaRica Data-Flow is a high level description language devoted to risk assessment studies [2]. It can be seen as a generalization of both Petri nets and Block Diagrams [3] and it has been created at the Institute of Mathematics of Luminy (IML, Marseilles) [4].

The GTS, Guarded Transitions Systems, which can be encapsulated into boxes, defines the semantics of this language. The principle is to make a hierarchy of boxes, which are called bricks, linked with flows. Bricks represent the components and flows are physical information exchanged between them. Each brick is characterized by one or several internal states, representative of its functional or health state. Events are modelled by deterministic or stochastic delays: each event occurrence generates transitions on the brick internal states. Furthermore, a propagation logic is implemented in each brick in order to define the output flows in function of the input flows and the internal states (see Fig. 1). Observers are defined by Boolean expressions, which can be function of flows or bricks internal states and used to facilitate model exploitation.

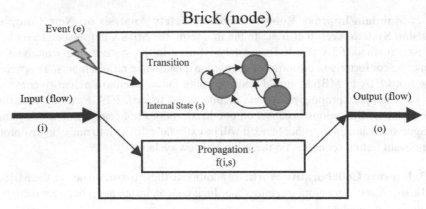

Fig. 1. AltaRica brick principle

SimfiaNeo, a software provided by APSYS [5], allows modelling graphically the AltaRica code in a clean and modular graphical interface. It builds the model of bricks and flows that define failure propagation and system reconfiguration. For a system, the followed method is: preliminary studies, model edition, model validation and then model exploitation [6]. The preliminary studies have been defined as follow:

1. Identify the failure conditions and their relevant observers.
2. Draft the model with the appropriated granularity, define the components and the different flows with their physical parameters, and then deduce domains associated.

According to the state of the art [1, 7], flows are modelled up to now by discrete states: a temperature could be *Nominal, Erroneous High* or *Erroneous Low* for example.

Afterwards, the model can be built on SimfiaNeo. The validation steps are performed for each brick created, then for the complete system.

The exploitation of the model is done thanks to different calculation modules. The two main tools are:

- Launch cutset and sequence computation to extract the minimal set of failures leading to a failure condition,
- Launch stochastic computations, or Monte-Carlo simulations, to extract indicators on the model.

2   Exploration of Approaches

In this section, we are going to focus on three different topics, to present tested approaches and to evaluate them. The first one aims to test and prove the efficiency of sequence generation and probability calculations on a pattern frequently encountered by propulsive system modelling. The second one addresses a crucial point for industrial deployment: re-use of existing models. The third one focuses on reliability study for multi-phased systems, and tests stochastic computation on a simple cold redundancy pattern.

2.1 Modelling a Physical Phenomenon with Effects Upstream

Needs. Occasionally, some dysfunctional phenomena can affect flow states upstream of the location where they are triggered. As mentioned in Sect. 1.3, the AltaRica language allows setting output flow states based on input flow states and internal states, but cannot change the input state after the appearance of a failure. AltaRica and other data flow languages reject models that include circular syntactic definitions such as loops or bidirectional flows [7]. Then how shall we model this kind of failures that propagate downstream and upstream?

Tested Approaches. In order to illustrate this specific dysfunctional phenomenon, a simple fuel filtering system has been studied by two approaches with SimfiaNeo. This system is composed of two components:

- The main filter which captures fuel contamination coming from aircraft or engine pumps before being injected in the engine combustion chamber,
- The bypass valve, which is closed during normal operation and turns open in case of clogged filter to continue to provide (contaminated) fuel flow in order to avoid engine shutdown.

First Approach. The first solution consists in modelling reverse flows to bring up fuel physical characteristics (flow, pressure, temperature, contamination) from the filter to the bypass valve (see Fig. 2). Reverse flows is a method used to model propagation of failures in mechanical continuous systems [7].

The nominal bypass valve behaviour will be coded so that in case of overpressure in the bypass valve input, the valve automatically opens; it remains closed otherwise.

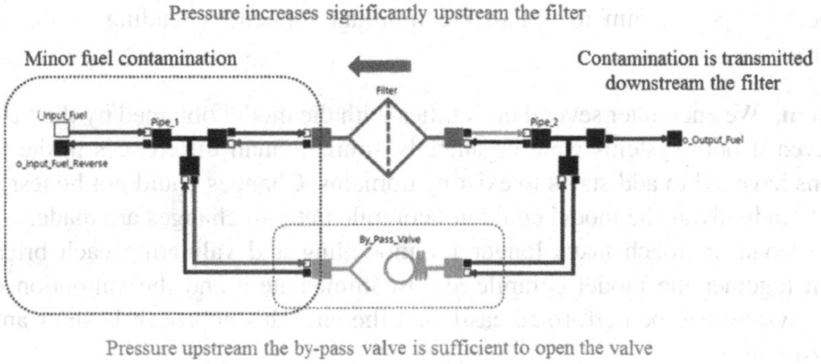

Pressure increases significantly upstream the filter

Minor fuel contamination

Contamination is transmitted
downstream the filter

Pressure upstream the by-pass valve is sufficient to open the valve

Fig. 2. Modelling a simple fuel filtering system by reverse flows

Second Approach. Another solution consists in using a feature of the AltaRica called synchronization, which allows triggering several events associated with different bricks at the same time after a same solicitation. When conditions are met to clog the filter, synchronize the clogging event in the filter and the opening event of the bypass valve only if the bypass valve is healthy.

Evaluation. Both solutions provided the same computation results. The second app-roach offers a better readability and a lower computation time. However, two points have led to abandon it. Firstly, the safety analyst identifies which components are affected, and models the propagation upstream. That means that we do not take advantage of AltaRica philosophy to model locally the behaviour of each component. Secondly, synchroniza-tion must be added in each new model, which jeopardise the re-use of existing models. The reverse flows approach is then preconized. However, this could be greatly improved by implementing bidirectional flows. The latest version of the language, AltaRica 3.0, can handle looped systems and the acausal component. We do not use it because there is not yet a graphical interface like SimfiaNeo adapted to our needs [8].

2.2 Re-use of Existing Models

Needs. We have modelled the fuel system of a given application in order to obtain the minimal sequences leading to several failure conditions. We want to perform the same study on the fuel system of another application. Failure conditions are similar and the system is well known in both cases. Which method should we follow to take the best benefit of the existing model?

Tested Approaches. We have considered two approaches.

The first one is to update the existing fuel system by modifying some bricks and flows in order to model the second fuel system.

The second one is to proceed in two steps. Firstly, we implement a library with all bricks modelled inside the existing fuel system model. Secondly, we model the second fuel system from scratch. As soon as possible, we use the bricks already existing in the library instead of modelling new ones.

In both cases, we aim to obtain the minimal sequences leading to the failure conditions.

Evaluation. We encounter several difficulties with the model obtained by the first app-roach. Even if both systems were organically similar, small differences in the failure conditions have led to add states to existing domains. Changes could not be tested and validated gradually as the model could not compile until all changes are made.

The second approach takes longer for modelling and validating each brick, but when put together the model compile almost immediately and the validation of the complete system can be performed easily. At the end, this approach is surer and less time-consuming.

2.3 Reliability of Dynamic Systems

Needs. We have to compute the reliability at the end of the mission of a system with the following characteristics: a long mission time, alternations of ON and OFF phases regularly during the mission, different failure rates for ON and OFF phases. Does the MBSA help to solve such an issue?

Tested Approach. Fault Tree Analysis do not allow answering such a question. Up to now, it was treated by analytical computation. To explore the ability of SimfiaNeo on such analysis, we have first modelled a very simplified system and validated it by step-by-step simulation. This pattern consists in a cold redundancy with alternation of ON and OFF phases (only for the active system; see Fig. 3). The failure condition is to loose both elements.

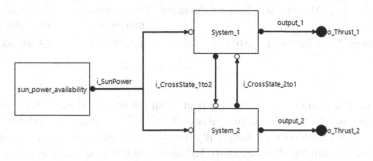

Fig. 3. Dynamic multi-phased system: model

System_1 and System_2 are implemented with the same AltaRica code. The only difference is the initial state: active for System_1 and passive for System_2. The mode automaton (see Fig. 4) for those systems is based on the pattern for spare units presented in [1] and updated for our needs. In this figure, i_SunPower and i_CrossState are the inputs of the System: their changes of state generate immediate transitions. Failure_On and Failure_OFF are stochastic transitions with given delay distributions. The state of the system is described by three variables: Nominal/Failed, ON/OFF, Active/Passive.

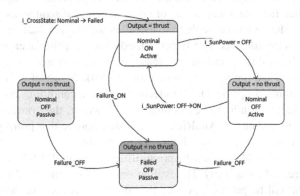

Fig. 4. A mode automaton to represent System_1 and System_2

Then, we have performed Monte-Carlo simulations by using SimfiaNeo stochastic simulation tool, and compared it with analytic result. Results and computation parameters are given in Table 1 below. The mean value is to compare with the one obtained by analytical way: 1,349E−04.

Table 1. Dynamic multi-phased system: results

Number of stories		10^8		
Running time (office computer)		152 min		
Mission time		8766 h		
Time ON/Time OFF		8 h/152 h		
	Mean value	Standard deviation	95% confidence min value	95% confidence max value
Loss of System_1 and System_2	1,346E−04	0,01160	1,323E−04	1,368E−04

Evaluation. The mean value obtained is near from the analytical one with a precision of 0.3%. However, the confidence interval is [−1.7%; 1.7%] around the analytical value. The release of SimfiaNeo v1.4.2 has greatly improved computation time performances, without however allowing drawing easily 10^9 stories in that case. Next step is to model the complete architecture and crosscheck the results with analytical ones.

3   New Challenges

To increase our maturity level on MBSA and to be able to model a whole propulsion system, we need to go further on several questions.

Firstly, how shall we model the temporal chain of events, especially when different events are modelled as simultaneous? In AltaRica, bricks change their states upon random events as upon deterministic events modelled by Dirac functions. SimfiaNeo fires each event separately, and allows attributing relative priorities to each deterministic event. We shall then find out a way to be sure that all relevant sequences are evaluated.

Secondly, how shall we validate that the model is well representative of the system? We could take advantage of tests already performed on test benches at engine and system level. This has to be evaluated and others ideas have to be explored.

Third, how could we improve the agility of the MBSA model of a given propulsion system throughout the project life? Indeed, the failure conditions are often slightly adapted, or new failure conditions can come out. However, the granularity of effects cannot yet be easily updated in AltaRica DataFlow. Improve that point would greatly help to use MBSA on products with a long lifetime as ours.

In conclusion, MBSA offers exciting possibilities to ensure RAMS studies on future products with increased complexity. The evaluations already conducted are very encouraging. Our efforts will be pursued, hoping that discussions and exchanges with other industrials interested in that method will help to build together a robust and certifiable method.

References

1. Bozzano, M., Cavallo, A., Cifaldi, M., Valacca, L., Villafiorita, A.: Improving safety assessment of complex systems: an industrial case study. In: Araki, K., Gnesi, S., Mandrioli, D. (eds.)

FME 2003. LNCS, vol. 2805, pp. 208–222. Springer, Heidelberg (2003). https://doi.org/10. 1007/978-3-540-45236-2_13

2. Boiteau, M., Dutuit, Y., Signoret, J.-P., Rauzy, A.: The AltaRica data-flow language in use: modeling of production availability of a multi-state system. Reliab. Eng. Syst. Saf. **91**(7), 747–755 (2006). ISSN 0951-8320

3. Rauzy, A.: Modes automata and their compilation into fault trees. Reliab. Eng. Syst. Saf. **78**(1), 1–12 (2002). ISSN 0951-8320

4. Prosvirnova, T.: AltaRica 3.0: a model-based approach for safety analyses. Doctoral thesis. Ecole Polytechnique (2014)

5. APSYS: SimfiaNeo User Manual, Version 1.4.2 (2022)

6. Machin, M., Sagaspe, L., De Bossoreille, X.: SimfiaNeo, complex systems, yet simple safety. In: Embedded Real Time Software and Systems, paper 9, Toulouse (2018)

7. Adeline, R., Darfeuil, P., Humbert, S., Cardoso, J., Seguin, C.: Toward a methodology for the AltaRica modelling of multi-physical systems. In: ESREL 2010, 05–09 September 2010, Rhodes, Greece (2010)

8. Batteux, M., Prosvirnova, T., Rauzy, A.: AltaRica 3.0 assertions: the whys and wherefores. Proc. Inst. Mech. Eng. Part O: J. Risk Reliab. **231**, 691–700 (2017)

Practical Application of Model-Based Safety Analysis to the Design of Global Operating System of New Rolling Stock on Automatic Metro Lines

Anthony Legendre[1]([⊠]) and Roland Donat[2]

[1] Fractus, Rue de la Croix Ronde, 91360 Epinay-sur-Orge, France
anthony.legendre@fractus.fr
[2] EdgeMind, Rue du départ, 75014 Paris, France

Abstract. System safety assessments are an integral part of system development, as indicated by EN 5012x railway standards. These activities are usually performed manually and rely on reviews and engineering judgments, with limited use of models to support the system assessment phase. In this paper, we present an application of Model-Based Safety Assessment to the Global Operating System (GOS) validation for automatic and semi-automatic metro lines. Safety assessment is a fundamental part of the development of railway systems and the use of model-based techniques provides an effective method for the formalization and analysis of such complex systems. A MBSA deployment methodology using AltaRica Wizard platform and its stochastic simulator is presented and results of the application of the automatic metro lines use-case are shown.

Keywords: Model based safety analysis · Integration in interdisciplinary processes · RAMS · Railway applications · Global operating system

1 Introduction of MBSA in Railway Context

Railway systems, especially for public transport in urban areas, are being transformed to meet the new challenges of increasing urbanization, climate change and other elements that influence public transport. They are asked to provide innovative transport offers, in particular by automating the operation of the railway system, while guaranteeing high efficiency, reliability and strong resilience.

For the densest urban areas, companies in charge of railway system operation in France target the highest level of automation, i.e. level GoA4 (Unattended Train Operation - UTO) [1]. This implies that:

– There is no driver or attendant required on board the rolling stock (train) for normal operation.
– The rolling stock does not require a control cabin: a hosting panel is deemed sufficient for rare manual movements.

© The Author(s), under exclusive license to Springer Nature Switzerland AG 2022
C. Seguin et al. (Eds.): IMBSA 2022, LNCS 13525, pp. 68–82, 2022.
https://doi.org/10.1007/978-3-031-15842-1_6

– The reliability of the system must be high enough to preclude the need for intervention by the rail operator, except in the event of very low probability failures.
– Manual movements of the rolling stock will be limited to maintenance, storage, preparation and uninstallation, or recovery following a significant breakdown.

Public transport companies that automate the operation of their railway system expect many advantages in terms of safety: significance reduction of risks linked to organizational and human factors (for example: Elimination of the harmful effects of driver inattention/distraction), reduce the occurrence of critical accident (to reduce the human damage). One of the main expected gains is delay reduction in order to improve the rail industry public image, to avoid legal proceedings resulting from incidents, to improve wayside working conditions during maintenance, etc.

Modernization of the railway system is accompanied by an increase in the complexity of the control-command systems managing the operation of lines and rolling stock. Thus, risks are taken into account in the design as one of the main concerns. In this situation, the RAMS team is therefore strongly included from the earliest stages of the design process. This major change necessarily implies a profound change in the risk analysis approaches and their collaboration mode with system architect and system engineer teams (intensity of the exchanges and collaborative techniques). Some companies choose to perform a model-based safety analysis/assessment (MBSA) to achieve an accurate representation of the system from a common understanding between system architects and RAMS engineers.

The MBSA, i.e. the use of computerized models to study and analyze RAMS, emphasizes several concepts, in particular:

– A change of approach from "classical formalisms-based" to "system model-based".
– Allows systems to be modeled at a high level of abstraction (closer to system specifications).
– Enable establishing traceability links between all items handled in Risks and RAMS models from beginning to end of the safety process.

It brings many benefits such as better complexity mastering, time savings in studies achievement, better discussion support with the design team. However, this change in approach implies a change in "know-how" among RAMS engineers:

– Refocus engineers on their primary technical functions (questioning, analyzing and interpreting).
– Actively participate (jointly with system architects adopting an MBSE approach) in capitalizing, exchanging, comparing, evaluating and sharing architectural views.
– Ensure traceability between the different models and concepts of dependability of the system of interest and with the models and concepts of other engineering disciplines involved in the design.

The purpose of this paper is to present the results of the MBSA approach deployment to assess a railway system: concepts, practices, and useful recommendations to implement in this industrial context. We introduced the context of our project in this section.

Section 2 presents the related works. Section 3 is devoted to the presentation of a simplified case study representing the automatic operation of a railway system. In Sect. 4, we detail the deployment process of the proposed MBSA approach. Then, Sect. 5 describes the tools and methods involved in our approach. Section 6 present AltaRica model and analysis on the case study. Finally, Sect. 7 presents our feedback, the main advantages and the limits of this work. The article ends with a short conclusion and perspectives.

2 Related Works

The context of this work is intended to support railway systems engineering and RAMS team where global views of systems are required and where interplay of different fields is crucial to capture common requirements and architecture definition. It also targets the elaboration of consistent solutions in an incremental and cooperative way. Model based safety analysis (MBSA) is one of the newest modeling approaches that promises to ease the exchange of information between safety engineers and system designers. The idea is to write models in high level modeling formalism, to keep them close to the functional and physical architecture of the system under study. Several modeling languages and tools support the MBSA approach, for instance, AltaRica [2, 3], Figaro [4], SAML [5], HiP-HOPS [6], AADL EMV2 [7], SOPHIA [8]. To apply MBSA approaches in accordance with MBSE (Model Based System Engineering), researchers explored several clues. Two approaches can be found in the literature. The first one tries to incorporate safety properties by extending formalism of system engineering domains. Those techniques are based on properties annotations (profile for SYSML, Error annex for AADL or EAST-ADL). The second approach consists in using two different domain specific modeling languages: the first one dedicated to system architecture, the second one to safety analyses. Consistency analysis between safety and system models is studied in [9] during the MOISE project, model synchronization has been studied [10, 11], models comparison tools, called SmartSync platform, have been developed in [12]. In 2020, the project S2C (system and safety continuity) was launched by IRT System X and IRT Saint Exupery [13]. These approaches may be criticized because they consider a unique system architecture design that will be transformed to a safety model for analysis. Most of the works are strongly tool oriented and not cooperative enough. In the railway field, applications have been done using the MBSA approach using the AltaRica framework, in particular S2ML [14] and ScOLA [15] for the CBTC system. SUN P. also proposes "MBSE for safety of railway critical systems" [16]. In this paper, we focus on the practical application of the MBSA deployment process dedicated to the Global Operating System of automatic metro lines for railway perspective.

3 Automatic Metro Lines System Case Study

To illustrate our work, we consider a simplified example design, taken from [17, 18], of an Operating Global System (GOS) of a public transport company operating collective mobility – bus, metro, trains and trams. A GOS is a safety-critical system designed to cover all functions that contribute to the realization of the transport offer, including all the systems, sub-systems, their interfaces and the human and organizational aspects (operating and maintenance procedures in particular).

The list of systems making up the GOS is as follows: Rolling Stock; Driving Automation; AVM (Audio Visual Means); Supervisory equipment; Data Transmission System; Railway signaling; Energy for traction and for remote control; Track; Platforms; Platforms facades; Infrastructure; Urban integration; External environment; Operation and Maintenance; Evacuation/Access/Fire safety including ventilation; Accessibility (tolls, ticketing, mobile telephony).

Based on this very broad definition, we are considering in this article only a few parts of this system in order to highlight the main features of the GOS. To sum up, the main GOS's objective is to ensure safe circulation of automatics railway systems in all modes and configurations respecting the daily operating program planned (by minimizing delay time).

The GOS case study, shown in Fig. 1, is dedicated to a tree-stations metro line. This system consists of four main interconnected devices: a line control room, a data transmission system allowing communication between all parts of the system, an energy supply and a set of tracks and platforms (itself containing stations, interstations and rolling stock). Figure 1 also depicts the different kinds of interconnections (communication flows in orange, energy flows in yellow and people flow in green). The station is composed of a remote control station, a set of railway signaling, two platforms, a traveler exchange system and sometimes rolling stock on the tracks.

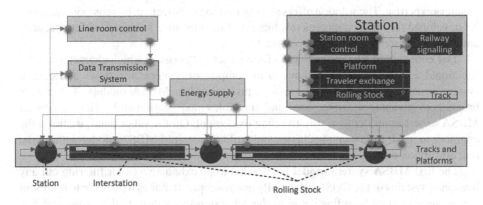

Fig. 1. Illustration of GOS case study.

The energy supply system distributes energy to each part of the GOS that requires it. In particular, rolling stock traction, signaling, control rooms, data transmission network, etc. Orders for the movement of rolling stock, the arrival and departure from the station, the start and end of passenger exchanges, the arrival or departure of rolling stock on the line are orchestrated by the remote control line which communicates to all necessary parts of the GOS system via the Data Transmission system.

4 Methodology of MBSA Deployment

The main objective of our project is to develop a system modeling tool capable of representing the functional and dysfunctional behavior of all systems and subsystems contained in the system of interest. In order to verify and validate the RAMS requirements, RAMS analyses are performed on a unique description of the system.

We have chosen to apply a high-level MBSA approach (also called "smart component" approach [19]) to provide a custom MBSA tool chain consisting of:

- A modeling library of basic railway system components.
- A functional and dysfunctional model of the system of interest built with the previous library of basic components.
- RAMS analyses obtained by system model simulations based on reliability data of system components.

The personalized MBSA tool chain consists of formalizing the dynamic and random behavior of the technical and environmental systems involved in the study of the GOS. The high-level approach makes it possible to build more intuitive models, close to the system architecture and to follow modular development methods using object-oriented concepts. Thus, MBSA tool chains promote readability and maintainability of models, unlike the use of an abstract dynamic modeling formalism (e.g. Markov chains, Petri nets, BDMP, etc.). Moreover, it is also facilitating the capitalization and reuse of business expertise. The solution offers a new valuation perspective, by reuse system models developed for others concerns (evaluation of maintenance strategies, safety/security analysis, integrated logistics support, etc.).

The component library enables defining a set of "classes" which characterizes the functional and dysfunctional behaviors of components, interaction flows and certain system structures. These classes are then instantiated in MBSA models. The library brings both advantages. On the one hand, it enables modification and enrichment by an MBSA expert in an iterative way to refine its content. On the other hand, it allows the engineer to use it to instantiate classes and build the desired MBSA model without the risk corruption on the structures or behaviors part of the library.

The first **MBSA system model** is intended to be exhaustive (after filtering out any irrelevant systems of the GOS) and initially macroscopic. It makes it possible to represent the entire system without fine detail of the subsystems (depth n, with $n \in \mathbb{N}^*$ and $n \leq 4$). The MBSA model produced is dynamic, it means that behavior of a component can change according to other components. This means that a component can sometimes switch from a nominal state to emergency or even be requested (solicitation) by certain systems based on the occurrence of events. In addition, MBSA models take into account the technical characteristics of each station and interstation. This degree of precision allows MBSA analyses to take into account the local specificities of a line.

It is worth noting that the delivery of these products (tools, component library, system models) requires a dedicated deployment approach to ensure relevant results for the system operators. The approach shall provide, in particular:

– Collaborative methods enabling to capture system architecture and the detailed behavior of the system (and parts of the systems) to be studied in perfect agreement with all stakeholders.
– Collaborative methods and tools to accurately characterize the model parameters.
– Visualization tools to represent analysis results.
– Intensive training to transmit the know-how to adjust system parameters, to use quantification tools, to enrich/adapt component library or change models.

To that end, we have defined the deployment approach illustrated in Fig. 2.

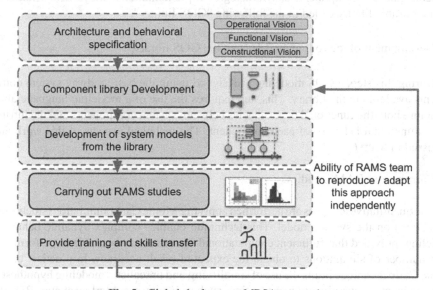

Fig. 2. Global deployment MBSA approach.

Our approach is based on the following steps:

1. Architecture and behavioral specification of the system of interest and matching between system architecture and RAMS architecture.

To design the specification of the MBSA models and the associated component library, we proceed in 3 steps. First, we conduct a collaborative system architecture approach in order to detail the operational, functional and constructional architecture of the studied system. In a second step, the analyses, such as PRA (Preliminary Risk Analysis), FMECA (Failure Mode and Effect Critical Analysis), and objectives (grid of criticality, grid of acceptability) defined from previous RAMS studies are collected. Finally, a cartography of the concepts from system design and RAMS analysis is iteratively built. This allowed us to clearly specify the component library and MBSA model to be developed. In addition, this cartography provides traceability relations between concepts/objects/components taken into account by both system architecture and RAMS domains. It also brings to light which concepts are considered by only one discipline, e.g. interstation lighting system is not taken into account in the RAMS models, failure modes are not dealt with in system architecture.

2. Development of component library.

    This step takes place in two parts:

– first phase of functional and dysfunctional specifications in order to formally describe the behavior of each component as well as its potential interactions.
– second phase of component behavioral logics implementation in the form of a modular and reusable library called in the following "GOS library".

3. Development of metro line models from the GOS library.

    During this step, a GOS modeling is designed using the basic railway system components available in the library. This step requires the use of a modeling language able to capture both the functional dependencies between system components and the intrinsic dysfunctional behavior of each component. The technical aspects of this work are discussed in Sect. 6.

4. Carrying out RAMS studies.

    The quantitative analyses are performed applying Monte Carlo simulation (stochastic simulation) on the system model. This technique enables complex dynamic behavior modeling, provided that sufficient computational resources are available to perform the right number of simulations to obtain the expected result accuracy. In practice, using Monte Carlo technique limits the use of simplifying and unrealistic modeling hypotheses imposed by other quantification approaches, such as Fault trees, Markov chains, BDMP, etc. Finally, the resulting RAMS studies consist of indicator estimations on different system points of interest to assess their reliability (e.g. downtime) and performance (e.g. availability) over time.

5. Provide training and skills transfer to the RAMS team.

    This step deals with the question of knowledge, know-how (skills) and the soft skills (attitudes) acquisition required for RAMS engineers to apply the proposed MBSA approach. In particular, the training addresses the general methodology as well as the use of the various techniques and tools involved in the approach.

5   Proposed and Used Tools and Methods

To deploy the MBSA approach for the GOS system as presented above, we relied on existing methods and tools along with complementary methods and developments. In this section, we detail the methods and tools used and developed for each step of the deployment.

5.1   Architecture and Behavioral Specification

We chose CESAM method [20] to model system architecture. Other methods may be appropriate, but our experience in this method allows us to master the building of system architecture.

To gather previous RAMS results, we study PRA and FMECA analyses achieved at components or subsystems level. Then, several workshops are organized with appropriate RAMS team members to get complementary information.

To build the cartography of the concepts from both system design and RAMS requirements, we define our own template that has been filled iteratively. In practice, we led several collaborative workshops with key players in the project. The template shown in Fig. 3 presents concepts that have been used. On the left, some useful system architecture diagrams are represented. On the right, few results of risk analysis are drawn in tables and diagrams. In the middle part, we build the model specification of the system by using system architecture and RAMS engineering concepts. For each item in the model specification panel (middle part), traceability links are added to indicate their source items (in system architecture or/and RAMS panels). The template, once completed, provides all the required information to define the specifications of the component library while ensuring consistency of modeling hypotheses collected from both system architecture and RAMS teams.

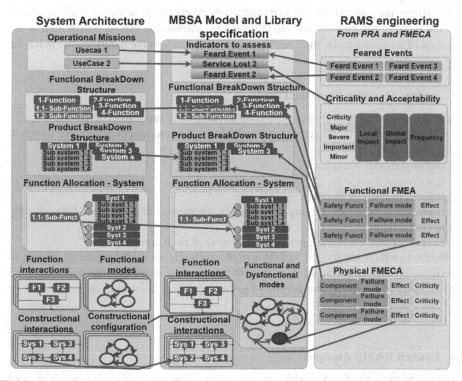

Fig. 3. Example of MBSE/MBSA concept cartography resulting from collaborative workshops.

5.2 GOS Component Library Development

We implemented the component library and system RAMS model using the AltaRica 3.0 modeling language. This language is based on structural concepts: S2ML, particularly well-suited to event-driven, hierarchical, compositional and implicit, reconfigurable and dynamic models; and a behavioral description language: GTS [21] allowing to generalize all the behavioral formalisms used by the industry (Fault trees, State machine, Markov chains, Petri nets, BDMP, etc.). In practice, the AltaRica Wizard [22] tools platform is used to implement classes representing component behavior. These classes consist of:

– State variables: these variables represent the state of the item, e.g. "failure", "reparation", etc.
– Flow variables: these variables represent the state of the physical or abstract flows circulating in the element, e.g. "power supply status", "control command request", etc.
– Transitions: the transitions are rules allowing the state of an element to be modified following an event whose occurrence may be random over time, e.g. if the platform facade system refuses to close, its repair will last on average 10 min during which the control command will be in a state preventing the rolling stock from leaving the platform. In other words, transitions represent the random (often dysfunctional) behavior of an element.
– Assertions: the assertions are deterministic flow propagation rules, e.g. if a flow arrives at the input of the element and the latter is operational, the flow is transmitted at the output of the element. In other words, assertions represent the deterministic behavior of an element.

5.3 System Modeling from the Library

A specific tool (written in Python) has been developed in order to generate the Altarica 3.0 code representing the target system model from the component library and a system configuration file.

The final model contains:

– Instances of each GOS component classes.
– System assertions, representing deterministic functional dependencies between system components.
– Reliability parameters (failure and repair rates) of each component.
– Observers which are special variables used to specify the components of interest to be monitored during simulation in order to estimate the study relevant indicators (e.g. probability of top event, availability of key components over time, etc.).

Figure 4 illustrates the model generation process.

5.4 Launch RAMS Analysis

RAMS studies of the GOS model can be performed with AltaRica Wizard. This tool provides features to configure stochastic simulation: observers to be estimated, number of simulations to be performed, mission time, etc.

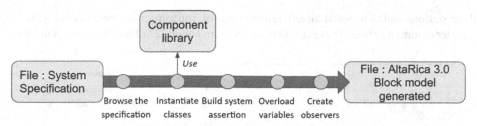

Fig. 4. Generation process of AltaRica model from Component library.

However, to ease study specifications and simulation process, a specific tool (written in Python) has been developed to automatically generate simulator configuration scripts and to post-process simulation raw results. Study results are finally depicted in a graphical dashboard enabling to bring light to relevant key indicators such as reliability, availability, rate of circulation on the line, cumulative delay, downtime, etc.

6 Case Study Analysis

The analyses were performed on a GOS model with the AltaRica Wizard platform. The model represents a generic automatic line composed of three stations and two interstations.

The AltaRica 3.0 model is organized in several files, as well as the AltaRica 3.0 library. The library consists of 9 modules representing sub-systems and dysfunctional behaviors (Travel Information, Energy, Failure Mode, Missions, Stations, Infrastructure, …). We define five AltaRica files as follows:

- Main block. The first module defines the line and remote control, the infrastructures, the energy system, traveler communication, …). It also defines all observers to be analyzed.
- Global parameters. The second module defines all global parameters. For example, it defines the target speed of rolling stock and the length of the line, etc.
- Line architecture. The third module defines stations and interstations, terminus, all sub-systems and associated failure modes.
- Missions. The fourth module defines the different target train frequencies for each period during a day of operation.
- The last module defines all failure rates and repair time parameters for each component of the GOS.

These 5 modules are automatically built by a python script from a data file that capitalize all architecture levels, components lists and all parameters to be defined by using the library.

To illustrate the result of AltaRica model generation, several AltaRica objects are presented: the system block (see Fig. 5), the signaling class (see Fig. 6) and two classes describing failure behaviors (see Fig. 7).

The main block, called "GOS_line_3_GOA4", represent the system GOS model is composed by 6 parts (as illustrated in the Fig. 5): set of missions, line (composed by three stations and two interstations), remote control, infrastructure, system energy, one traveler communication. These sub-systems contain about 227 elementary components.

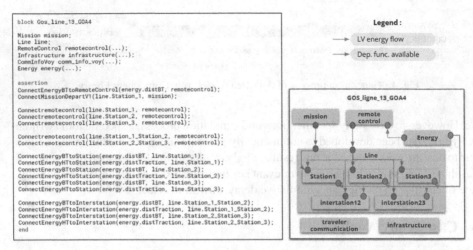

Fig. 5. Generated GOS Main Block Module in AltaRica 3.0.

The signaling AltaRica class is shown in Fig. 6. It contains signal processors and a logical spacing maneuver. It receives information from remote control and energy. This system allows remote control to proceed to the automatic train circulation at each parts of the line.

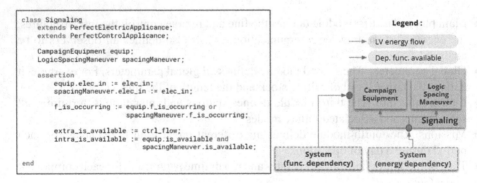

Fig. 6. Signaling system class in GOS library AltaRica 3.0.

For instance, GOS AltaRica library includes 2 kinds of failure modes:

1. The "Failure in-operation" (ATM2StateExp class) that occurs during normal operation when the component is working. For example: railway switch problem, broken track, signaling break, etc.
2. The "Failure on demand" (ATM2StateGammaExp class). For example: - Refusal to leave the station on PLC order, Refusal to close on landing door, etc.

```
class ATM2StateExp                                    class ATM2StateGammaExp
extends ATM2State;                                    extends ATM2State;

parameter Real lambda = 0;                            parameter Real gamma = 0;
Real lambda_t (init = lambda);                        Real gamma_t (init = gamma);
parameter Real mu = 0;                                parameter Real mu = 0;
Real mu_t (init = mu);                                Real mu_t (init = mu);

event ev_true (delay = exponential(lambda_t), expectation = 0);   event ev_true (delay = constant(gamma_t), expectation = 1);
event ev_false (delay = exponential(mu_t));           event ev_false (delay = exponential(mu_t));
event ev_true_reset (delay = Dirac(0), expectation = 0);   event ev_true_reset (delay = Dirac(0), expectation = 0);
event ev_false_reset (delay = Dirac(0), expectation = 0);   event ev_false_reset (delay = Dirac(0), expectation = 0);

assertion                                             assertion
ev_true_spec := lambda_t > 0;                         ev_true_spec := gamma_t > 0;
ev_false_spec := mu_t > 0;                            ev_false_spec := mu_t > 0;
end                                                   end
```

Fig. 7. Failure Mode classes in GOS library AltaRica 3.0.

The GOS model was partially presented. It will now be used to perform stochastic simulations of AltaRica Wizard. This analyzes enable to quantify the reliability, the availability and various performance indicators of the system, such as expected train flows in each station over the mission time. The state of the system and the subsystems are captured by observers in the AltaRica model (it represents the Performance Key Indicators to quantify).

For reasons of confidentiality, failure data and repair times provided here are fictitious. This is why the results presented are illustrative.

We performed 1000 simulations for this example. Indicators are calculated over a period of 19 h (typical operating day) considering an average of 10 trains in operation. The Table 1 shows indicators estimated at functions level and component level. Indicators are defined as follows:

- **failure_occ:** Estimation of the number of intrinsic failures of the function over the period.
- **failure_time:** Estimation of the intrinsic failure time of the function over the period.
- **up_time:** Estimation of the availability time of the function over the period.
- **Avail_intrin:** Estimation of the intrinsic availability of the function over the period.

  Avail_ope: Estimation of the operational availability of the function over the period.

7 Discussion

At our knowledge, the work presented in this paper is the first attempt to deploy a comprehensive high level MBSA methodology relying on the AltaRica 3.0 language in the railway sector at industrial level. In this section, we report on our feedback, difficulties encountered and the unexpected opportunities in the project.

Here are our findings on the organizational and human levels. During the workshops, we noted the following key success factors:

- Sharing common definitions of handled system architecture and RAMS concepts.
- Promote collaborative work during the workshops by organizing practical exercises to get consensus with all stakeholders.

Table 1. Result of stochastic simulation of AltaRica GOS model.

Level		Indicators				
Function	date	failure_occ	failure_time	up_time	Avail intrin.	Avail ope.
Power systems	19	0,0286	0,0043231	18,958	99,977%	99,778%
Manage traveler exchange	19	0,3101	0,102241	18,826	99,462%	99,086%
Ensure the train movement	19	0,0712	0,0650361	18,886	99,658%	99,400%
Guide the train	19	0,0269	0,04122	18,887	99,783%	99,406%
Supervise train movements	19	0,0566	0,0494811	18,913	99,740%	99,542%
Visualize and communicate with travelers	19	0,0021	0,0201613	18,957	99,894%	99,775%
System	date	failure_occ	failure_time	up_time	Avail intrin.	Avail ope.
Energy	19	0,023	0,0003533	18,961	99,998%	99,799%
Traveler transfer system	19	0,307	0,0867923	18,841	99,543%	99,167%
Remote Control	19	0,1241	0,0756468	18,924	99,602%	99,602%
Signaling	19	0,0302	0,0270008	18,935	99,858%	99,659%

– Explain the benefits of collaborative work to people who do not initially grasp the interest. Nevertheless, the choice of the CESAM method was of great help in this work, because it brought a lot of structure to the work accomplished.

Here are our observations on the realization of the technical work. First, the deployment approach brings the both following major benefits to system operators:

– The developed tool chain solution limits user interactions with the code as much as possible. As a consequence, no development skill is required for engineers in charge of performing studies.
– The approach only demands Python and AltaRica 3.0 development skills for the people (in general one person) in charge of library and models maintenance, e.g. to add new component or new behavioral concerns, or to integrate change in system models, etc.

The proposed MBSA methodology brings a RAMS analysis tool capable of analyzing the target system in a comprehensive manner, which consists in a significant practice change for RAMS teams in most industries. Indeed, RAMS teams are used to follow bottom-up approaches, starting from low-level FMEA analyzes and trying to obtain system conclusions with few (often no) collaborations between teams in charge of supervising different part of the systems. Our approach encourages stakeholders to collaborate and share information to build faithful system representations, especially at sub-systems interaction level.

8 Conclusion and Future Works

In this paper, we first describe our proposed MBSA deployment approach for the railway industry. We present a simplified use-case dedicated to automatic railway system modeling. Then, the proposed MBSA deployment process is detailed for the railway use-case, along with the tools and methods involved in this process. Application on case study is presented. Finally, feedbacks, benefits, and limits of our work are given.

The deployment of our approach and the deliveries of the various models and component library make it possible to carry out serene change management for the RAMS team. This step must be accompanied by a training phase, appropriation of the tools and the approach by the engineers. This step must be accompanied by a training phase, appropriation of the tools and the approach by the engineers. We plan to organize training sessions in 2022 or 2023.

After a certain time, the models will become more stable and the development of solutions such as model synchronization [9] will become possible. It will be able to benefit the design team to carry out trade-off studies on several architectural solutions. It can also be used in operation to study modifications to architecture, configurations, or equipment changes.

Finally, our high-level modeling approach aimed at representing and forecasting the behavior of a complex system as a whole can be leveraged in the digital twins framework. Indeed, one major concern in the digital twin design process deals with system representation and synchronization with the physical system state. Our approach offers an interesting perspective to be explored providing both a formal modeling methodology to represent system behaviors and stochastic analysis tools to predict future system states under uncertainties.

Acknowledgments. Fractus and EdgeMind work on a project to deploy tailor-made MBSA methods and tools dedicated to a railway Global Operating System (GOS) for a GOA4 metro line for a major urban public transport company in France.

References

1. Implications of Increasing Grade of Automation. https://www.apta.com/wp-content/uploads/RC17-Keevill_Dave.pdf. Accessed 24 Apr 2022
2. Point, G., Rauzy, A.: AltaRica: constraint automata as a description language. Eur. J. Autom. Syst. **33**(8–9), 1033–1052 (1999)
3. Prosvirnova, T., Batteux, M., Brameret, P.A., Cherfi, A., Friedlhuber, T., et al.: The AltaRica 3.0 project for model-based safety assessment. In: 4th IFAC Workshop on Dependable Control of Discrete Systems, DCDS 2013, York, UK (2013)
4. Bouissou, B., Bouhadana, H., Bannelier, M., Villatte, N.: Knowledge modelling and reliability processing: presentation of the FIGARO language and associated tools. In: Proceedings of SAFECOMP 1991, Trondheim, Norway (1991)

5. Güdemann, M., Ortmeier, F.: A framework for qualitative and quantitative model-based safety analysis. In: Proceedings of the 12th High Assurance System Engineering Symposium (HASE 2010), pp. 132–141 (2010)
6. Adachi, M., Papadopoulos, Y., Sharvia, S., Parker, D., Tohdo, T.: An approach to optimization of fault tolerant architectures using HiP-HOPS. Softw. Pract. Exper. **41**(11), 1303–1327 (2011)
7. Feiler, P.H., Gluch, D.P., John, J.H.: The architecture analysis & design language (AADL). In: Conference ERTS 2006, Software Engineering Institute, Toulouse, France (2006)
8. Cancila, D., Terrier, F., et al.: SOPHIA: a modeling language for model-based safety engineering. In: ACES-MB@MoDELS 2009 Workshop Proceedings, Denver, USA (2009)
9. Prosvirnova, T., Saez, E., Seguin, C., Virelizier, P.: Handling consistency between safety and system models. In: Bozzano, M., Papadopoulos, Y. (eds.) IMBSA 2017. LNCS, vol. 10437, pp. 19–34. Springer, Cham (2017). https://doi.org/10.1007/978-3-319-64119-5_2
10. Legendre, A., Lanusse, A., Rauzy, A.: Toward model synchronization between safety analysis and system architecture design in industrial contexts. In: Bozzano, M., Papadopoulos, Y. (eds.) IMBSA 2017. LNCS, vol. 10437, pp. 35–49. Springer, Cham (2017). https://doi.org/10.1007/978-3-319-64119-5_3
11. Batteux, M., et al.: Synchronization of system architecture, multi-physics and safety models. In: Boy, G.A., Guegan, A., Krob, D., Vion, V. (eds.) CSDM 2019, pp. 37–48. Springer, Cham (2020). https://doi.org/10.1007/978-3-030-34843-4_4
12. Batteux, M., Choley, J.Y., Mhenni, F., Prosvirnova, T., Rauzy, A.: Synchronization of system architecture and safety models: a proof of concept. In: IEEE International Symposium on Systems Engineering, ISSE 2019, Edinbourg, UK (2019). hal-02357379
13. Validation des architectures de Système via les modèles MBSE-MBSA "Intégration des approches MBSE/MBSA pour la prévision, le suivi et l'optimisation des performances de systèmes pendant leur cycle de vie: couplage avec les Data Science". http://afis.community/wp-content/uploads/2019/07/JT-19-06_APSYS_MBSE-MBSA.pdf. Accessed 24 Apr 2022
14. Batteux, M., Prosvirnova, T., Rauzy, A.: System Structure Modeling Language (S2ML) (2015). hal-01234903
15. Issad, M., Kloul, L., Rauzy, A., Berkani, K.: Modeling the CBTC railway system with ScOLA. In: ITS World Congress, Bordeaux, France (2015). https://doi.org/10.1007/s13177-017-0146-2
16. Sun, P.: Model based system engineering for safety of railway critical systems. Automatic. Ecole Centrale de Lille (2015). NNT: 2015ECLI0018. tel-01293395
17. Vauquier, D.: Modeling transportation systems: a case study with the open method Praxeme. In: Aiguier, M., Caseau, Y., Krob, D., Rauzy, A. (eds.) Complex Systems Design & Management, pp. 73–89. Springer, Heidelberg (2013). https://doi.org/10.1007/978-3-642-34404-6_5
18. Zing, C., Iningoue, V.: Methodology for carrying out a RAM study on a complete metro line. In: 22nd Risk Management and Dependability Congress λμ22, Le Havre (2020)
19. Yanar, D.: System structuring for risk analysis using object oriented methodology. In: Proceedings of the Fourth International Conference on Probabilistic Safety Assessment and Management (PSAM IV), New York, vol. 1, pp. 227–232 (1998)
20. Krob, D.: CESAM: CESAMES Systems Architecting Method, A Pocket Guide. CESAM Community, Paris, France (2017)
21. Rauzy, A.: Guarded transition systems: a new states/events formalism for reliability studies. In: Proceedings of the Institution of Mechanical Engineers, Part O-journal of Risk and Reliability, vol. 222 (2008). https://doi.org/10.1243/1748006XJRR177
22. Batteux, M., Prosvirnova, T., Rauzy, A.: AltaRica wizard: an integrated modeling and simulation environment for AltaRica 3.0. In: Congrés Lambda Mu 21 «Maîtrise des risques et transformation numérique: opportunités et menaces», Reims, France, October 2018 (2018)

Plug-and-Produce... Safely!

End-to-End Model-Based Safety Assurance for Reconfigurable Industry 4.0

Daniel Hillen[1]([✉]) [ID], Tom P. Huck[2] [ID], Nishanth Laxman[1] [ID],
Christoph Ledermann[2] [ID], Jan Reich[1] [ID], Patrick Schlosser[2],
Andreas Schmidt[1] [ID], Daniel Schneider[1] [ID], and Denis Uecker[1] [ID]

[1] Fraunhofer Institute for Experimental Software Engineering (IESE),
Kaiserslautern, Germany
{Daniel.Hillen,Nishanth.Laxman,Jan.Reich,Andreas.Schmidt,
Daniel.Schneider,Denis.Uecker}@iese.fraunhofer.de
[2] Karlsruhe Institute of Technology (KIT), Institute for Anthropomatics
and Robotics - Intelligent Process Automation and Robotics Lab (IAR-IPR),
Karlsruhe, Germany
{Tom.Huck,Christoph.Ledermann,Patrick.Schlosser}@kit.edu

Abstract. To enable resilient, innovative, and sustainable industrialization, adopting the Industry 4.0 (I4.0) paradigm is essential, as it enables distributed, reconfigurable production environments. Fast reconfiguration, and hence flexibility, is further achieved by employing human-robot-collaborations—but this poses challenges with respect to human worker safety that currently assumes only static systems. While industrial practice is moving towards service-oriented approaches for the nominal function (producing goods), the safety assurance process is not yet ready for this new world that demands continuous, collaborative, on-demand assurance [21]. In this paper, we present an end-to-end model-based safety assurance lifecycle (using Conditional Safety Certificates [30]) to bring the assurance process closer to the demands of I4.0 and overcome this paradigm mismatch. We give details on the different steps of our approach and provide a worked example for an industrial human-robot-collaboration use case.

Keywords: Safety · Production · Assurance · Collaborative systems

1 Introduction

Industry 4.0 (I4.0) is the fourth industrial revolution that enables distributed and flexible production environments, including on-demand, lot-size-1 manufacturing.This transition from conventional mass-manufacturing involves turning the assembly line into individual work cells—allowing fast reconfiguration.Individualisation is further increased by employing *human-robot-collaboration* (HRC), where humans work alongside robots.However, exploiting the full I4.0 potential is not possible due to unresolved questions regarding

© The Author(s), under exclusive license to Springer Nature Switzerland AG 2022
C. Seguin et al. (Eds.): IMBSA 2022, LNCS 13525, pp. 83–97, 2022.
https://doi.org/10.1007/978-3-031-15842-1_7

human worker safety in a fast changing industrial environment [21].

Broadly speaking, ensuring human worker safety when working with heavy machinery (i.e. robots), typically leads to the following two safety requirements:(1) The employed individual systems and machines must have certified safety functions, if they are potentially dangerous or serve as a safety measure.(2) The composition of systems and machines must reduce the risk of an injury to acceptable levels. This includes proper choice, installation, and configuration.While I4.0 has no impact on fulfilling the first requirement, the second requirement poses a challenge due to frequent reconfiguration.

The Safety-Engineering Process for Robotic Workplaces. According to legal guidelines (e.g. the EU machinery directive [9]), safety assurance is required before commissioning a machine or robotic work cell in a factory. As a basis of this safety assurance processes, a hazard and risk analysis (HARA) is performed. While there are different safety standards and thus, different kinds of HARA, the goal is—generally speaking—the same: To identify potential hazards of a system, to assess the associated risks, and to implement safety measures to mitigate the hazards. As the safety measures themselves can lead to additional hazards, this leads to an iterative process, until all hazards have been mitigated to an acceptable level. This process can be time consuming, and the resulting HARA-document is only valid for the exact configuration of machines and systems. Thus, if there is any change to the system, a requalification is necessary. This results in costs for a qualified safety engineer, as well as larger downtimes, making it economically prohibitive and limiting the true potential of I4.0 for cost-efficient small batch size production.

Traditionally, the HARA is mostly based on human reasoning, expert knowledge, and simplistic tools such as checklists [18]. To keep up with the ever-increasing complexity of safety-critical systems, esp. HRC workplaces, several new HARA approaches were proposed. Semi-formal analysis methods support human reasoning through system models and guide words [14,16,26]. Formal verification methods, which analyze a safety-critical system on the basis of mathematical models, can help safety engineers to identify hazards that might arise from unintended system behavior and/or faulty specifications [2]. Finally, simulation-based testing has also been adopted as a method to support hazard analysis by identifying potential failure scenarios before a system is deployed in the real world [7,15,25].

While these methods can help speed up the process of the HARA, they are still only valid for the one fixed system configuration considered in the analysis, and therefore not suitable for systems whose configuration may vary every few days or even during operation. There are methods which can cope with certain, domain-specific kinds of variabilities (e.g. [27]), but there is currently no general solution available to deal with the challenges brought by I4.0.

We propose a change in the safety assurance process regarding the composition of systems and machines: Similar to service-driven manufacturing [32], safety-relevant components shall no longer be treated as specific components, but abstracted by the safety-services they can provide and/or the safety-demands they have. This abstraction will be implemented using so-called *Conditional Safety Certificates* (ConSerts)—a model-based safety engineering approach [30]. The task of the safety engineer will shift to formulate a composition of service-level demands that allows for safe operation when fulfilled (the *integration responsibility* identified in [21]). Consequently, the exchange of devices with comparable capabilities and/or demands will become possible without a full re-qualification, as long as they can fulfill the composition of service-level demands. So whenever a change is made, e.g. a safety laser scanner is substituted, no safety engineer is required to check and verify the safety, but instead, the new (pre-qualified) device itself will tell the system that it is capable of the required safety measure. Furthermore, ConSerts provide support for formulating which runtime properties must be monitored, to ensure safety under changing conditions (note that changing conditions are different from changing collaborations due to reconfiguration).

Contribution and Structure. Our contribution is three-fold: (1) We describe an *End-to-End Safety Assurance Approach* for I4.0 environments. (2) We show how the ConSerts methodology and artifacts are used throughout the approach, including the *Domain Engineering, Derivation from Assurance Case*, and *Runtime Usage*. (3) We show the application of our approach to a HRC use case.

The remainder of the paper is structured as follows: In Sect. 2 we give background and related work. Our use case is described in Sect. 3, followed by details on our I4.0-compatible safety assurance process in Sect. 4. This process is applied to the use case in Sect. 5, before we conclude the paper in Sect. 6.

2   Background and Related Work

Model-Based Safety-Engineering. Due to the core I4.0 concept of establishing distributed value-creation networks (instead of chains), the respective safety engineering should be *modular, on-demand*, and *continuous* [21]. [21] further highlights how responsibility for the safety of the overall production system is distributed among different parties, such as integrators, cloud service providers, as well as the producers of "things". While our paper does not address these challenges directly, we show how an end-to-end assurance process could support in overcoming these challenges.

Furthermore, model-based (safety) engineering is increasingly getting relevant, to which the large body of literature on both *modeling languages in Industry 4.0* (e.g., [5,34]) as well as *model-based safety engineering* [33] is testament. This is in line with an *industrial roadmap for dependable DevOps* [35], enabling *continuous safety engineering* that relies on suitable *modular safety models*. In the paper, we are going to leverage *Assurance Cases* (AC) [11], as well as *Asset Administration Shells* (AAS) [1]. AAS are a tool to support building digital twins. In I4.0, AAS represent assets digitally. Each AAS contains so called Sub-models that represent functionalities and properties of the asset. While ACs are used for various use cases, in this paper we focus on the purposes of a sound argumentation why the system is safe and the derivation of sub-claims, which the system components must fulfill in order to result in a safe system. For AAS, in this paper we focus on their features of *interoperability* (Type I,"passive" AAS) and *executability* (Type III, "pro-active" AAS).

ConSerts. *Conditional Safety Certificates (ConSerts)* [30] have been developed to support the safe integration of systems along the supply chain (e.g. supplier components being integrated into an OEM system), at a deployment site (e.g. integrating devices in a production facility) or even in the field (e.g. cooperative autonomous vehicles or machines). ConSerts are akin to the idea of *Safety Element out of Context* (SEooC), but provide a concrete and comprehensive framework as well as a number of extensions, e.g. for supporting automated and continuous determination of current guarantees in heterarchical system structures.To apply the ConSerts framework in a given domain, it is necessary to first set the stage in terms of defining a service type system including safety properties.Moreover, for utilizing ConSerts at runtime, corresponding evaluation mechanisms either need to be integrated as aspects across participating systems and/or directly in the distribution platform or middleware that is used.Up to now ConSerts have been applied in several domains such as agriculture, automotive, ambient assisted living, medical devices, and production.The ConSert approach uses a metamodel (only informally described here, more details are given in [30]) consisting of various *Elements* that are marked in italics in the following.The coarsest element of our metamodel are *Systems*. In the I4.0 context, this can be devices (e.g. sensors or actuators), installations (e.g. fences), or human actors.Any system can have any number of *ProvidedServices* and/or *RequiredServices*.These elements each have a type that is uniquely defined by the domain. *Guarantees* are part of a provided service, i.e. Guarantees ensure a specific quality of a service.*Demands* are part of required services, i.e. the System requires a matching Guarantee that is capable of fulfilling the demand.In addition to Guarantees/Demands, which are exchanged between systems, a Guarantee of a system can depend on internal conditions. These internal conditions are formalized as *Runtime Evidence*.Finally, a *ConSert Tree* is a success tree, where a *Guarantee* is the root, while *Demands* and *Runtime Evidence* are the leaves.In between, we find logic gates (And and Or).Note that demands and runtime evidence can be shared between ConSert trees of a system, but each guarantee has a unique tree.

HRC and Safety. In general, Human Robot Collaboration (HRC) scenarios can be classified as one of four categories [3]: (1) *Coexistence:* Human and robot do not share a common workspace. (2) *Sequential Cooperation:* Human and Robot share a workspace, but perform tasks one after another. (3) *Parallel Cooperation:* Human and Robot share a workspace and perform tasks at the same time without direct interaction. (4) *Collaboration:* Human and Robot share a workspace and perform tasks with direct interaction.

To ensure human safety in HRC scenarios, there are different approaches, formulated in the standard ISO TS 15066 [20]: (1) *Safety Stop (SS):* The robot has to stop before a human can reach it. (2) *Speed and Separation Monitoring (SSM):* The distance between the robot and human is monitored. The robot has to slow down and finally stop when the distance decreases or has to move away from the human. (3) *Hand Guidance (HG):* Different parameters of the robot are heavily restricted (e.g. maximum force/maximum speed) to allow it being guided by hand. (4) *Power and Force Limiting (PFL):* Measures are taken to limit the maximum force that a robot can exert on the human to enable direct interaction.

Depending on the HRC scenario, only a subset of safety approaches is viable: For example, employing SSM in a collaboration scenario where the human works directly together with the robot is not possible. Independent from the scenario and chosen safety approach, it is necessary that each safety-critical device conforms to Performance Level d (PL d), as legally required by safety standard ISO 10218 [17]. Systems qualified under PL d can cause sever damage to humans while they are exposed to the danger often and/or for longer time periods. In comparison to PL e, the danger of PL d systems can be controlled and prevented, As with any machinery in industrial settings, there is also a safety assessment necessary before commissioning. However, there are no additional regulations for the safety assessment in HRC scenarios, so the process defined by general standard ISO 12100 [18] has to be followed.

Related Work. With respect to *model-based (safety) engineering for I4.0*, we are not the first to propose solutions.SOTER [8] is an architecture (programming framework and a domain-specific language for communication) to do runtime assurance via monitoring, but does not address reconfiguration activities. [8]'s contribution is providing a simplex architecture to provably provide safety of SEooCs (System Elements out of Context), using safeguards. [12] is also on runtime monitoring in I4.0, where AWS IoT infrastructure is used to host safety functions—employing *Metric Temporal Logic*, which is a more powerful approach than the *Boolean Trees* we provide with ConSerts. However, ConSerts are a methodological approach that is closer to the state of practice in safety engineering that relies on a pre-assured fixed set of configurations between which one can switch. [10] is similar in that it leverages more powerful abstractions to model safety requirements—but is farther away from practice. Finally, [22] presents monitor-based oracles to detect certain kinds of faults during operation of a black-box component—which is comparable to our runtime assurance activities. The SmartFactory initiative has published several white papers on safety of modular production processes[1]. Their focus is more on self-awareness

---

[1] https://smartfactory.de/wp-content/uploads/2018/04/SF_WhitePaper_Safety_3-1_DE_XS.pdf
https://smartfactory.de/wp-content/uploads/2019/03/Whitepaper_AG1_englisch_042019.pdf
https://smartfactory.de/wp-content/uploads/2020/12/SF_WhitePaper-082020_EN_PRINT-2.pdf.

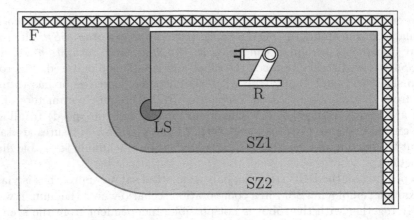

Fig. 1. Schematic bird view of a common HRC robot cell layout. To the top and right, access to the workcell is denied by fence F, preventing humans from reaching the robot R and its workspace (in grey). To the left and bottom, a safety laser scanner LS is used to detect approaching humans, resulting in a slowdown of the robot when safety zone 2 (SZ2) is violated and a full stop of the robot when safety zone 1 (SZ1) is violated. (Color figure online)

with respect to safety (similar to DDIs [28,31]) and not on a safety engineering lifecycle that spans from product conception down to operation. In [6], an ontology-based data management approach is described, which is similar to our domain engineering process—though they focus on control systems IEC 62264-1, while we have safety aspects in mind. Furthermore, they do not consider assurance activities. Formal methods for reconfigurable cyber-physical systems in production are discussed in [13], which provide model-checking and testing-generation approaches for validating systems. [23] proposes a runtime safety analysis approach based on a Safety Analysis Module at Run-time (SAM-RT). This concept is envisioned to perform context-relevant analysis at runtime using different safety-relevant information from integrated machine components and thereby facilitating monitoring of different variables at runtime.

The aforementioned approaches provide benefits for their use cases. However, for our use case, ConSerts are better suited to provide a modular safety concept for reconfigurable and interconnected systems in the I4.0 environment. Additionally, due to the proximity of ConSerts to current safety processes, they can be integrated in an established safety lifecycle naturally.

3   Use Case

For exemplary purposes, we are going to use a simple, yet typical, sequential cooperation HRC application: A robot, that is performing assembly tasks in its own robot cell. The necessary parts are provided by a human worker, who is also responsible for retrieving finished parts and inspecting the robot's work. This makes it necessary for the human to enter the robot's workspace, involving the inherent risk of injury—making a suitable safety concept necessary.

To develop such a safety concept, a risk assessment and mitigation procedure according to ISO 12100 [18] is performed. This includes: (1) Defining limits of the system and its use. (2) Identifying potential hazards. (3) Assessing and evaluating the risks related to those hazards. (4) Defining risk-reduction measures to mitigate unacceptable risks.

On the basis of this procedure, and guided by additional specifications from ISO/TS 15066 [20], an SSM safety strategy (cf. Sect. 2) is chosen. A fence prevents access to the work space from two sides, and the inner gap between fence and robot workspace is small enough so that no human can fit in between. The other two sides are monitored by a safety laser scanner. This monitoring includes setting up safety zones. Their dimensions depend on various factors, like the reaction time of the laser scanner or the stopping time of the robot. If a safety zone gets violated, an appropriate action of the robot (slowdown for outer zones, safety stop for the most inner zone) is triggered (cf. Fig. 1).

As required by ISO 10218 [17], all safety-critical devices and software functions (i.e., laser scanner, robot control functions for safety stop/velocity reduction) need to be safety-rated to performance level d (PLd in ISO 13849 [19]).

The combination of all safety measures must result in an overall safe setting, and the composition of the individual components must be suitable so that the human cannot reach the robot while it is still operating. Before commissioning, these and other properties have to be validated by a safety engineer.

This validation process has the major issue that it is bound to the specific setup. Any change invalidates the previously performed safety analysis, forces a reevaluation, and ultimately leads to a new iteration of the development process—making it incompatible with I4.0 demands. For instance, in some situations, frequent changes of the robot gripper may be necessary. These changes can also alter the safety properties of the robot slightly (e.g., slightly different stopping time due to different payloads), making a whole reevaluation of the workcell necessary despite only minor changes being performed.

4 I4.0-enabled Safety Engineering

Lifecycle. A major promise of I4.0 is to bring *Service Orientation* [4]—a common design paradigm in computing—to industrial manufacturing. Naturally, having a service-oriented nominal function, i.e. creating products, while using a "monolithic" safety assurance approach is bound to cause issues due to paradigm mismatch (cf. Sect. 1). Hence, we first look at the *Safety Lifecycle* we propose (depicted in Fig. 2), which is a derivation of the lifecycle in IEC 61508 [16] and compatible with robotic standards [18,19]. We use the IEC 61508, which is generally considered the mother standard from which most other safety standards are derived. Although we refer to other, more domain-specific standards in our use case, the overall safety engineering approach is comparable.

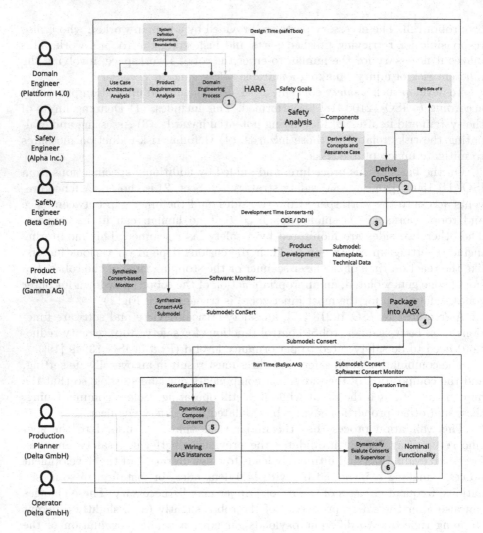

Fig. 2. Our proposed adaptation of the IEC61508 Safety Lifecycle (changes in yellow). (Color figure online)

In Fig. 2, we see that the different development activities are executed by various actors, employed by various organizations—allowing for a truly distributed and decentralized process of safety assurance though maintaining traceability. Within the lifecycle, we distinguish between *Design-*, *Development-* and *Run-Time*. *Design Time* activities beyond the current practice are *Domain Engineering* (1) and the *Derivation of ConSerts* (2). An additional *Development Time* activity is the synthesis of I4.0 compatible models (AAS Submodels [1]) as well as runtime monitors (in container form). Finally, these artifacts are documented/packaged into an AASX file[2]. *Run-Time* is completely different from the current practice: Assembling the production line is done in accordance with I4.0 principles for reconfigurable production. On the safety side, ConSerts of collaborating systems are composed and their conceptual safety is assured at the *Reconfiguration Time*. During operation, the runtime monitor is used to fill the "conditionals" in the ConSerts with runtime information.

Domain Engineering is concerned with finding a common, formalized terminology across the domain (cf. [24]). For I4.0, there are existing ontologies, such as the *Common Data Dictionary* (IEC 61360-2/ISO 13584-42) to foster vendor interoperability. For safety, there is no such ontology yet, but it is mandatory for our approach to work—especially when vendors want to collaboratively build safe systems. We envision vendors of safety devices (e.g. sensors) to formalize their product features (e.g. measurement modes, and integrity levels) and leverage non-safety-specific concepts (e.g. sharing geometry concepts with other tasks such as navigation). While vendors are reluctant to share too much information about their products to protect their intellectual property, we believe that a common understanding for commonly implemented concepts is key to achieve interoperability and fast reconfiguration. In consequence, we think the *Plattform Industrie 4.0* is an organization that is predestined in supporting the creation of such a common terminology—or should help in assembling a *Safe I4.0* initiative.

Assurance Cases and ConSert. The assurance cases are created by having ConSerts in mind such that goals, strategies, and solutions can be mapped to ConSert elements such as guarantees, demands, and runtime evidence. The modularity of ConSerts are represented by different assurance cases, which are referenced through *AwayGoals*. An AwayGoal is used here as a placeholder to reference a suitable assurance case of a subsystem or a component. This modularity enables the integration or modification of subsystems and components without changes to the remaining assurance case. Components or system vendors must provide an assurance case with a top-level goal that is compatible with the AwayGoal and the vendor must be trustworthy. This decreases the effort for changing the system or the system environment, because only a minimal part of the safety argumentation must be checked. These AwayGoals correspond to demands of ConSerts. The demands must be fulfilled to provide a specific guarantee and they specify which guarantees a lower level ConSert must provide. In our assurance cases, the top-level goals correspond to guarantees. While a ConSert can usually provide several guarantees of different qualities, the assurance case will only have one top-level goal. This goal is then parameterized i.e. variables are used to describe the safety goal. Such a goal can then depict these different levels of qualities. Last, solutions of the assurance case are mapped to runtime evidence of the ConSert.

---

[2] https://github.com/admin-shell-io/aasx-package-explorer.

Supporting Safety via Type Systems. Eventually, the question is why our approach assures the safety of the collaborating systems. *Domain Engineering* is one measure to ensure that systems have the same understanding of the world. The *Composition Process* ensures that only matching services are combined. Whether a system faithfully implements a service has to be validated by an authority and is out of scope here.

Dimensions are a means to encode the semantics of guarantees and demands. ConSerts support *Binary, Categorical,* and *Numerical* dimensions. While we work with Strings in our example, a *Dimension Type* can be the URL of a matching *Ontology Concept.* Categorical dimensions implement established integrity level frameworks (e.g. Safety Integrity Level (SIL) or Performance Level). Numerical dimensions can also have a *Unit of Measure.* ConSerts ensure that dimensional analysis is carried out and only truly matching guarantees and demands are used. Furthermore, the runtime monitor code requires properly annotating data before insertion, providing a straightforward location to validate adequate handling of units of measure. Additionally, dimensions carry a *Subset Relationship* which defines whether the guarantee's set of covered values (numerical or categorical) should be subset of the demand or the other way round. Finally, ConSerts are provided as Submodels of the AAS [1]—making them compatible with the remaining I4.0 ecosystem.

5   A Worked Example

Now that our generic approach has been described, we apply it to the use case outlined in Sect. 3. In order to keep the description brief, we only provide fragments of the assurance artifacts here and the full artifacts online[3].

While following standards during development is an important strategy to ensure safety for industrial systems, it is also important to argument why these measures are sufficient such that the remaining risk of the system is acceptable—e.g. using ACs [11]. Here, we created first an AC for the overall system which provides a safety argument according to the ISO 12100 [18]. At some point within the AC, a safety goal is created that reflects the technical and control measures mentioned in the ISO 12100. In this branch, the safety goal is to reduce the risk of collisions of the robot arm with a human. As described in Sect. 2, this risk highly depends on the speed of the robot arm, the environment occupation and the reaction time. Reaction time here means the time between perceiving a human until reaching a safe operation mode. Therefore, several environmental and system conditions must be fulfilled during runtime. As a control measure, ConSerts are used to monitor the environment and the system state during runtime and to evaluate safety guarantees. Those guarantees are mapped to the velocity of the robot arm movement as shown in Fig. 3 on the left hand side. At the bottom, one solution specifies that environmental occupation service must be provided with a specific time guarantee. This solution can be fulfilled and thus the service could be provided by a workspace ConSert. This service must be

---

[3] https://gitlab.cc-asp.fraunhofer.de/schmidt2/plug-and-produce-safe.

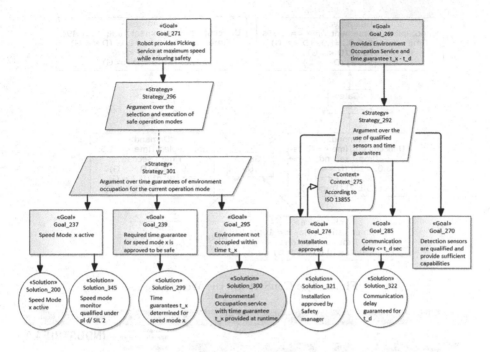

Fig. 3. Fragments of the Robot (left) and Workspace (right) Assurance Cases

reliable and fulfill certain safety requirements itself. In Fig. 3, on the right hand side, the workspace safety argumentation is visualized. When composing both ACs, the solution could be changed into an AwayGoal to formally connect both ACs. Here, a solution was chosen to enable modularity. A specific workspace has its own AC that addresses all safety-related requirements. If the workspace changes, then only the workspace AC must be changed accordingly. The new AC can then be integrated and linked to the Robot AC. Finally, our approach results in a ConSert model (cf. Fig. 4), which is then used to automatically generate a ConSerts *AAS Submodel* (cf. Fig. 5) and the *Run-Time Monitor* (cf. [29]). In the AC (Fig. 3) the top level goal (Goal_269) ensures a variable time guarantee for the environment to be unoccupied. Within the ConSert (Fig. 4) this variability is represented through two different guarantees. Here, the guarantee ensures a time in seconds that is required by a human, who is moving with less than $3m/s$, to reach the robot. The left hand guarantee in Fig. 4 therefore provides a higher quality guarantee. Runtime evidence and demands can be tracked to solutions in the AC similarly.

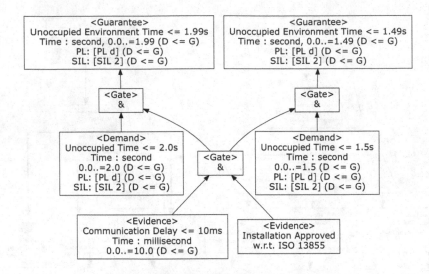

Fig. 4. The ConSert for the Workspace

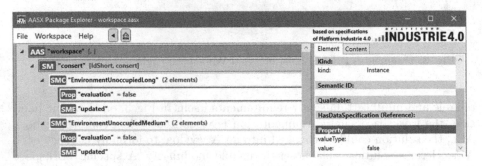

Fig. 5. The automatically generated AAS Submodel in AASX Package Explorer.

Discussion. As introduced in Sect. 4, modular service-oriented I4.0 also requires a corresponding modular safety approach that covers the design, development, and runtime phases. In the design time, modular safety arguments can be created in the way presented by means of assurance cases. An important prerequisite, however, is a formalized function type system that describes functions, data, and safety properties for the overall system in a uniform semantic way. In addition, different variants must be thought through in advance and created as an AC, if they are to be available later as options. All development-time activities, which include the creation of synthesized AAS submodels, runtime monitors, and packaging, are subject to the process requirements of the corresponding safety standards and must pass through the entire safety lifecycle. At runtime, many aspects can be checked automatically, such as configuration and current values. Our approach can especially help to accelerate the approval processes through automation. However, some processes cannot be automated and acceptance by a safety engineer is still required. This concerns, for example, the inspection of structural conditions as well as the correct installation of the system. In turn, the confirmation of the correct approval can be stored digitally and the system can only be put into operation if the approval is given. Nevertheless, this presupposes that it is taken into account and intended during the creation of the assurance case and the transfer to ConSerts. An evaluation at runtime requires a safe exchange of the safety property information between communication partners, which must be guaranteed by a suitable communication channel. There are also safety requirements for the entire runtime environment, which consists of software and hardware for operating the system. This applies in particular to ensuring the integrity of data, compliance with timing requirements, the detection of errors, and the development process of the hard- and software itself.

6 Conclusion

In this paper, we presented an end-to-end model-based safety assurance process for reconfigurable Industry 4.0 environments. We describe how our approach combines *Assurance Cases, Conditional Safety Certificates* as well as *Asset Administration Shells* to support engineers throughout the safety engineering lifecycle from design-time safety activities over product development to operation in the factory. We showcase the usage of our approach for an industrial human-robot collaboration use case, where we create an assurance for the modular and reconfigurable system. In future work, we plan to partner with industry and apply this approach to real-world case studies. Furthermore, we will investigate ways to overcome the issues we have outlined in Sect. 5.

Acknowledgment. The German Federal Ministry for Economic Affairs and Climate Action (BMWK) supported this work within the research project "FabOS" under grant 01MK20010A.

References

1. Details of the asset administration shell - part 1. https://www.plattform-i40.de/PI40/Redaktion/DE/Downloads/Publikation/Details_of_the_Asset_Administration_Shell_Part1_V3.html
2. Askarpour, M., Mandrioli, D., Rossi, M., Vicentini, F.: SAFER-HRC: safety analysis through formal vERification in human-robot collaboration. In: Skavhaug, A., Guiochet, J., Bitsch, F. (eds.) SAFECOMP 2016. LNCS, vol. 9922, pp. 283–295. Springer, Cham (2016). https://doi.org/10.1007/978-3-319-45477-1_22
3. Behrens, R.: Biomechanische Grenzwerte für die sichere Mensch-Roboter-Kollaboration. Springer (2019). https://doi.org/10.1007/978-3-658-26996-8
4. Bell, M.: Service-Oriented Modeling: Service Analysis, Design, and Architecture. Wiley, Hoboken (2008)
5. Brauner, P., et al.: A computer science perspective on digital transformation in production. ACM Trans. Internet Things **3**(2), 1–32 (2022). https://doi.org/10.1145/3502265

6. Brecher, C., Buchsbaum, M., Ziegler, F., Storms, S.: Ontology-based data management for adaptable safety functions in cyber-physical production systems. Procedia CIRP **104**, 194–199 (2021)
7. Corso, A., Moss, R., Koren, M., Lee, R., Kochenderfer, M.: A survey of algorithms for black-box safety validation of cyber-physical systems. J. Artif. Intell. Res. **72**, 377–428 (2021)
8. Desai, A., Ghosh, S., Seshia, S.A., Shankar, N., Tiwari, A.: SOTER: a runtime assurance framework for programming safe robotics systems. In: 49th International Conference on Dependable Systems and Networks (DSN), pp. 138–150 (2019)
9. EU: Directive 2006/42/ec of the European parliament and of the council of 17 May 2006 on machinery, and amending directive 95/16/ec (recast) (2006)
10. Göbe, F., Ney, O., Kowalewski, S.: Reusability and modularity of safety specifications for supervisory control. In: 21st International Conference on Emerging Technologies and Factory Automation (ETFA), pp. 1–8 (2016)
11. Graydon, P.J.: The many conflicting visions of 'safety case'. In: 47th International Conference on Dependable Systems and Networks Workshops (DSN-W) (2017)
12. Grochowski, M., Kowalewski, S., Buchsbaum, M., Brecher, C.: Applying runtime monitoring to the industrial internet of things. In: 24th International Conference on Emerging Technologies and Factory Automation (ETFA), pp. 348–355 (2019)
13. Grochowski, M., et al.: Formale Methoden für rekonfigurierbare cyber-physische Systeme in der Produktion. Autom.-Tech. **68**(1), 3–14 (2020)
14. Guiochet, J.: Hazard analysis of human-robot interactions with HAZOP-UML. Saf. Sci. **84**, 225–237 (2016)
15. Huck, T.P., Ledermann, C., Kröger, T.: Testing robot system safety by creating hazardous human worker behavior in simulation. IEEE Robot. Autom. Lett. **7**(2), 770–777 (2021)
16. International Electrotechnical Commission: IEC 61508:2010 - Functional safety of electrical/electronic/programmable electronic safety-related systems (2010)
17. International Organization for Standardization: ISO 10218:2011 - Robots and robotic devices - Safety requirements for industrial robots (2011)
18. International Organization for Standardization: ISO 12100:2011 Safety of machinery - General principles for design - Risk assessment and risk reduction (2011)
19. International Organization for Standardization (ISO): ISO 13849:2015 - Safety of machinery - Safety-related parts of control systems (2015)
20. International Organization for Standardization (ISO): ISO/TS 15066:2016 - Robots and robotic devices - Collaborative robots (2016)
21. Jaradat, O., Sljivo, I., Habli, I., Hawkins, R.: Challenges of safety assurance for industry 4.0. In: 13th European Dependable Computing Conference (EDCC) (2017)
22. Kane, A., Fuhrman, T., Koopman, P.: Monitor based oracles for cyber-physical system testing: practical experience report. In: 44th International Conference on Dependable Systems and Networks, pp. 148–155 (2014)
23. Koo, C., Laxman, N., Möhrle, F.: Runtime safety analysis for reconfigurable production systems. In: 30th European Safety and Reliability Conference (ESREL) (2020)
24. Kretschmer, F., Lechler, A., Verl, A.: Gelbe Seiten für Industrie 4.0 - Aufbrechen statischer Produktionsstrukturen mittels eines übergeordneten Verzeichnisdienstes, pp. 109–110. AUTOMATION 2016: 17. Branchentreff der Mess- und Automatisierungstechnik, VDI Verlag, Düsseldorf, 1 edn. (31012022 2016)
25. Lesage, B.M.J.R., Alexander, R.: SASSI: safety analysis using simulation-based situation coverage for Cobot systems. In: SafeCOMP (2021)

26. Leveson, N.: Engineering a Safer World. MIT Press, Cambridge (2011)

27. Rathmair, M., et al.: Formal verification of safety properties of collaborative robotic applications including variability. In: 30th International Conference on Robot & Human Interactive Communication (RO-MAN), pp. 1283–1288 (2021)

28. Reich, J., Zeller, M., Schneider, D.: Automated evidence analysis of safety arguments using digital dependability identities. In: Romanovsky, A., Troubitsyna, E., Bitsch, F. (eds.) SAFECOMP 2019. LNCS, vol. 11698, pp. 254–268. Springer, Cham (2019). https://doi.org/10.1007/978-3-030-26601-1_18

29. Schmidt, A., Reich, J., Sorokos, I.: Live in ConSerts: model-driven runtime safety assurance on microcontrollers, edge, and cloud practical. In: 17th European Dependable Computing Conference (EDCC), pp. 61–66. IEEE (2021)

30. Schneider, D., Trapp, M.: Conditional safety certification of open adaptive systems. ACM Trans. Auton. Adapt. Syst. (TAAS) **8**(2), 1–20 (2013)

31. Schneider, D., Trapp, M., Papadopoulos, Y., Armengaud, E., Zeller, M., Höfig, K.: WAP: digital dependability identities. In: 26th International Symposium on Software Reliability Engineering (ISSRE), pp. 324–329. IEEE (2015)

32. Schnicke, F., Kuhn, T., Antonino, P.O.: Enabling industry 4.0 service-oriented architecture through digital twins. In: Muccini, H., et al. (eds.) ECSA 2020. CCIS, vol. 1269, pp. 490–503. Springer, Cham (2020). https://doi.org/10.1007/978-3-030-59155-7_35

33. Trapp, M.: Assuring functional safety in open systems of systems (2016)

34. Wortmann, A., Barais, O., Combemale, B., Wimmer, M.: Modeling languages in industry 4.0: an extended systematic mapping study. Softw. Syst. Model. **19**(1), 67–94 (2020)

35. Zeller, M., Ratiu, D., Rothfelder, M., Buschmann, F.: An industrial roadmap for continuous delivery of software for safety-critical systems. In: 39th International Conference on Computer Safety, Reliability and Security (SAFECOMP) (2020)

Causal Models and Failure Modeling Strategies

Strategies for Modelling Failure Propagation in Dynamic Systems with AltaRica

Tatiana Prosvirnova[1(✉)], Christel Seguin[1], Christophe Frazza[2],
Michel Batteux[3], Xavier de Bossoreille[4], Frédéric Deschamps[5], Jean Gauthier[6],
and Estelle Saez[7]

[1] ONERA/DTIS, Université de Toulouse, Toulouse, France
{Tatiana.Prosvirnova,Christel.Seguin}@onera.fr
[2] SaToDev, 25 rue Marcel Issartier, 33700 Mérignac, France
christophe.frazza@satodev.fr
[3] IRT SystemX, Palaiseau, France
michel.batteux@irt-systemx.fr
[4] APSYS Airbus, 37 Avenue Escadrille Normandie Niemen, 31700 Blagnac, France
xavier.debossoreille@apsys-airbus.com
[5] LGM, Euclide B4 - ZAC St Martin du Touch, 1 Rue Emmanuel Arin,
31300 Toulouse, France
frederic.deschamps@lgm.fr
[6] 5 Dassault Aviation, 54 AV Marcel Dassault, 33700 Mérignac, France
Jean.Gauthier@dassault-aviation.com
[7] IRT Saint-Exupéry, B612, 3 rue Tarfaya, 31405 Toulouse, France
estelle.saez@irt-saintexupery.com

Abstract. The AltaRica modelling language has been designed to facilitate failure propagation modelling and safety analyses of complex technical systems. Indeed, it makes it possible to model the functional dynamics (change of control mode, reconfiguration of equipment, etc.) and failures (cascades of failures, hidden failures, etc.) of the systems.

The objective of this article is to provide guides to make the best use of this dynamic modelling capability. We focus on the modelling of potentially problematic dynamic phenomenon - continuous control of a physical process with a feedback loop.

We propose different strategies to model this phenomenon illustrated by a simple example. We discuss the advantages and drawbacks of the proposed solutions.

Keywords: Model Based Safety Assessment · Dynamic systems · Failure propagation models · AltaRica

1 Introduction

The AltaRica language [2] was designed to facilitate failure propagation modelling and safety analyses of complex technical systems. Thus, it makes it possible

Supported by French Institutes of Technology Saint Exupéry and SystemX.

more particularly to model the functional dynamics (change of control mode, reconfiguration of equipment, etc.) and failures (cascades of failures, hidden failures, etc.) of the systems.

The objective of this article is to provide guides to make the best use of this dynamic modelling capability for control systems. The proposed guides were developed by a panel of classical safety and MBSA (Model Based Safety Assessment) experts as part of the S2C (System & Safety Continuity) project of the French Institutes of Technology (FIT) Saint Exupéry and SystemX.

The S2C working group extracted from the participants' MBSA feedback the commonly encountered pitfalls and the modelling strategies adopted to overcome the difficulties. The paper focuses on potentially problematic dynamic phenomenon: continuous control of a physical process with feedback loops.

The modelling guide endeavours to give for this case:

- an example of a very simple system and a failure condition which illustrates the need for modelling;
- the usual modelling errors of this type of system and the resulting malfunctions;
- good modelling practices in the form of AltaRica modelling strategies;
- the results of qualitative analyses (simulations, search for the causes of failure conditions) which provide confidence in the behaviour, modelled according to the strategies;
- the general assumptions under which the modelling strategies are valid.

The modelling of dynamic systems in dependability has mainly been studied to evaluate the usual probabilistic indicators of reliability or safety (see for example [18]). This paper characterises strategies for modelling dynamic systems that also allow the calculation of sequences of events that lead to failure conditions. This type of modelling is in the process of being standardised in aeronautics and the communication also contributes to clarifying the modelling choices made to deal with the aircraft braking system in the future document ED-135 [1].

The remainder of this article is organised as follows. Section 2 describes the case study. Section 3 gives an overview of the related works. Section 4 presents issues raised by failure propagation modelling of systems with control loops and discusses different strategies to solve them. Section 5 concludes this article and gives some perspectives.

2   Case Study Description

In order to illustrate how to deal with failure propagation modelling of systems with control feedback loops, let us consider a simple example illustrated in Fig. 1. In that example, we consider a system composed of an equipment under control and a controller that builds a command from the information provided by a sensor and from the initial order sent, for instance, by an operator. The sensor acquires data of the equipment output and sends it to the controller, which is used to control the equipment. This example is a simplified control loop, and we can easily replace the equipment by a valve or an actuator.

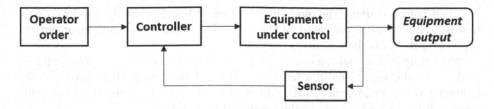

Fig. 1. Case study: an equipment under control.

We consider that all the components (operator order, controller, equipment under control and sensor) have two failure modes:

- fail_loss: leads to the loss of the component;
- fail_err: leads to the erroneous behaviour of the component.

From a safety point of view, the evaluated failure conditions are the following:

- FC1: Loss of equipment output;
- FC2: Erroneous equipment output.

The equipment output is monitored by the sensor that sends its acquired information to the controller. The equipment output depends on the equipment input data. The controller computes a re-evaluated order from its two inputs (the operator order and the sensor acquisition information) and controls the equipment based on the order.

The component failures and the corresponding system output and effects are described in Table 1.

Table 1. Component failure and their safety effects.

Component	Failure mode	Safety effects
Order	fail_loss	Leads to the loss of control and the loss of equipment output
	fail_err	Leads to an erroneous command of the equipment and an erroneous equipment output
Equipment	fail_loss	Leads to the loss of equipment output
	fail_err	Leads to an erroneous equipment output. The erroneous data is acquired by the sensor
Sensor	fail_loss	Leads to the loss of the sensor acquisition sent to the controller leading to the loss of the equipment output
	fail_err	Leads to an erroneous information from the sensor acquisition, leading to an erroneous equipment output

Equipment Output, on Fig. 1, is a safety artefact, an observer of the failure conditions.

To compute the order and to control the equipment, the controller needs the output of the equipment under control sent by the sensor.

Even before starting the modelling, one can identify that the modelled system is a control loop: the input of the controller depends on the sensor output depending itself on the controller output.

Modelling systems with a control loop using classical Fault Tree approach can lead to circular equations in a fault tree. If the fault tree is structured strictly following the dependencies of the different inputs and outputs of the system, there will be a circular logic in the produced fault tree.

In practice, most of the time, the circular equations in fault trees are solved by the analysts, who make assumptions on the behaviour of the system and adapt a modelling strategy to remove the circular equations from the fault tree. Nevertheless, when a circular equation appears in a fault tree, it is always worth analysing the possible impacts of the simplification performed to solve it.

Modelling systems with a control loop using high level modelling languages supporting MBSA (Model-Based Safety Assessment) approach may lead to similar problems. Different strategies to solve them are discussed in the following sections.

3 Related Works

3.1 Static and Dynamic Failure Propagation Models

Failure propagation modelling formalisms can be divided in two categories: combinatorial models (for example, Fault Trees or Reliability Block Diagrams) and discrete-event models (for example, Markov chains or Generalized Stochastic Petri Nets).

Combinatorial models are static models, i.e. all the events are assumed to be independent and may occur in any order. In other words, the order of occurrence of events has no influence on the occurrence of the Failure Conditions. In this case, models are assessed by solving systems of Boolean equations to calculate Minimal Cut Sets (MCS) and probabilistic indicators (for instance, the probability of the Failure Condition). Efficient assessment algorithms have been developed for static models [16], which enable to assess industrial scale models.

Discrete-event models may be static, and in that case the occurrence order of the events has no influence on the resulting state. But it is not always the case. We say that a discrete-event model is dynamic if it exists at least one couple of sequences that are constituted with the same events and result in different states. For dynamic models, the order of occurrence of events is important.

Static discrete-event models can be assessed by generation and solving of Boolean equations. For dynamic discrete-event models, the compilation into Boolean equations is not always possible and may lose information. In that cases, it is possible to generate sequences of events leading to the Failure Conditions. The generation of sequences partially explores the failure scenarios of the model. Note that, the computation time greatly increases compared to the generation of Boolean equations and their assessment.

There are different high-level modelling languages supporting the MBSA approach. Amongst them we can cite AltaRica (AltaRica LaBRI [2], AltaRica DataFlow [7] and AltaRica 3.0 [4]), Figaro [8], SAML [9], HiP-HOPS [12], Component Fault Trees [11], Generalised Stochastic Petri nets with predicates implemented in GRIF [17]. The list is not exhaustive.

Amongst the cited modelling formalisms HiP-HOPS and Components Fault Trees are combinatorial formalisms and enable to create static models. To model failure propagation of systems with control loops using these formalisms the analyst needs to make assumptions on the system behaviour in order to create a static model.

AltaRica, Figaro, SAML and Petri nets are based on discrete-event models and enable to describe static and dynamic models. Continuous control of a physical process with a feedback loop is a dynamic phenomenon. Different strategies can be adopted for failure propagation modelling of systems with control loops. Some of them are presented and discussed using AltaRica DataFlow in the remainder of this article.

3.2   AltaRica Modelling Language

AltaRica is a high level textual formal domain specific modelling language dedicated to Safety Analysis created at the end of nineties [2]. AltaRica is an event-centric language. The behaviour of components is described by means of state machines. The state of a component is represented by variables (the so-called state variables) and their values. The changes of state are possible when, and only when, events occur. The occurrence of an event updates the values of the variables, by the firing of a transition: a triple $<guard, event, action>$, where a guard is a Boolean expression built over the variables and an action is an instruction which modifies the values of state variables. AltaRica distinguishes two types of variables: state variables and flow variables. State variables can be modified only through the firing of transitions. Flow variables are used to model information circulating between nodes of a model. Their values are calculated from the values of state variables thanks to a mechanism described by means of the so-called assertion.

When a transition is fired, first its action is executed to compute the values of state variables, second the assertion is executed to compute the values of flow variables.

The behaviour of components is described inside nodes. Nodes can be assembled into hierarchies, their input and output flows can be connected and their transitions can be synchronised. Nodes can be stored in the libraries of reusable components and are reused by instantiation, like in structured programming languages. AltaRica is an asynchronous language: only one transition can be fired at a time. However, it offers a mechanism to synchronise events. For example, common cause failures, shared repair crews, broadcasts can be represented by means of synchronisations. There are three versions of AltaRica modelling language:

- AltaRica LaBRI, the first version of the language developed by LaBRI [2];
- AltaRica DataFlow, the second version of the language implemented in several industrial tools [7];
- and AltaRica 3.0 implemented in the OpenAltaRica platform by AltaRica Association and IRT SystemX [4].

Acausal and Causal Models. The main difference between the three versions of the language is the semantics of the assertion (calculation of values of flow variables).

In the first version of the language, AltaRica LaBRI, the assertion is a set of constraints. There is no input or output variables and in that way, it is possible to represent acausal models. Each time a transition is fired, first the action of the transition is executed, second a set of constraints (the assertion) is resolved to calculate the values of flow variables. Constraints have a big expressive power. However, in general, solving constraints involves multiple computation iterations and may be very resource consuming. A set of constraints may have several acceptable solutions resulting in non-deterministic model. In addition, there may be no solution. In this case, the initial model is incorrect.

To be able to assess industrial scale models, a second version, AltaRica DataFlow, has been created, reducing the expressive power of the assertion [7]. Its semantics is based on Mode Automata [14]. In this version of the language, the assertion is a set of DataFlow assignments. Each flow variable is assigned only once in the model and there is no circular definition. So, it is only possible to represent causal models. The order of the execution of the DataFlow assignments is calculated only once during the compilation of the model. When a transition is fired, first, the values of state variables are calculated; second, the values of the flow variables are calculated by executing the DataFlow assignments only once, which is more efficient than resolving constraints.

The semantics of the third version of the language, AltaRica 3.0, is defined in terms of Guarded Transition Systems [3]. To be able to model easily some kind of looped systems, for instance networks or electrical systems, AltaRica 3.0 introduces the concept of bidirectional assignment. If x and y are variables, $x :=: y$ is a bidirectional assignment, which is equivalent to two assignments: $x := y$ and $y := x$. The assertion is an instruction, where each variable may be defined in several assignments and there may be circular definitions. After each transition firing, first the action of the transition is executed, second, the values of flow variables are calculated by fixpoint solving of the assertion. In general, fixpoint solving of the assertion is more resource consuming than calculation of DataFlow assignments, but less resource consuming than resolving constraints.

Note that loops encountered in communication networks or electrical systems are different from the feedback control loops introduced in Sect. 2 and fixpoint solving does not resolve the modelling problems. Modelling techniques presented in this article should be used in that case for both AltaRica DataFlow and AltaRica 3.0 modelling languages.

AltaRica DataFlow. In the remainder of this article we focus on AltaRica DataFlow. It is used as a description language of several industrial modelling tools: Cecilia Workshop (Dassault Aviation, Satodev), Simfia V3 and SimfiaNeo (Apsys). Many industrial scale experiments have been conducted with this version of the language [5,6,13]. It has been used to assess the safety of the flight control system in the frame of the certification of the Dassault Aviation Falcon 7X. A set of efficient assessment tools has been developed, including a Fault Tree compiler [14], a generator of critical sequences of events, and a stepwise simulator. The definition of timed and stochastic semantics of AltaRica DataFlow made it possible to develop a compiler to Markov chains [15], a probabilistic model-checker [19] and a Monte Carlo simulator [10].

4 Case Study Modelling and Analysis Using AltaRica DataFlow

4.1 Issues Raised by Failure Propagation Modelling of Systems with Control Feedback Loops

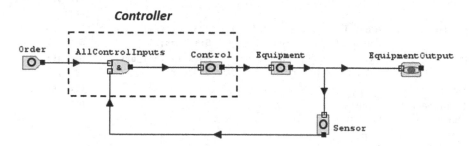

Fig. 2. Graphical representation of the AltaRica DataFlow model of the Case study.

Figure 2 shows a graphical representation of the AltaRica DataFlow model of the case study. The behaviour of each component is represented by an AltaRica node. The node **Sensor** represents the behaviour of the sensor, the node **Order** - the behaviour of the operator order, the node **Equipment** - the behaviour of the equipment under study, nodes **AllControlInputs** and **Control** represents the behaviour of the controller. The node **EquipmentOutput** is a safety artefact, it is an observer on the status of the equipment output and models the Failure Conditions.

The internal state of each node is represented by three values: $\{ok, lost, err\}$, where ok represents the nominal behaviour, $lost$ represents the loss of the component, err represents the erroneous behaviour of the component.

Nodes **Order, Control, Sensor** and **Equipment** have two events **fail_err** and **fail_loss** representing the failure modes of these components.

The node **AllControlInputs** is a logical node, it does not have any internal state. If at least one of the inputs is erroneous, then the output is erroneous. If not, if at least one of the inputs is lost then the output is lost. Otherwise the output is *ok*.

The details of the AltaRica nodes are given in Table 2.

Table 2. AltaRica DataFlow modelling framework.

Component	Input and output flows	State variables	Transitions	Assertions
Order	Input: N/A Output: O Type: $\{ok, lost, err\}$	$S \in \{ok, err, lost\}$ Initially ok.	`S=ok |- fail_loss ->` `S:= lost;` `S=ok |- fail_err ->` `S:= err;`	`O=S;`
AllControl- Inputs	Input: I1, I2 Output: O	N/A	N/A	`O = case{` `I1=err or` `I2=err :` `err,` `I1=lost` `or I2=lost` `:lost, else` `ok};`
Control Sensor Equipment	Input: I Output: O Type: $\{ok, lost, err\}$	$S \in \{ok, err, lost\}$ Initially ok.	`S=ok |- fail_loss ->` `S:= lost;` `S=ok |- fail_err ->` `S:= err;`	`O =case {` `S=ok: I,` `S=lost:` `lost,` `else err};`
Equipment- Output	Input: I Output: O Type: $\{ok, lost, err\}$	N/A	N/A	`O=I;`

The AltaRica DataFlow model given Fig. 2 is not correct because the assertion of this model is not DataFlow.

We say that, there is a cycle of equations in the assertion if there is a flow variable which depends on itself in the assertion. In other words, there is a circular definition in the assertion. In practice, cycles of equations can be detected during a compilation thanks to the dependency graph of the assertion. If the dependency graph of the assertion has cycles, then there is a cycle in the equations of the assertion.

Indeed, in our example there is a cycle in the equations of the assertion, the output of the node **Equipment** depends on itself.

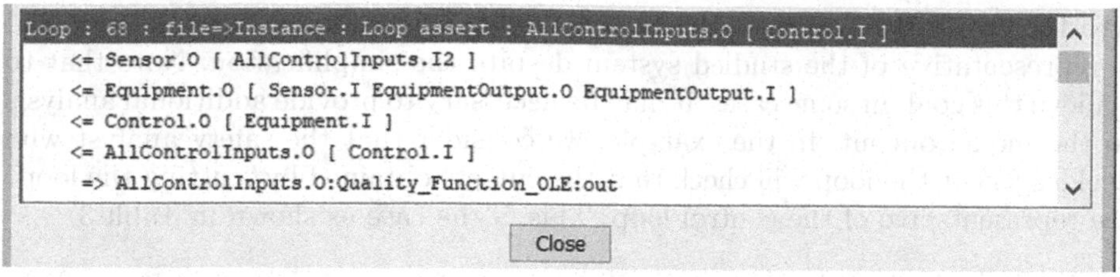

Loop : 68 : file=>Instance : Loop assert : AllControlInputs.O [Control.I]
<= Sensor.O [AllControlInputs.I2]
<= Equipment.O [Sensor.I EquipmentOutput.O EquipmentOutput.I]
<= Control.O [Equipment.I]
<= AllControlInputs.O [Control.I]
=> AllControlInputs.O:Quality_Function_OLE:out
Close

Fig. 3. Example of an error: cycle in the assertion.

During the compilation of the model an error is detected (see for example Fig. 3), that should be corrected. There are different strategies to solve this problem. They are presented below.

4.2 "Cut the Loop" Solution

The simplification or "cut the loop" solution modifies the model in order to solve the equation cycle by "cutting" the control loop in the system, and by ensuring the safety model analysis is still representative of the studied system. Most of the time, it is necessary to add assumptions and explanations in order to achieve this goal. For instance, instead of analysing the control loop illustrated Fig. 1 we can choose to perform the analysis on a model with a simplified control loop as illustrated Fig. 4.

Order
AllControlInputs
&
Control
Equipment
EquipmentOutput
ok
Const_ok
Sensor

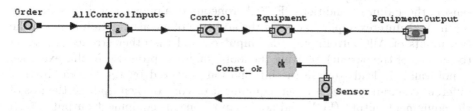

Fig. 4. Illustration of the "cut the loop" solution.

In our example, the existing control loop is "cut" using a safety artefact shown in green in Fig. 4. The purpose of the "Const_ok" node is to use the same Sensor node than the one previously defined. It is a numerical "cap" that sends an "Ok" input to the Sensor. This is equivalent to use a Sensor node with no Input.

The key point in this solution is to ensure that the analysis performed with the simplified model is as representative as the one performed with the complete model.

Model Validation and Analysis. This solution is valid if the simplified model is representative of the studied system despite the simplification. Note that to achieve this goal, in some cases, it may be necessary to provide additional analysis to the model output. In the example, we consider that the safety analyst who decides to cut the loop will check that the cutsets obtained by "cutting the loop" are representative of the control loop. This is the case as shown in Table 3.

Table 3. Cutsets for the "Cut the loop" solution.

Cutsets for FC1: Loss of equipment output	Cutsets for FC2: Erroneous equipment output
Control.fail_loss	Control.fail_err
Order.fail_loss	Order.fail_err
Equipment.fail_loss	Equipment.fail_err
Sensor.fail_loss	Sensor.fail_err

In particular, we check that the Sensor failures (fail_loss and fail_err) lead to the Failure Conditions as it is expected (loss of the Sensor leads to the Loss of equipment output and erroneous Sensor leads to an erroneous equipment output). In addition, the others components' failures effects are unchanged. Indeed, the failures of the order, control or equipment (fail_loss and fail_err) directly lead to the equipment output corresponding failures. In this example, the Sensor State ("ok" or "failed") has a direct effect. In other words, in case of an erroneous sensor, the Failure Conditions "FC2: Erroneous equipment output" is directly reached. Counterexample: In case of the addition of a consolidation between the two inputs of AllControlInputs (one input ok and the other erroneous leading to the loss of the output), "cutting the loop" solution, proposed in this example, is not valid. It leads to lose the information captured by the Sensor. In that different case, an erroneous order, equipment or control then leads to the loss of the equipment output (FC1) and not to an erroneous equipment output (FC2). It is still possible to "Cut the loop" by linking directly the AllControlInputs to the EquipmentOutput and by cutting the loop right before the Control node, nevertheless the resulting model is very far from the initial system.

Advantages and Drawbacks of the Approach. The interest of this approach is to solve the equation cycle in the assertion by using a static modelling. Compared to dynamic modelling, static modelling enables shorter cutset computation time. In addition, it is possible to generate Boolean equations from static models without loss of information. In that case, this modelling choice can allow solving huge industrial scale models. Eventually, in addition, for static models the probabilities computation is straightforward.

Nevertheless, the simplification of the model leads to a model closer to what the safety specialist has in mind (and could write down using Fault Tree Analysis approach) than to the initial system description. Modellers can choose to make the model look like the system, for instance by adding some graphical artefacts or "empty" links. In that case, they introduce an artificial consistency between the safety and the system models that may lead to misunderstandings and future mistakes.

Only the output just before the "loop cut" is affected by all the failure modes. Consequently, this approach is only valid (in terms of resulting cutset) when the control loop has only one output (here **EquipmentOutput**). When the control loop has several outputs (to the FCs or to the other parts of the model) some information may be missing. In our example, if Control output is an input for a monitoring positioned after the sensor, this new node does not see the impact of the failures of equipment. This approach is efficient when the loop can be "cut" before nodes (the sensor here) that only affect the system when they fail (State ok or failed here). Its use is limited when the components are involved in the functional description of the system (for instance in the monitoring).

4.3   The "Dirac" Solution

The "Dirac" solution introduces a safety artefact to handle the equation cycle. It allows the modelling of all dependencies between the output and input flows by introducing a state variable. In order to solve the equation cycle in the example illustrated in Fig. 5, we introduce this safety artefact through the modelling unit named "FeedbackDelay".

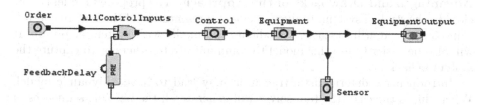

Fig. 5. Illustration of the "Dirac" solution.

The "FeedbackDelay" modelling unit contains:

- A state variable `prev_val` (previous value) that is initially ok;
- Two flow variables: `I` and `O`;
- An assertion: `O = prev_val`;
- An immediate deterministic event called "update", associated with the probability distribution Dirac(0);
- A transition `not (I = prev_val) |- update -> prev_val:=I;`, which allows to remove the direct flow dependency between the output value (`O`) of the node and its input value (`I`) and to introduce a dependency between the input `I` and the state variable `prev_val`.

The defined transition can be read: when the condition (input value I is different from the state value prev_val), the deterministic event update is instantaneously triggered (because it follows a Dirac(0) law). As a result, prev_val is assigned to the current value of I. Because of the assertion the output O takes immediately the same value, resulting in the propagation of the failure mode.

The introduction of a state variable set to "ok" initialises the problem to be solved when no failure is triggered. This solves the equation cycle for the initial state. At this stage it is interesting to note that the state variable introduces a "memory" effect on the transition. Indeed, the state value of prev_val will change only when the transition conditions are fulfilled. This is why the modelling artefact we have presented is often called a "Delay". It does not refer to quantitative time (e.g. measured in second) but to sequential time, i.e., the order in which the different updates happen.

Model Validation and Analysis. The minimal cutsets calculated for the model given in Fig. 5 are the same as the ones obtained for the previous solution given in Table 3.

The "Dirac" solution does not require specific validation, except for the local validation of the dedicated component. The stepwise simulator can be used to validate the model behaviour. In addition, we can also outline that special care shall be taken when several immediate (Dirac(0)) transitions are introduced in the model that can be enabled at the same time.

Advantages and Drawbacks of the Approach. The proposed model is very close to the studied system. It allows a close representation of the system control. Consequently, it will be easier to validate the model with system engineers. It will also be easier to use this model to communicate to others or to capture the system behaviour.

Introducing a deterministic transition may lead to have a dynamic model. When this is the case, the tool solver will generate all the possible sequences of failures leading to the top events while for a static model it would be sufficient to generate all the combinations of failures (i.e. cutsets) or to solve directly a Boolean equation. Consequently, the computation time becomes more important than for a static model. At worst, for very huge industrial scale systems this computation time can be a blocking point. In addition, when there are several deterministic transitions, their synchronisation and priority of triggering need to be handled. This adds complexity to the model.

4.4 The "Double Flow" Solution

The "double flow" solution relies on the addition of artificial flows to deal with the dependencies in the model. As shown in Fig. 6, the dependencies between the variables are modelled through two different paths.

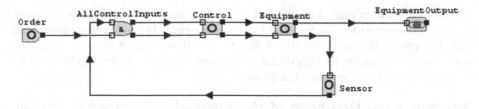

Fig. 6. Illustration of the "double flow" solution.

Firstly, failure modes of all components are "collected" by the flows from Order to Sensor (underneath path). In this underneath path, the output of All-ControlInputs does not depend on the Sensor output. Then, **AllControlInputs** gets a second output. Each **AllControlInputs** output is related to an input (see Table 4).

Table 4. AltaRica DataFlow modelling framework for the "double flow" solution.

Component	Input and output flows	State variables	Transitions	Assertions
AllControl-Inputs	Input: I1, I2 Output: O1, O2	N/A	N/A	O1 = I1; O2 = I2;
Control	Input: I1, I2 Output: O1, O2	$S \in \{ok, err, lost\}$	S=ok |- fail_loss -> S:= lost;	O1 =case { S=ok: I1, S=lost: lost,
	Type: $\{ok, lost, err\}$	Initially ok.	S=ok |- fail_err -> S:= err;	else err}; O2 =case { S=ok: I2, S=lost: lost, else err};
Equipment	Input: I1, I2 Output: O1, O2	$S \in \{ok, err, lost\}$	S=ok |- fail_loss -> S:= lost;	O1 =case { S=ok: I1, S=lost: lost, else err
	Type: $\{ok, lost, err\}$	Initially ok.	S=ok |- fail_err -> S:= err;	O2 =case { S=ok: I2, S=lost: lost, else err};

Model Validation and Analysis. The validation of this approach is the same as the one discussed for the "cut the loop" approach. It is needed to demonstrate that the model is representative of the modelled system. Additional analyses may be required to justify this choice. The cutsets are as expected (the same as given in Table 3) and validate the model outputs.

Advantages and Drawbacks of the Approach. The interest of this approach is to solve the equation cycle using a static modelling. This choice can thus reduce the model computation time. In addition, the probabilities computation is straightforward. This approach is usable in case of control loops with several outputs (when several downstream components depend on the control loop output).

This approach is the one requiring the more safety artefacts, making the model and the justifications heavier. As a consequence, it is mostly used for local loops, with few involved components.

4.5 Summary

We presented three different solutions that can be used to solve an equation cycle in the assertion of AltaRica DataFlow models. All of them have their advantages and drawbacks.

The "Cut the loop" solution is simple and conserves static modelling. But it is not always possible to use and needs additional validation by the analyst.

The "Dirac" solution is always possible. The model can be validated using stepwise simulation. The model in most of the cases is dynamic which may greatly increase computation time for large scale models. In addition, when several immediate transitions are used in the model, this greatly increases the model complexity and its validation.

The "Double flow" solution adds some artificial flows. But the model stays static and conserves the efficiency of calculations. However, additional validation of the model should be provided by the analyst.

5 Conclusion and Perspectives

In this article we presented different strategies that can be used to represent control loops with AltaRica DataFlow modelling language. We show that there is no best solution to solve the problem. All the proposed solutions have their advantages and drawbacks.

Our future works will focus on the identification of other types of modelling problems raised in the domain of dynamic failure propagation modelling and on the definition of modelling strategies for these problems.

References

1. EUROCAE ED-135 guidelines and methods for conducting the safety assessment process on civil airborne systems and equipment

2. Arnold, A., Griffault, A., Point, G., Rauzy, A.: The AltaRica language and its semantics. Fund. Inform. **34**, 109–124 (2000)
3. Batteux, M., Prosvirnova, T., Rauzy, A.: AltaRica 3.0 assertions: the why and the wherefore. J. Risk Reliab. (2017, article accepted)
4. Batteux, M., Prosvirnova, T., Rauzy, A.: AltaRica 3.0 in 10 modeling patterns. Int. J. Crit. Comput.-Based Syst. **9**(1–2), 133–165 (2018). https://doi.org/10.1504/IJCCBS.2019.098809
5. Bernard, R., Aubert, J.J., Bieber, P., Merlini, C., Metge, S.: Experiments in model-based safety analysis: flight controls. In: Faure, J.M. (ed.) Proceedings of IFAC Workshop on Dependable Control of Discrete Systems, Cachan, France, pp. 43–48. Curran Associates Inc. (2007). ISBN 9781617389948
6. Bieber, P., et al.: Integration of formal fault analysis in assert: case studies and lessons learnt. In: Proceedings of 4th European Congress Embedded Real Time Software, ERTS 2008. SIA (Electronic Proceedings), Toulouse, France (2008). Code R-2008-01-2B04
7. Boiteau, M., Dutuit, Y., Rauzy, A., Signoret, J.P.: The AltaRica data-flow language in use: assessment of production availability of a multistates system. Reliab. Eng. Syst. Saf. **91**, 747–755 (2006)
8. Bouissou, M., Bouhadana, H., Bannelier, M., Villatte, N.: Knowledge modelling and reliability processing: presentation of the Figaro modelling language and associated tools. In: Proceedings of Safecomp 1991 (1991)
9. Güdemann, M., Ortmeier, F.: A framework for qualitative and quantitative model-based safety analysis. In: Proceedings of 12th High Assurance System Engineering Symposium, pp. 132–141 (2010)
10. Khuu, M.: Contribution à l'accélération de la simulation stochastique sur des modèles AltaRica Data Flow. Thèse de doctorat, Université de la Méditerranée (Aix-Marseille II) (2008)
11. Mohrle, F., Zeller, M., Hofig, K., Rothfelder, M., Liggesmeyer, P.: Automated compositional safety analysis using component fault trees. In: 2015 IEEE International Symposium on Software Reliability Engineering Workshops (ISSREW), pp. 152–159. IEEE (2015)
12. Papadopoulos, Y., et al.: Engineering failure analysis and design optimization with hip-hops. Eng. Fail. Anal. **18**, 590–608 (2011)
13. Quayzin, X., Arbaretier, E.: Performance modeling of a surveillance mission. In: Proceedings of the Annual Reliability and Maintainability Symposium, RAMS 2009, Fort Worth, Texas, USA, pp. 206–211. IEEE (2009). ISBN 978-1-4244-2508-2
14. Rauzy, A.: Mode automata and their compilation into fault trees. Reliab. Eng. Syst. Saf. **78**, 1–12 (2002)
15. Rauzy, A.: An experimental study on iterative methods to compute transient solutions of large Markov models. Reliab. Eng. Syst. Saf. **86**(1), 105–115 (2004)
16. Rauzy, A.: Probabilistic Safety Analysis with XFTA. AltaRica Association, Les Essarts le Roi, France (2020)
17. Signoret, J.P., Dutuit, Y., Cacheux, P.J., Folleau, C., Collas, S., Thomas, P.: Make your petri nets understandable: reliability block diagrams driven Petri nets. Reliab. Eng. Syst. Saf. **113**, 61–75 (2013). https://doi.org/10.1016/j.ress.2012.12.008
18. Signoret, J.-P., Leroy, A.: Reliability Assessment of Safety and Production Systems. SSRE, Springer, Cham (2021). https://doi.org/10.1007/978-3-030-64708-7
19. Teichteil-Königbuch, F., Infantes, G., Seguin, C.: Epoch probabilistic model-checking. In: Model Based Safety Assessment Workshop, Toulouse, France (2011)

Towards Causal Model-Based Engineering in Automotive System Safety

Robert Maier[✉][iD], Lisa Grabinger[iD], David Urlhart[iD], and Jürgen Mottok[iD]

Regensburg University of Applied Sciences, 93053 Regensburg, Germany
{robert.maier,lisa.grabinger,david.urlhart,
juergen.mottok}@oth-regensburg.de

Abstract. Engineering is based on the understanding of causes and effects. Thus, causality should also guide the safety assessment of complex systems such as autonomous driving cars. To ensure the safety of the intended functionality of these systems, normative regulations like ISO 21448 recommend scenario-based testing. An important task here is to identify critical scenarios, so-called edge and corner cases. Data-driven approaches to this task (e.g. based on machine learning) cannot adequately address a constantly changing operational design domain. Model-based approaches offer a remedy – they allow including different sources of knowledge (e.g. data, human experts) into safety considerations. With this paper, we outline a novel approach for ensuring automotive system safety. We propose to use structural causal models as a probabilistic modelling language to combine knowledge about an open-context environment from different sources. Based on these models, we investigate parameter configurations that are candidates for critical scenarios. In this paper, we first discuss some aspects of scenario-based testing. We then provide an informal introduction to causal models and relate their development lifecycle to the established V-model. Finally, we outline a generic workflow for using causal models to identify critical scenarios and highlight some challenges that arise in the process.

Keywords: SOTIF · Causality · Probabilistic reasoning ·
Model-based engineering · Scenario identification

1 Introduction

"A picture is worth a thousand words", this saying best describes the idea behind Model-based Testing (MBT) [16]. In MBT, it is essential to abstract a system, process, or any other part of reality in a structured and comprehensible manner. This can be achieved with models. They provide a common language for communicating assumptions, relationships, and concepts among experts [5,16]. MBT is assumed to increase both, the efficiency and effectiveness of test case specification, through a high degree of automation. It also benefits from the fact that models can be reused or split into sub-models. This allows to add further levels of detail iteratively while remaining transparent and modular.

C. Seguin et al. (Eds.): IMBSA 2022, LNCS 13525, pp. 116–129, 2022.
https://doi.org/10.1007/978-3-031-15842-1_9

In the automotive industry, the increasing complexity of modern vehicles challenges both, engineers and authorities. One of these challenges is how to ensure system safety. There are standards for managing Functional Safety (FS) [10] or the Safety Of The Intended Functionality (SOTIF) [11], but their application in practice is not trivial. In SOTIF, safety assurance is based upon scenarios. Creating, detecting, or specifying a sufficient set of those scenarios is an active area of research [1,8,13,17–19,26]. The difficulty lies primarily in the open-context environment that comes with real-life situations. A test set of scenarios should include so-called corner and edge cases, critical combinations of environmental and vehicle conditions. Discovering them by chance from real-world test drive data is very unlikely. This creates the need for a new approach to uncover scenarios, which takes multiple sources of knowledge into account.

MBT is very useful for describing and managing test cases during the development of a system. Nevertheless, it is missing some capabilities required for scenario-based approaches. One such capability is being able to reason under uncertainty. Probabilistic reasoning makes it possible to partially compensate for imperfect knowledge about an Operational Design Domain (ODD) by providing likelihoods for a conclusion. Vice versa, statistical learning uses data generated by real systems to build or improve models [22]. Probabilistic reasoning and statistical learning, show that models do not only provide a compact representation of a system. Instead, they also serve to gain valuable insights into a system. Note that, in both cases, human experts are needed to specify goals or provide missing domain knowledge.

An implicit assumption for building most models is causality. Many interactions among random variables encoded in a model can be interpreted as cause-effect pairs. Depending on the use case, these relationships represent triggering conditions or temporal dependencies. If models obey causality, the insights derived from them also become causal. This is crucial in the context of ensuring system safety, where one of the main interests is to gain causal insights, e.g. about causes of malfunctioning behaviour, triggering events, or the nature of influences between system components.

If the relationships in a model are deterministic and stochastic, it can be framed as a Probabilistic Graphical Model (PGM) [12,20]. Throughout many domains, Bayesian Networks (BNs) are the most widely used PGMs. As [3,20] show, BNs can also represent causality and can be linked to a more generic representation called Structural Causal Models (SCMs) [20]. Both approaches are based on sound formalism and an intuitive interpretation of the underlying formal concepts, such as independence among variables.

In this paper, we propose a novel approach for ensuring automotive system safety: causal model-based engineering. We use SCMs to specify an ODD and derive scenario parameters for testing a system according to SOTIF. The paper is structured as follows: we start by reviewing selected contributions to scenario-based testing. Thereby, we take a closer look at problems that arise in the open-context domain of automotive system safety. Next, we focus on the theoretical foundation of our method. We present how causal probabilistic models are built and what constitutes an SCM. With that, we create an intuition for causal model-based engineering in the automotive area. We proceed by discussing several touchpoints of our method with FS and SOTIF and give a high-level view of a modelling process. After outlining a workflow for identifying edge and corner case scenarios, we point out some challenges in implementing our approach in practice. Finally, we conclude with a summary as well as suggestions for future research.

2   Related Work

The development of new techniques for (partial) autonomous driving vehicles has made enormous progress in the last decade. This is attributable mostly to the extensive use of software and, more recently, Machine Learning (ML) methods. It is possible to build a vehicle operating on state-of-the-art technology. To actually deploy such a system, it has to be proven to be functionally safe [10]. As autonomous driving cars face a versatile and constantly changing environment [13], the plain validation of technical requirements is not sufficient. In response, ISO 21448 proposes the concept of desired and predefined intended functionality and advocates scenario-based testing to complement requirements-based testing [11]. This renders the definition of appropriate scenarios a key element for many verification and validation approaches.

2.1   Terminology of Scenarios

Bagschik et al. [2] suggest dividing the level of detail of scenarios into three categories. Functional scenarios describe the objects and environmental conditions considered in a scenario – its parameters. Logical scenarios enhance the semantic definition of these parameters by specifying their potential values. Finally, concrete scenarios constitute a specific instantiation of the parameter space defined by a logical scenario. The particular scenario parameters can be linked to different layers of abstraction as discussed in [1,24,28].

Based on a test objective, scenarios can be further categorized into common, edge, and corner cases [9,14]. The latter two are usually distinguished by their predictability. While edge cases are rare but often known in advance (e.g. boundary values), corner cases depict unforeseen combinations of several parameters with non-extreme values. In the context of SOTIF, it is necessary to consider all three scenario categories. Whereas common scenarios can be easily captured by a test drive or requirements, the specification of edge and corner cases is more challenging.

In practice, scenarios are represented in a suitable data format such as traffic sequence charts [6], ontologies [18], or object-oriented classes [25]. Due to their widespread use in industry, the *ASAM e. V.* standardized exchange formats, OpenDRIVE[1] for managing road networks, and OpenSCENARIO[2] for describing dynamic properties of scenario entities, are of particular interest.

---

[1] https://www.asam.net/standards/detail/opendrive/.
[2] https://www.asam.net/standards/detail/openscenario/.

2.2   Sources of Knowledge

A lot of work in scenario-based testing focuses on ML techniques and available real-life data [4,8,9,26]. These approaches provide promising results, yet they do not meet the challenge of an open-context environment. If the available data are too sparse (in either scope or diversity), edge and corner cases can hardly be detected. Moreover, the identified scenarios may only be valid for existing systems. When new vehicles with different sensors or algorithms are deployed, the available data may become obsolete. In other words: data alone is not sufficient for scenario-based testing.

Neurohr et al. [19] outline, that a reliable safety-case argumentation should involve human experts and data-driven methodologies. Experts are well suited to specify causal relationships between scenario parameters on a qualitative level. These informal descriptions can then be structured using linguistic methods such as ontologies [1]. In contrast, data constitutes an objective source for a reliable, quantitative system parametrization. Sampling, clustering, or counterexample selection among many others are established methods for drawing information from data [23]. As described before, due to a highly complex ODD, recorded data will lack information, which can be provided by experts.

Only by relying on both, data and domain experts, a comprehensive test database can be created. Ideally, these two sources of knowledge should be consulted iteratively. As either semantic frameworks or plain data suffer from including complementary information, a new methodology for describing a large and constantly evolving ODD is needed.

3   Causal Models

All model-based approaches use *some* notation as a common language to convey information about a system. In PGMs, this information consists of a set of random variables, their stochastic information (e.g. probability distribution) as well as their probabilistic relationships graphically represented as nodes and edges [12,20]. PGMs like BNs not only provide a graphical notation, but also define a mathematical framework for making use of the structural information encoded in the model.

3.1   Terminology of Causal Models

The edges in a BN represent relationships of random variables. Thereby, they encode additional information, such as dependencies and (conditional) independencies among model elements. If two random variables are directly connected by an edge, they are dependent. For non-adjacent nodes, the structure of subgraphs (so-called junctions, i.e. chains, forks, and colliders) needs to be considered. The corresponding concept is referred to as d-separation [7]. In short: the random variables in a BN influence each other based on the respective graph topology. If data is consistent with this topology, dependence between random variables found as correlation can also be identified graphically (i.e. d-separation). Any inference (i.e. calculating probabilistic information) in BNs is based on Bayes' rule [12]. Independencies among random variables may simplify inference. Because of the link between graph topology and independencies, the joint probability distribution $P(\mathbf{X})$ entailed by the model may be factorized as a special case of the chain rule of probability as shown in formula 1. The operator pa_i ("parents of the variable x_i") refers to all random variables, which are directly connected to x_i by an edge pointing into x_i in the graph.

$$P(\mathbf{X}) = \prod_i P(x_i | pa_i) \tag{1}$$

BNs can be created by algorithms working on data [27] or by human experts [15]. In the case of algorithmic model creation, the link between (in)dependency assumptions in the data and their interpretation as junctions is exploited (i.e. d-separation).

The graphical representation of a BN is built upon directed edges and represents a Directed Acyclic Graph (DAG). Whereas BNs by definition only model associational relationships [3], they can also be used for modelling cause-effect relations. In this case, the directed edges are given a causal interpretation [20] and their graphical representation is called a causal diagram. Stochastic information linking parent nodes to their children (i.e. the configuration of the parent states affects the resulting conditional distribution of the child node) is then considered as a probabilistic causal mechanism [3,20].

SCMs formalize a causal mechanism between a random variable x_i and its parents pa_i by so-called structural equations $x_i := f_i(pa_i, u_i)$ [3,20]. A formal definition of SCMs can be given as:

Definition 1 (Structural Causal Model (SCM) [20, p. 203]).
A SCM is a triple $M = \langle \boldsymbol{U}, \boldsymbol{V}, \boldsymbol{F} \rangle$ where:

1. *$\mathbf{U}$ is a set of background variables (also called exogenous), that are determined by factors outside the model;*
2. *$\mathbf{V}$ is a set $\{V_1, V_2, ..., V_n\}$ of variables, called endogenous, that are determined by variables in the model – that is, variables in $\mathbf{U} \cup \mathbf{V}$; and*
3. *$\mathbf{F}$ is set of functions $\{f_1, f_2, ..., f_n\}$ such that each f_i is a mapping from (the respective domains of) $U_i \cup PA_i$ to V_i, where $U_i \subseteq \mathbf{U}$ and $PA_i \subseteq \mathbf{V} \setminus V_i$ and the entire set $\mathbf{F}$ forms a mapping form $\mathbf{U}$ to $\mathbf{V}$. In other words, each f_i in $v_i = f_i(pa_i, u_i), \quad i = 1, ..., n$,assigns a value to V_i that depends (on the values of) a selected set of variables in $\mathbf{V} \cup \mathbf{U}$, and the entire set $\mathbf{F}$ has a unique solution $V(u)$.*

Figure 1 exemplary visualizes the graphical notation of a causal diagram: three junctions, an exemplary DAG, and its corresponding representation by structural equations.

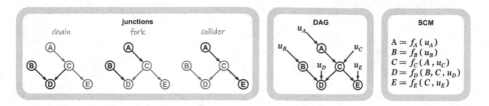

Fig. 1. On the left side, the junctions chain, fork, and collider are depicted. In the middle, an exemplary causal diagram (i.e. a BN structure) is shown including exogenous influences u_i of each random variable. On the right side, this diagram is represented by its structural equations.

3.2   Inference in Causal Models

The probabilistic definition of a system (e.g. by an SCM) together with the causal diagram (implied by this definition) forms a causal model. Causal models define how the probability distributions of random variables change, if causal mechanisms are modified. With that, causal models enable causal reasoning (i.e. estimating causal effects of random variables among each other) [3,20].

Depending on the type of model used (e.g. BN, causal BN, or SCM), different levels of causal expressiveness [3] can be addressed. This is commonly pictured as the "ladder of causation" [21]. The three distinct levels are defined as associational (i.e. insights gathered by "seeing"), interventional (i.e. insights gathered by "doing"), and counterfactual (i.e. insights gathered by "imagining") reasoning. For our application, results gained by counterfactual queries are of great interest. Counterfactual metrics such as the probability of necessity (PN) or the probability of sufficiency (PS) allow distinguishing the *kind* of cause-effect relationship between (non-adjacent) random variables based on a likelihood [20, p. 283].

4   Causal Models and Scenario-Based Testing

In the following, we examine the link between the normative regulations ISO 26262 and ISO 21448, causal models, and scenario-based testing. Moreover, we present a possible approach for deriving corner and edge cases.

4.1   Models in Automotive Safety Engineering

The term *model* can be interpreted differently depending on the context of use. In model-based design, models specify the functional properties of a system and therefore are the central element of a development cycle. In software development, models are often associated with MBT. There, one of the central goals "is to formalize and automate as many activities related to test case specification as possible" [16, p. 2]. In automotive system safety, models are often used to describe the dynamic behaviour of a component (e.g. Markov-Model, Petri Net)

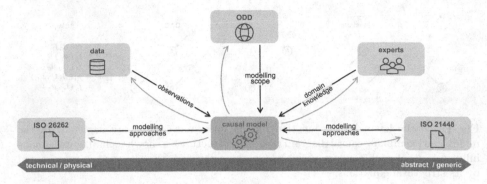

Fig. 2. A causal model interacts with different knowledge bases: data, experts, and normative regulations such as ISO 26262 or ISO 21448. Their modelling approaches and promoted artefacts contribute to building a model of an ODD. On the other hand, the knowledge bases benefit from the causal insights gained through the model.

or a logical connection of events (e.g. Fault Tree Analysis (FTA), Event Tree Analysis (ETA)). Thereby, the focus is on decomposing a complex system or process into tractable components or events and their interactions. Across all areas, models can be viewed as a standardized way of describing a use case. As a common language (i.e. visual representation and/or mathematical specification), they simplify and improve engineering.

While standards like ISO 26262 rely on requirement-based testing and analysis methods such as Hazard Analysis and Risk Assessment (HARA) or Failure modes, effects, and diagnostic analysis (FMEDA), ISO 21448 advocates giving attention specifically to the ODD. Systems are typically designed, developed, and tested with an ODD in mind. Yet, there is no model-based framework for explicitly specifying elements of an ODD and their interactions. Following the considerations in Sect. 2, such a model-based framework should take into account different sources of knowledge and allow for an iterative construction and continuous adaptation of models. Causal models as described in Sect. 3 meet those demands.

Figure 2 visualizes the different knowledge bases that interact with a causal model. These interactions are two-sided. Data, expert knowledge, ODD specifications, and artefacts from standard-encouraged analysis approaches (e.g. results of an FMEDA) can help to build a causal model. A model may then be used as an approximation of an ODD, or provide insights to improve data collection, fault management, or the design of associated systems.

4.2   Development of Causal Models

Causal models follow an iterative development lifecycle [15], as outlined in Fig. 3. This process can be roughly divided into the following steps:

Desired Insight (step 1): The intended use of the causal model is specified.

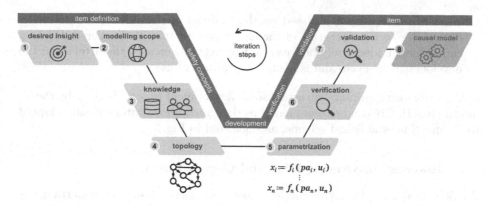

Fig. 3. On a high-level view, the iterative development lifecycle for causal models can be divided into distinct steps. The outlined process can be related to the established V-model (grey envelope) approach as specified by ISO 26262 and ISO 21448.

Modelling Scope (step 2): Depending on the use case, the required expertise of domain experts and potential data sources are identified. Target variables (i.e. effects of interest) are identified.

Knowledge (step 3): Domain experts are introduced to the use case and the basic concepts of causal modelling. This includes organizing an introductory session, creating a first model draft through guided creativity techniques (e.g. brainstorming), and enabling access to relevant data. As mentioned in Sect. 4.1, many artefacts of normative modelling approaches (e.g. results of an FMEDA, HARA, or FTA) might be re-used as sources of knowledge. Already generated insights can speed up the process of causal model creation. Moreover, they allow uncovering gaps in the system and ODD specifications.

Topology (step 4): Relevant random variables, their properties (e.g. value types, units, or ranges), and their relationships with each other are identified. A causal diagram representing this information is created either through expert elicitation, algorithmic approaches [27], or a combination of both.

Parameterization (step 5): The causal diagram is enhanced by the probability distributions of its random variables and by structural equations as a formalization of causal mechanisms. This is done based on either expert knowledge, data, or a combination of both. Since any change in the model topology requires a re-evaluation of the parameters, the causal diagram should be developed as far as possible before starting the current step.

Verification (step 6): The current version of the causal model is tested for internal consistency. This includes checking the (in)dependence assumptions implied by the model against the data and comparing inference estimates to expected results.

Validation (step 7): The current version of the causal model is tested for its fit to the use case. With regard to the intended use, the completeness and level of detail are examined.

Causal Model (step 8): Based on the findings of the verification and validation step, a new iteration of the entire process may be triggered. When a causal model adequately addresses a use case, it becomes the artefact of the development lifecycle and is ready for productive use.

In the automotive industry, an established development process is given by the V-model [10,11]. Creating causal models as described above can be easily adapted to fit into this established scheme, as suggested in Fig. 3.

4.3   Towards Discovering Edge and Corner Cases

As described in Sect. 2, identifying edge and corner cases is important for scenario-based testing. A common approach to find suitable scenario candidates is to use ML methods [9,29]. Due to their data-driven nature, three major problems arise. First, because of an open-context environment, a full description of an ODD is not possible. Second, even with a constrained model, the number of potentially relevant combinations of scenario parameters is intractable. Finally, the available data may not be suited to the use case: for example, real-world test drives carried out by human drivers may encounter critical situations, which are not necessarily relevant for autonomous systems. Those problems already show that purely data-driven methods are not enough to identify edge and corner cases. Instead, different sources of domain knowledge are to be used.

As argued before, SCMs constitute a suitable framework for modelling an ODD from different knowledge sources. Above that, SCMs allow for causal reasoning (e.g. computing counterfactual estimates such as PS and PN) [20]. Recall that those causal metrics can provide information about the causal relationships of random variables in the model. This allows exploring, which random variables (i.e. scenario parameters) influence a variable of interest (i.e. the effect we care about).

Edge or corner cases are not limited to one influencing factor, but can result from a combination of two or more parameters. Moreover, only certain value combinations of contributing parameters may result in a critical scenario. Because of that, we need to consider each configuration of parameters (tuple) in the model. By using causal metrics, all tuples and their respective parameter spaces are evaluated. The resulting hot spots (i.e. local and global extrema) can be interpreted as candidate areas for edge or corner case parameter combinations. Figure 4 builds intuition for the overall process.

To better understand the potential of our approach, suppose we are interested in whether a sensor system can detect an obstacle or not. Based on domain knowledge, we can build a causal model that describes the impact of environmental effects, occlusions, or hardware failure rates on this system. Finding a critical scenario (i.e. detection failed) amounts to finding a configuration of model parameters that causally affect the modelled detection capability.

The presented approach can be framed by the engineering process shown in Fig. 5. The individual steps are defined as follows:

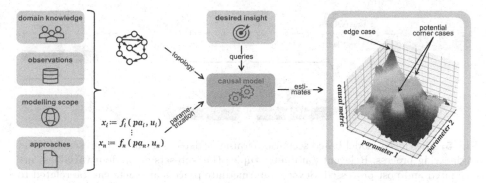

Fig. 4. A fully specified causal model (i.e. an SCM) is queried with regard to a parameter of interest (e.g. ability to detect an obstacle). The estimates of these queries relate to a parameter space for every combination of parameters. Hot spots in these parameter spaces can be interpreted as candidates for edge or corner cases.

Causal Model (step 1): Based on a use case (e.g. investigating detection issues), a relevant part of the related ODD is modelled in an iterative process (see Sect. 4.2) or an already available causal model (i.e. an SCM) is selected.

Target Variable (step 2): According to the present use case, a suitable random variable (i.e. the parameter of interest) is chosen. This random variable will serve as a query target, for which all causal metrics are evaluated.

Tuples (step 3): A sub-set of random variables (i.e. parameter tuple) is chosen based on the causal diagram and the testing scopes. By selecting the parameter combinations to be considered, we implicitly specify functional scenarios. Since an underlying SCM assigns value ranges for the selected parameters, we additionally gain potential logical scenarios [2].

Causal Metrics (step 4): Causal metrics like PN and PS are computed for the selected parameter tuples (i.e. potential causes) with regard to the selected target variable (i.e. effect of interest).

Relevant Tuples (step 5): The evaluated tuples are post-processed. This includes the detection of edge and corner cases (see Fig. 4) as well as the evaluation of the involved parameters in the context of safety (e.g. SOTIF relevance). Critical candidates implicitly describe concrete scenarios, as they represent a specific instantiation of the modelled parameter space.

In the automotive domain, elements of a scenario (as defined by [11]) can be broken down into several layers [2]. Each layer comprises different scenario entities, ranging from road networks to environmental influences. Various exchange formats for automated testing (e.g. [18,25]) build on this decomposition. Ideally, we want to provide scenario parametrizations for use in e.g. simulations. The results obtained with the above methodology must therefore remain compatible with the layer decomposition. This can be achieved by adjusting the modelling scope.

In general, the random variables in a causal model can be specified arbitrarily. Because of that, parameter configurations discovered from causal models can

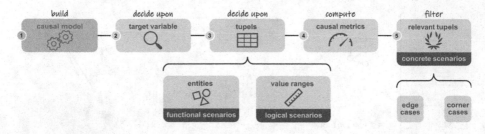

Fig. 5. The causal model-based scenario parameter detection can be represented as an engineering process. Relevant parameter tuples (i.e. sub-sets of random variables) are evaluated and post-processed. Several intermediate process artefacts can be related to functional, logical, or concrete scenarios.

usually not be linked directly to a specific exchange format (e.g. OpenDRIVE or OpenSCENARIO). This is in large part a semantic problem. To solve it, causal models need to be developed with the scenario layer entities in mind.

As exchange formats usually define a set of parameters, it is enough to simply include those defined parameters as required building blocks of the causal model. The parameter configurations resulting from such scenario-centric causal models can then be mapped automatically to a common scenario exchange format.

With that, our approach bridges the gap to model-based testing by providing a model-driven parametrization for executable scenarios (e.g. for simulation). This allows a joint evaluation and verification of a system. Figure 6 depicts the resulting adjustment of the engineering process with a focus on executable scenario exchange formats.

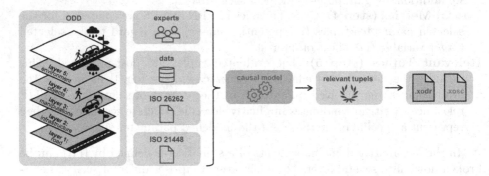

Fig. 6. In the automotive domain, scenario entities can be categorized into several layers [2]. To allow scenario-based testing according to [11], causal models need to include those entities. This allows mapping generated results to established exchange formats, which can then be used for system simulation and verification.

5 Conclusion

Causal models can be used to abstract an ODD. When they are described with probabilistic frameworks like SCMs, causal inference is enabled. Various sources of information (e.g. data, experts) can be jointly used for the creation of causal models, compensating for the limitations of using a sole knowledge source. As the associated development lifecycle can be related to the V-model, causal model-based engineering can be integrated into established industrial processes.

Scenario-based testing is considered an integral part of evaluating SOTIF. Scenarios can be described and abstracted in different ways. Besides the demand to cover a wide range of common situations (e.g. by a scenario database), critical scenarios are of great interest. Discovering such critical scenarios (i.e. edge and corner cases) is non-trivial.

In this paper, we outline an approach for identifying edge and corner cases based on causal models. We propose to use causal metrics such as the probability of necessity or the probability of sufficiency to identify critical parameter configurations. Ideally, discovered candidate tuples can serve as an input for simulation environments. This requires that the causal model itself contains scenario-centric entities. Once these random variables match with the parameters defined in model exchange formats like OpenDRIVE or OpenSCENARIO, an automated mapping of results becomes feasible.

When using causal models, the common problem of test case explosion based on potential parameter combinations remains. Even though concepts like d-separation seem promising to restrict some combinatorics, an evaluation of candidate tuples still suffers from the curse of dimensionality. Furthermore, in our approach, the decision for or against critical candidate scenarios is based on thresholds for causal metrics. The exact definition of these thresholds is an open research topic. Above that, in the context of automotive systems, additional safety considerations (e.g. severity, exposure, controllability, or potential resulting loss) of contributing factors must be taken into account. Additional research is needed to refine the proposed process with regard to these open challenges.

With this paper, we hope to encourage researchers to participate in the development of causal model-based engineering – a methodology where all types of knowledge contribute to a better understanding of safety issues.

Acknowledgment. The present paper is supported by *Bayerisches Staatsministerium für Wirtschaft, Landesentwicklung und Energie* through the granting of the funding project *HolmeS*[3] (FKZ: DIK0173/03). Moreover, we thank Daniel Ebenhöch from *e:fs TechHub GmbH*, Tilo Linz from *imbus AG*, and their respective team members for valuable insights and discussions.

References

1. Bagschik, G., Menzel, T., Maurer, M.: Ontology based scene creation for the development of automated vehicles. In: 2018 IEEE Intelligent Vehicles Symposium (IV), pp. 1813–1820 (2018). https://doi.org/10.1109/IVS.2018.8500632

2. Bagschik, G., Menzel, T., Reschka, A., Maurer, M.: Szenarien für Entwicklung, Absicherung und Test von automatisierten Fahrzeugen. In: 11th Workshop Fahrerassistenzsysteme (Uni-DAS e. V.), pp. 125–135 (2017)
3. Bareinboim, E., Correa, J.D., Ibeling, D., Icard, T.: On Pearl's hierarchy and the foundations of causal inference, 1st edn., pp. 507–556. Association for Computing Machinery, New York (2022). https://doi.org/10.1145/3501714.3501743
4. Bogdoll, D., et al.: Description of corner cases in automated driving: goals and challenges. In: 2021 IEEE/CVF International Conference on Computer Vision Workshops (ICCVW), Montreal, BC, Canada, pp. 1023–1028. IEEE (2021). https://doi.org/10.1109/ICCVW54120.2021.00119
5. Bringmann, E., Kramer, A.: Model-based testing of automotive systems. In: 2008 1st International Conference on Software Testing, Verification, and Validation, pp. 485–493 (2008). https://doi.org/10.1109/ICST.2008.45
6. Damm, W., Kemper, S., Möhlmann, E., Peikenkamp, T., Rakow, A.: Using traffic sequence charts for the development of HAVs. In: European Congress on Embedded Real Time Software and Systems 2018. 9th European Congress on Embedded Real Time Software and Systems (ERTS 2018) (2018). https://hal.archives-ouvertes.fr/hal-01714060
7. Geiger, D., Verma, T., Pearl, J.: d-Separation: from theorems to algorithms. In: Machine Intelligence and Pattern Recognition, vol. 10, pp. 139–148. Elsevier Science Inc. (1990). https://doi.org/10.1016/B978-0-444-88738-2.50018-X
8. de Gelder, E., et al.: Scenario parameter generation method and scenario representativeness metric for scenario-based assessment of automated vehicles. arXiv:2202.12025 [cs] (2022)
9. Heidecker, F., et al.: An application-driven conceptualization of corner cases for perception in highly automated driving. In: 2021 IEEE Intelligent Vehicles Symposium (IV), pp. 644–651 (2021). https://doi.org/10.1109/IV48863.2021.9575933. arXiv:2103.03678
10. ISO Central Secretary: Road vehicles - Functional safety. Standard ISO 26262-2:2018, International Organization for Standardization, Geneva, CH (2018)
11. ISO Central Secretary: Road vehicles - Safety of the intended functionality. Standard ISO 21448:2022, International Organization for Standardization, Geneva, CH (2022)
12. Koller, D., Friedman, N.: Probabilistic Graphical Models: Principles and Techniques. Adaptive Computation and Machine Learning. MIT Press, Cambridge (2009)
13. Koopman, P., Fratrik, F.: How many operational design domains, objects, and events? In: SafeAI@AAAI (2019)
14. Koopman, P., Kane, A., Black, J.: Credible autonomy safety argumentation. In: 27th Safety-Critical Systems Symposium (2019)
15. Korb, K.B., Nicholson, A.E.: Bayesian Artificial Intelligence, 2nd edn. CRC Press Inc., (2010). https://doi.org/10.1201/b10391
16. Kramer, A., Legeard, B.: Model-Based Testing Essentials: Guide to the ISTQB® Certified Model-Based Tester Foundation Level. Wiley, Hoboken (2016). https://doi.org/10.1002/9781119130161
17. Kramer, B., Neurohr, C., Büker, M., Böde, E., Fränzle, M., Damm, W.: Identification and quantification of hazardous scenarios for automated driving. In: Zeller, M., Höfig, K. (eds.) IMBSA 2020. LNCS, vol. 12297, pp. 163–178. Springer, Cham (2020). https://doi.org/10.1007/978-3-030-58920-2_11

18. Menzel, T., Bagschik, G., Isensee, L., Schomburg, A., Maurer, M.: From functional to logical scenarios: detailing a keyword-based scenario description for execution in a simulation environment. In: 2019 IEEE Intelligent Vehicles Symposium (IV), Paris, France, pp. 2383–2390. IEEE (2019). https://doi.org/10.1109/IVS.2019.8814099

19. Neurohr, C., Westhofen, L., Henning, T., de Graaff, T., Möhlmann, E., Böde, E.: Fundamental considerations around scenario-based testing for automated driving. In: 2020 IEEE Intelligent Vehicles Symposium (IV), pp. 121–127 (2020). https://doi.org/10.1109/IV47402.2020.9304823

20. Pearl, J.: Causality: Models, Reasoning and Inference, 2nd edn. Cambridge University Press (2009)

21. Pearl, J., Mackenzie, D.: The Book of Why: The New Science of Cause and Effect, 1st edn. Basic Books Inc. (2018)

22. Peters, J., Janzing, D., Schölkopf, B.: Elements of Causal Inference - Foundations and Learning Algorithms. Adaptive Computation and Machine Learning Series. The MIT Press, Cambridge (2017)

23. Riedmaier, S., Ponn, T., Ludwig, D., Schick, B., Diermeyer, F.: Survey on scenario-based safety assessment of automated vehicles. IEEE Access 8, 87456–87477 (2020). https://doi.org/10.1109/ACCESS.2020.2993730

24. Schuldt, F.: Ein Beitrag für den methodischen Test von automatisierten Fahrfunktionen mit Hilfe von virtuellen Umgebungen, Ph.D. dissertation (2017). https://doi.org/10.24355/dbbs.084-201704241210

25. Steimle, M., Menzel, T., Maurer, M.: Toward a consistent taxonomy for scenario-based development and test approaches for automated vehicles: a proposal for a structuring framework, a basic vocabulary, and its application. IEEE Access 9, 147828–147854 (2021). https://doi.org/10.1109/ACCESS.2021.3123504

26. Steimle, M., Weber, N., Maurer, M.: Toward generating sufficiently valid test case results: a method for systematically assigning test cases to test bench configurations in a scenario-based test approach for automated vehicles. IEEE Access 10, 6260–6285 (2022). https://doi.org/10.1109/ACCESS.2022.3141198

27. Vowels, M.J., Camgöz, N.C., Bowden, R.: D'ya like DAGs? A survey on structure learning and causal discovery. CoRR abs/2103.02582 (2021)

28. Weber, H., et al.: A framework for definition of logical scenarios for safety assurance of automated driving. Traffic Injury Prev. 20(sup1), S65–S70 (2019). https://doi.org/10.1080/15389588.2019.1630827. pMID: 31381437

29. Xinxin, Z., Fei, L., Xiangbin, W.: CSG: critical scenario generation from real traffic accidents. In: 2020 IEEE Intelligent Vehicles Symposium (IV), Las Vegas, NV, USA, pp. 1330–1336. IEEE (2020). https://doi.org/10.1109/IV47402.2020.9304609

Performance Assessment of an Offshore Windmill Farm with AltaRica 3.0

Michel Batteux[1], Tatiana Prosvirnova[2(✉)], and Antoine Rauzy[3]

[1] IRT SystemX, Palaiseau, France
`michel.batteux@irt-systemx.fr`
[2] ONERA/DTIS, Université de Toulouse, Toulouse, France
`tatiana.prosvirnova@onera.fr`
[3] Norwegian University of Science and Technology, Trondheim, Norway
`antoine.rauzy@ntnu.no`

Abstract. In this publication, we present how the AltaRica 3.0 modelling language can be used to efficiently design a model of an offshore windmill farm and evaluate its performance. The system we consider is composed of combinations of series-parallel components, combining different states for components and different modes for parts of the system and implements complex reconfiguration strategies.

Knowing the syntax and semantics of languages such as AltaRica 3.0 is however not sufficient to efficiently design models. First, models should make it possible to efficiently calculate performance indicators. Second, individual models should be designed quickly (and without bugs!) and modelling knowledge should be capitalized from models to models. With both respects, architectural and behavioural modelling patterns are of great help. The AltaRica 3.0 model we propose in this article for the assessment of an offshore windmill farm achieves both goals. We show that the design of the model is very efficient thanks to the advanced structural constructs of the AltaRica 3.0 modelling language. Finally, we use assessment tools available for AltaRica 3.0, e.g. the stochastic simulator, to evaluate the model of the system.

Keywords: AltaRica 3.0 · Offshore windmill farm · Production availability

1 Introduction

In this article we study how to assess the production availability, over a given period of time, of an offshore windmill farm by means of AltaRica 3.0 [6]. Such an industrial production system is composed of several production lines, uses complex reconfiguration and maintenance strategies and so on. Furthermore, on the one hand the power production follows a demand based on houses and industries consumption, which depends on the seasons (spring, winter, autumn, summer) and the different parts of the day (morning, day, evening, night). On the other hand, the power production also depends on the force of the wind.

As of today, AltaRica 3.0 is probably the most advanced modelling language dedicated to probabilistic risk and safety analyses. AltaRica 3.0 results from the combination of a powerful mathematical framework, guarded transition systems, and a versatile and coherent set of model structuring constructs stemmed from object- and prototype-oriented programming, S2ML [5]. Guarded transition systems provide the expressive power required for the analysis of such production systems [3,15].

Knowing the syntax and semantics of languages such as AltaRica 3.0 is however not sufficient to efficiently design models. First, models should make it possible to efficiently calculate performance indicators. What is feasible in reliability engineering is actually over-determined by computational complexity issues, see [17] for an in-depth discussion. Second, individual models should be designed quickly (and without bugs!) and modelling knowledge should be capitalised from models to models. With both respects, architectural and behavioural modelling patterns are of great help. Modelling patterns can be thought as ways of organising the model, in a similar way design patterns are used to organise software, see [12] for a seminal book. The AltaRica 3.0 model we propose in this article achieves both goals.

Thus, in this publication, we show how the AltaRica 3.0 modelling language can be used to efficiently design models of production systems like an offshore windmill farm. The model combines the use of different modelling patterns: multi-state components, maintenance policies with shared resources, reconfiguration of the system taking into account the power demand and so on.

Finally, we use assessment tools available for AltaRica 3.0, e.g. the stochastic simulator [2], to evaluate performance indicators of the system.

The contribution of this publication is thus twofold: first, it shows how to efficiently design AltaRica 3.0 models of production systems; second it demonstrates the interest of AltaRica 3.0 advanced modelling constructs. Furthermore it continues the presentation of "how to model some features with AltaRica 3.0" started with [6] presenting several modelling patterns, [9] presenting a modelling pattern for phased-mission systems, [7] presenting the modelling of maintenance policies, and [8] presenting how to model large scale Markov chains with AltaRica 3.0.

The remainder of this article is organised as follows. Section 2 presents the case study, an offshore windmill farm that we use throughout the publication. Section 3 briefly presents the AltaRica 3.0 modelling language and its assessment tools. Section 4 explains how to model the case study with AltaRica 3.0. Section 5 provides the results of experiments with stochastic simulation. Finally, Sect. 6 concludes the article.

2 Case Study: An Offshore Windmill Farm

In order to illustrate how the AltaRica 3.0 modelling language can be used to efficiently model and assess performance of large scale technical systems, we consider an offshore windmill farm depicted Fig. 1.

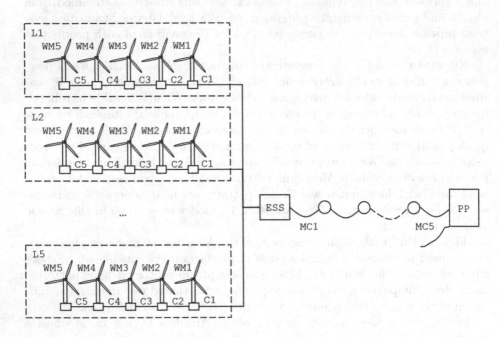

Fig. 1. An offshore windmill farm.

The system producing power is composed of five lines of five wind turbines WM1, WM2, ..., WM5 connected in series by cables C1, C2, ..., C5 to an electrical substation ESS located at sea. The cables connecting the wind turbines to each other and the first wind turbine to the electrical substation ESS may be lost. When a wind turbine is out of service, the power can still be transmitted from the wind turbines located upstream to the substation ESS. If a cable is failed, it isolates the wind turbines located upstream. The substation ESS is itself connected to the power plant PP by a series of five cables, which can be failed.

We assume that the failures of wind turbines and cables follow exponential distributions with a failure rate $\lambda = 10^{-5}$. The wind turbines may fail when they are stopped with a failure rate $\lambda^* = 10^{-6}$.

There is a limited number of repairers. If a repair crew is available, the maintenance starts as soon as a line is failed. The end of the maintenance follows a uniform distribution with two parameters: $\alpha = 12\,h$ (start of the maintenance) and $\beta = 72\,h$ (end of the maintenance).

The power production of the windmill farm depends on the force of the wind and the power production demand. When the wind is too weak or too strong, the wind turbines do not produce power because they must be stopped. Otherwise, the power production depends on the force of the wind (in first approximation, we consider that it is a linear function).

The power production demand depends on the season of the year and the time of the day.

We would like to estimate the power production of the offshore windmill farm over a year and the difference between the power demand and the power production over a year.

3   AltaRica 3.0 Modelling Language and Assessment Tools

AltaRica 3.0 is a high level and stochastic event based modelling language, initially dedicated to the assessment of complex critical systems [6]. The language is based on the mathematical framework GTS (for Guarded Transition Systems [15]- [3]) to describe the behaviour of the system under study. The execution of an AltaRica 3.0 model is quite similar to other event-based formalisms. It means that when a transition is enabled, it is scheduled and will be potentially fired after its associated delay (see [10] and [18] for introductions of such executions of Discrete Event Systems). This behavioural part of AltaRica 3.0, based on GTS, is combined with a structural part named S2ML. S2ML stands for System Structure Modelling Language [5], and gathers in a coherent way structuring constructs stemmed from object-oriented programming, (see, e.g., [1]), and prototype-oriented programming, (see, e.g., [13]).

The AltaRica 3.0 modelling language comes with a versatile set of assessment tools to design and evaluate models:

- The integrated modelling environment AltaRica Wizard [4], which provides the expected functionalities of a code editor and a project management;
- An interactive simulator to simulate, by hand, AltaRica 3.0 models;
- A compiler to fault trees in Open-PSA format [14] and ch10epstein2008psam, this compiler is chained with the fault tree engine XFTA [16];
- A generator of critical sequences of events leading from an initial state to failed states;
- Finally, a stochastic simulator [2].

The design of advanced AltaRica 3.0 models relies on the application of modelling patterns [6]. The pattern-based approach in model-based safety assessment is strongly inspired from the corresponding approach in software engineering [12]. Not only patterns make it possible to avoid the "blank page syndrome", i.e. not to know where and how to start a model, but they unify modelling styles (alleviating maintenance tasks) and they prove to be a very good way to document and to share models.

4   Case Study Modelling and Assessment

Figure 2 shows the global architecture of the model. It is composed of the model of the environment, the model of the technical system under study and the observers.

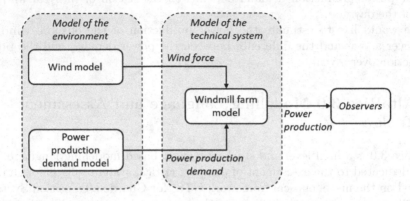

Fig. 2. Model structure diagram of an offshore windmill farm.

Observers are quantities of the model that we would like to evaluate. Basically, in our example it is the power production and the difference between the power demand and the power production.

The model of the environment includes the simplified models of the wind and of the power production demand. The model of the wind provides the wind force to the windmill farm model. The model of the power production demand provides the value of the production demand or need to the technical system.

The model of the technical system includes the model of the windmill farm detailed below. It transmits the value of the power production to the observers.

4.1   Modelling the Technical System

First, we start with modelling of the basic classes representing the behaviour of the wind turbines, the cables and the electrical station. Second, we assemble these classes to create the model of the lines. Finally, we define controllers to implement reconfiguration and maintenance strategies.

AltaRica 3.0 Classes of the Wind Turbines and Cables. We model the behaviour of the wind turbines by a state machine StandbyRepairableUnit represented in Fig. 3a. Stochastic transitions are represented with plain arrows while the deterministic ones, labeled by the events start and stop, are represented with dashed arrows.

The AltaRica 3.0 model of the class StandbyRepairableUnit is given Fig. 4. It first defines a domain UnitState containing four values. It will be used to

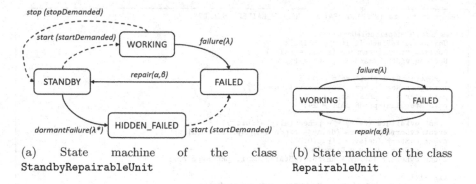

(a)   State   machine   of   the   class   (b) State machine of the class
StandbyRepairableUnit   RepairableUnit

Fig. 3. Behaviour of the generic classes

define the state of a `StandbyRepairableUnit`. Then this class is defined. An AltaRica 3.0 class is an on-the-shelf modelling component that can be instantiated as many times as necessary in the models. This class declares several elements: a state variable `vsState` of type `UnitState`, Boolean flow variables `vfStartDemanded` and `vfStopDemanded`, and several parameters and events. All these elements are used in the transition part to define the behaviour of a `StandbyRepairableUnit`, i.e. the changes of values of the state variable according to the occurrences of the events, as represented in Fig. 3a.

An AltaRica 3.0 transition starts with the name of the event, also called a label, then there is a guard (i.e. a Boolean condition on variables), and finally the action, which is an instruction that changes the value of (some of) the state variables. For example, in Fig. 4, the first transition defines the failure of the component. Its label is the event `evFailure`, which is associated with a delay obeying the inverse of a negative exponential distribution of parameter `pFailure`. To fire this transition the unit state must be working, so the guard imposes that the state variable `vsState` must be equal to the value `WORKING`. Finally, when the transition is fired the unit is failed, and the action sets the state variable `vsState` to the value `FAILED`.

A wind turbine may be started or stopped when it receives an order represented by flow variables `vfStartDemanded` and `vfStopDemanded`. It is modelled by two immediate events `evStart` and `evStop`. The transitions labeled by these events should be fired as soon as the their guards become satisfied.

A wind turbine may also fail when it is in standby mode. It is represented by the event `evDormantFailure`, which is associated with a delay obeying the inverse of a negative exponential distribution of parameter `pDormantFailure`.

A wind turbine may be repaired. The event `evRepair` is associated with a uniform distribution with parameters `pStartRepair` and `pEndRepair`. The values of the parameters can be changed at will while performing experiments with models.

The AltaRica 3.0 model of the class `WindTurbine` is given Fig. 5. It extends the class `StandbyRepairableUnit` and defines other parameters, flow variables

```
domain UnitState {WORKING, FAILED, HIDDEN_FAILED, STANDBY}

class StandbyRepairableUnit
    UnitState vsState (init = WORKING);
    Boolean vfStartDemanded (reset = false);
    Boolean vfStopDemanded (reset = false);

    parameter Real pFailure = 1.0e-5;
    parameter Real pDormantFailure = 1.0e-6;
    parameter Real pStartRepair = 12;
    parameter Real pEndRepair = 24;

    event evFailure (delay = exponential(pFailure));
    event evDormantFailure (delay = exponential(pDormantFailure));
    event evStart (delay = Dirac(0.0));
    event evStop (delay = Dirac(0.0));
    event evRepair (delay = uniform(pStartRepair, pEndRepair));

    transition
        evFailure: vsState == WORKING -> vsState := FAILED;
        evDormantFailure: vsState == STANDBY -> vsState := HIDDEN_FAILED;
        evStart: vsState == STANDBY and vfStartDemanded -> vsState := WORKING;
        evStart: vsState == HIDDEN_FAILED and vfStartDemanded -> vsState := FAILED;
        evStop: vsState == WORKING and vfStopDemanded -> vsState := STANDBY;
        evRepair : vsState == FAILED -> vsState := STANDBY;
end
```

Fig. 4. AltaRica 3.0 class `StandbyRepairableUnit`.

```
class WindTurbine
    extends StandbyRepairableUnit;

    parameter Real pLowProduction = 40.0;
    parameter Real pNormalProduction = 70.0;
    parameter Real pHighProduction = 100.0;

    Real vfProductionOut(reset = 0.0);
    WindForce vfWindForceIn (reset = NULL);

    assertion
        vfProductionOut := if vsState == WORKING then
                           (if (vfWindForceIn == NULL or vfWindForceIn == STORM) then 0.0
                            else if vfWindForceIn == LOW then pLowProduction
                            else if vfWindForceIn == NORMAL then pNormalProduction
                            else pHighProduction) else 0.0;
end
```

Fig. 5. AltaRica 3.0 class `WindTurbine`.

and an assertion. The production of a wind turbine depends on the wind force, which is represented by a flow variable `vfWindForce`. The dependency is expressed in the assertion. An assertion is an instruction which modifies the value of flow variables. It is executed after each transition firing.

The values of parameters (e.g. `pLowProduction`, `pNormalProduction`) are arbitrary. They can be changed while performing experiments with the model.

The behaviour of the cables and the electrical station is represented by a state machine given Fig. 3b. They may be failed and repaired. Their AltaRica 3.0 model is quite similar to the model of the wind turbines given Fig. 5. It uses the same principles: we, first, define a generic class and then a class which extends it, and define its flow variables and its assertion.

Modelling Reconfiguration and Maintenance Strategies. Figure 6 shows the structural diagram of the block `WindmillFarm`. It is composed of 5 lines of wind turbines `Line1, ..., Line5`, an electrical station `ESS`, a series of cables `MC1, ..., MC5` and a global controller `Controller`.

The global controller is used to implement reconfiguration and maintenance strategies. It receives the diagnosis on the state of each line, the power production demand and the production of the lines. Based on these data, it sends the commands to start or to stop the line to the local controllers of each line.

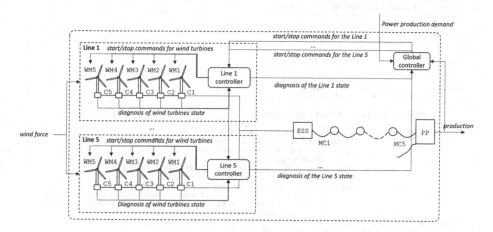

Fig. 6. Structure diagram of the block `WindmillFarm`.

We assume that there is a priority between the lines. The controller always starts with the Line 1, then if the demand is not satisfied, it starts the Line 2, and so on. If the demand gets lower, the controller first stops the Line 5, then the Line 4 and so on in the reverse order.

The global controller also implements the maintenance policy. There is a limited number of repairers. We assume that if a line is failed, and a repairer is available then the maintenance of the line can start immediately. The end of the maintenance is modelled by a uniform distribution with two parameters `pEndMaintenanceTimeMin` equal to 24 h and `pEndMaintenanceTimeMax` equal to 72 h. To implement this maintenance policy we use a modelling pattern presented in [7].

Modelling the Lines. The structure of the AltaRica 3.0 model of the class `Line` is given Fig. 7. Each line is composed of 5 wind turbines, 5 cables and a local controller. Connections between cables and wind turbines are defined in the assertion part. First, each wind turbine WM_i receives the value of the wind force. Second, each wind turbine WM_i is connected to its cable C_i. Finally, the production of the line `vfProductionOut` is calculated taking into account

```
class Line
// System composition
    WindTurbine WM1, WM2, WM3, WM4, WM5 (vsState.init = STANDBY, evRepair.hidden = true);
    Cable C1, C2, C3, C4, C5(evRepair.hidden = true);

// Flow input variables
    WindForce vfWindForceIn (reset = NULL);
    Boolean vfStartDemanded (reset = false);
    Boolean vfStopDemanded (reset = false);

// Flow output variables
    Real vfProductionOut (reset = 0.0);

// Flow output variables for diagnosis
    Integer vfNumberOfWorkingWM (reset = 0);
    Integer vfNumberOfFailedWM (reset = 0);
    Integer vfNumberOfStoppedWM (reset = 0);
    Boolean vfIsFailed (reset = true);

// Controller
    block Controller
// ...
    end

    assertion
// assertions to connect components
    WM1.vfWindForceIn := vfWindForceIn;
// ...
    C1.vfProductionIn := WM1.vfProductionOut;
// ...
    vfProductionOut := if not C1.vfWorking then 0.0
                        else if not C2.vfWorking then C1.vfProductionOut
                        else if not C3.vfWorking then C2.vfProductionOut +
                                C1.vfProductionOut
                        else if not C4.vfWorking then C3.vfProductionOut +
                                C2.vfProductionOut + C1.vfProductionOut
                        else if not C5.vfWorking then C4.vfProductionOut +
                                C3.vfProductionOut + C2.vfProductionOut + C1.vfProductionOut
                        else C5.vfProductionOut + C4.vfProductionOut + C3.vfProductionOut
                                + C2.vfProductionOut + C1.vfProductionOut;
// assertions to start or stop wind turbines implementing the priority
    WM1.vfStartDemanded := vfStartDemanded;
    WM2.vfStartDemanded := vfStartDemanded and not (WM1.vsState == STANDBY);
// ...

    WM1.vfStopDemanded := vfStopDemanded and not (WM5.vsState == WORKING) and not
        (WM4.vsState == WORKING) and not (WM3.vsState == WORKING) and not (WM2.vsState
        == WORKING);
    WM2.vfStopDemanded := vfStopDemanded and not (WM5.vsState == WORKING) and not
        (WM4.vsState == WORKING) and not (WM3.vsState == WORKING);
// ...

// assertions implementing the diagnosis
    vfNumberOfStoppedWM := #(WM1.vsState == STANDBY, WM2.vsState == STANDBY, WM3.vsState
        == STANDBY, WM4.vsState == STANDBY, WM5.vsState == STANDBY );

    vfIsFailed := (WM1.vsState == FAILED or WM2.vsState == FAILED or WM3.vsState ==
        FAILED or WM4.vsState == FAILED or WM5.vsState == FAILED
                        or C1.vsState == FAILED or C2.vsState == FAILED or C3.vsState ==
                        FAILED or C4.vsState == FAILED or C5.vsState == FAILED) ;
// ...

end
```

Fig. 7. AltaRica 3.0 class Line.

the fact that if a cable C_i is failed then the wind turbines located upstream $WM_{i+1}, WM_{i+2}, \ldots$ are isolated.

The line receives the orders to stop and to start the wind turbines from the global controller. We assume that there is a priority between the wind turbines. First, the wind turbine WM_1 is attempted to start, then the wind turbine WM_2, and so on. This priorities are implemented in the assertion part of the class

Line, when the variables `WMi.vfStartDemanded` and `WMi.vfStopDemanded` are assigned.

The diagnosis part is also defined in the assertion. The value of the variables `vfNumberOfStoppedWM`, `vfIsFailed` and others are calculated in the assertion and sent to the global controller. Then these values are used to define global reconfiguration and maintenance strategies.

The block `Controller` is used to define when the maintenance can be started and stopped. It uses synchronisations as explained in [7].

4.2 Modelling the Environment

Simplified Model of the Wind. The wind force can be modelled by a discrete-time Markov chain.

In our model we assume that the wind force may be NULL, LOW, NORMAL, HIGH and STORM. When the wind force is NULL or STORM, the wind turbines must be stopped. The wind force changes every 4 h. The discrete-time Markov chain modelling the force of the wind is given Fig. 8.

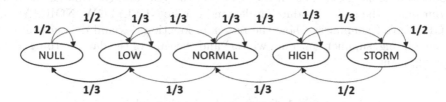

Fig. 8. Discrete-time Markov chain representing the wind force.

In AltaRica 3.0 this Markov chain is partially represented Fig. 9. First, we define a domain `WindForce`, which is an enumeration of five values: NULL, LOW, NORMAL, HIGH, STORM. Second, we define a class `Wind`. This class declares a state variable `vsWindForce`, which takes its values in the domain `WindForce`, to represent the internal state of the class, i.e. the wind force. It declares a flow variable `vfWindForceOut` which takes the same value. The parameter `pWindChangePeriod` is used to represent when the force of the wind changes. Its value can be changed to perform experiments. Events `evStayNull`, `evStayStorm`, ... and transitions represent how the state changes. The probability of the event is given by the attribute `expectation`. For instance, if the wind force is NULL, then there is a probability of 0.5 for the events `evStayNull` and `evIncreaseLow` to occur. The values of expectations may be declared using parameters and can be changed at will.

Of course, it is possible to use a more realistic model of the wind force taking into account real data coming from weather reports for a given region.

```
domain WindForce {NULL, LOW, NORMAL, HIGH, STORM}

class Wind
    WindForce vsWindForce (init = NORMAL);
    WindForce vfWindForceOut (reset = NULL);

    parameter Real pWindChangePeriod = 4; // hours

    event evStayNull(delay = Dirac(pWindChangePeriod), expectation = 1.0/2.0);
    event evStayStorm(delay = Dirac(pWindChangePeriod), expectation = 1.0/2.0);
    event evIncreaseLow (delay = Dirac(pWindChangePeriod), expectation = 1.0/2.0);
    event evDecreaseHigh (delay = Dirac(pWindChangePeriod), expectation = 1.0/2.0);
    event evStay (delay = Dirac(pWindChangePeriod), expectation = 1.0/3.0);
    event evIncrease (delay = Dirac(pWindChangePeriod), expectation = 1.0/3.0);
    event evDecrease (delay = Dirac(pWindChangePeriod), expectation = 1.0/3.0);

    transition
// ...
    assertion
        vfWindForceOut := vsWindForce;
end
```

Fig. 9. AltaRica 3.0 model of the Wind.

Model of the Power Production Demand. We assume that the power production demand depends on the season of the year and the time of the day. In our model the power production demand can be NULL, LOW, NORMAL or HIGH. Table 1 summarises how the power production demand depends on the season (spring, summer, autumn, winter) and the time of the day (morning, day, evening, night).

Table 1. Power production demand.

Heading level	Spring	Summer	Autumn	Winter
Morning (5a.m. - 9a.m.)	NORMAL	LOW	NORMAL	HIGH
Day (9a.m. - 4p.m.)	LOW	LOW	LOW	NORMAL
Evening (4p.m. - 10p.m.)	NORMAL	LOW	NORMAL	HIGH
Night (10p.m. - 5a.m.)	LOW	NULL	LOW	NORMAL

To represent this demand in AltaRica 3.0 we use a deterministic model. It can also be modeled by a discrete-time Markov chain by adding some uncertainties to the events.

5 Experiments

As previously introduced in part 3, the AltaRica 3.0 modelling language comes with a versatile set of assessment tools to design and evaluate models. Thus for our specific offshore windmill farm case study, we use the stochastic simulator to perform evaluations. Of course, the modelling environment AltaRica Wizard, and the interactive simulator are used during the design and evaluation to get qualitative and quantitative information about the model.

Table 2 resumes the quantitative information about the model. We consider the designed AltaRica 3.0 model and the flattened one resulting from the compilation process. The main interpretation of these quantitative information is the huge difference between the number of models elements. In fact, when designing the AltaRica 3.0 model, we intensively used the powerful mechanisms of the language: the classes and the inheritance, the synchronisation of events, etc. For instance, the design of the fives lines, each one composed of five wind turbines and five cables is realised with different classes: a class for wind turbines with 5 atomic variables, a class for cables with 3 atomic variables, and a class Line (instantiating five wind turbines and five cables) with 8 atomic variables. The number of declared atomic variables is thus 16, whereas the real number of variables for all the lines, when the classes are instantiated, is 80.

Table 2. Quantitative information about the model.

AltaRica 3.0 model	Designed	Flattened
Number of lines	450	1260
Number of classes	5	–
Number of state variables	6	67
Number of flow variables	26	244
Number of parameters	25	175
Number of events	39	159
Number of transitions	46	190
Number of instructions in assertion(s)	60	244

Quantitative results are obtained with the AltaRica 3.0 stochastic simulator. We define different observers in the model and indicators to evaluate these observers. Then statistics are made on the indicators by the stochastic simulator. Figure 10 defines the three main observers used to obtain the results. The two observers oProd and oDiffProdNeed are real observers. oProd gets the value of the production, whereas oDiffProdNeed gets the difference between the value of the production and the value of the need. Finally the observer oNeedSatisfied is Boolean and checks if the production is more than the demand, meaning "the demand is satisfied".

```
block WindmillFarm
  block ProductionNeed
    // ...
  end
  block ProductionSystem
    // ...
  end
  // ...
  observer Real oProd = ProductionSystem.out;
  observer Real oDiffProdNeed = ProductionSystem.out - ProductionNeed.need;
  observer Boolean oNeedSatisfied = ProductionSystem.out >= ProductionNeed.need;
end
```

Fig. 10. AltaRica 3.0 observers.

We define indicators on these observers. For the two real observers oProd and oDiffProdNeed, we define mean-value indicators, meaning the mean value of the observer through the time period $[0, t]$, with t representing a time instant (the mission time for these experiments). For the Boolean observer oNeedSatisfied, it is a sojourn-time with the value **true**, meaning the time the observer had the value **true** from the time instant 0 to the time instant t (the mission time for these experiments). Then mean, standard deviation and confidence range are computed for these indicators.

The stochastic simulator produced 100000 runs for a mission time of 43800 h (representing 5 years). It calculated statistics on indicators not only at the end of the mission time, but also at intermediate time instants: every year at 8760 h 17520 h, 26280 h and 35040 h). Table 3 presents these results divided in two parts.

Table 3. Quantitative results.

Fired events	Mean	Min	Max
	128943.0	123381	134143
Indicator	Date	Mean	Standard deviation
Mean-value(oProd)	8760	770.871	18.7466
	17520	770.562	13.2972
	26280	770.457	10.868
	35040	770.391	9.38924
	43800	770.384	8.39527
Mean-value(oDiffProdNeed)	8760	−434.722	18.7466
	17520	−435.031	13.2972
	26280	−435.137	10.868
	35040	−435.203	9.38924
	43800	−435.209	8.39527
Sojourn-time(oNeedSatisfied)	8760	5100.25	135.047
	17520	10200.6	191.6
	26280	15300.6	234.779
	35040	20400.2	271.06
	43800	25501.0	302.954

Table 4. Sojourn times for a given wind force and a maximum production.

		Wind force				
		NULL	LOW	NORMAL	HIGH	STORM
Production	NULL	501.3	749.69	740.6	731.59	496.79
	LOW	3174.73	4774.95	4757.46	4738.58	3184.28
	NORMAL	2385.97	3548.67	3558.77	3565.07	2391.52
	HIGH	695.66	1039.13	1036.85	1036.18	692.17

The first part indicates the number of fired events: 128943 on average. This number seems high, but it can be explained by the fact that after each modification of the demand, starts or stops of wind turbines are fired. For instance, at the beginning of each simulation, the need is set to 2000 and with an initial wind force set to NORMAL, all the 25 wind turbines must be started, which means that 25 events are triggered.

The second part indicates statistics for the different indicators at every year. We only consider the mean and the standard deviation. What one can observe is that the need is satisfied only during 25501 h for the five years (43800), and the difference between the production and the power demand is always negative (on average). To analyse these results, we can consider the Table 4 summarising the sojourn times for a given wind force and a maximum production (when the 25 wind turbines are started). We indicate in gray when the production is lower than the power demand during the 5 years. By summing all these sojourn-times in gray, we obtain the sojourn-time when the need is not satisfied. Thus it means that during a certain period of time (the sum of the sojourn-times) the wind force is not sufficient to satisfy the power demand with all the 25 wind turbines started.

6 Conclusion and Perspectives

In this publication, we presented how the AltaRica 3.0 modelling language can be used to efficiently design models of large scale reconfigurable systems and to assess their performances using the stochastic simulation. The presentation was based on an example of an offshore windmill farm composed of several lines of wind turbines connected in series. We have shown that the advanced constructs of AltaRica 3.0 help to easily model several different features of such a system: combination of multi-states, resource sharing, reconfiguration, maintenance, etc. We calculated some indicators on this model using the stochastic simulator.

Modelling of these features involved a pattern based approach: resource sharing, limited number of repairers, reconfiguration, etc. This not only increases the set of already presented AltaRica 3.0 modelling patterns but it also confirms that modelling patterns are a very efficient mean to design models and, more fundamentally, they are a way to reason about the system under study.

Finally, the designed AltaRica 3.0 model can be easily extended so to introduce new elements, such as new lines or more repairers, or new features, such as different maintenance policies or more quantitative production values of the units according, for instance, to their degradation and failures. Different experiments may be conducted with different models of the wind force, of the power production demand, with different number of lines and different number of wind turbines per line, and of course with different values of parameters.

References

1. Abadi, M., Cardelli, L.: A Theory of Objects. Springer-Verlag, New-York, USA (1998)
2. Aupetit, B., Batteux, M., Rauzy, A., Roussel, J.M.: Improving performance of the AltaRica 3.0 stochastic simulator. In: Podofillini, L., Sudret, B., Stojadinovic, B., Zio, E., Kröger, W. (eds.) Proceedings of Safety and Reliability of Complex Engineered Systems: ESREL 2015, pp. 1815–1824. CRC Press (2015)
3. Batteux, M., Prosvirnova, T., Rauzy, A.: Altarica 3.0 assertions: the why and the wherefore. J. Risk Reliab. **231**(6), 691–700 (2017). https://doi.org/10.1177/1748006X17728209
4. Batteux, M., Prosvirnova, T., Rauzy, A.: Altarica wizard: an integrated modeling and simulation environment for Altarica 3.0. In: Actes du congrès Lambda-Mu 21 (actes électroniques). IMdR, Reims, France (2018)
5. Batteux, M., Prosvirnova, T., Rauzy, A.: From models of structures to structures of models. In: 4th IEEE International Symposium on Systems Engineering, ISSE 2018. Rome, Italy (2018)
6. Batteux, M., Prosvirnova, T., Rauzy, A.: Altarica 3.0 in 10 modeling patterns. Int. J. Crit. Comput. Based Syst. **9**(1–2), 133–165 (2019). https://doi.org/10.1504/IJCCBS.2019.098809
7. Batteux, M., Prosvirnova, T., Rauzy, A.: Modeling patterns for the assessment of maintenance policies with AltaRica 3.0. In: Papadopoulos, Y., Aslansefat, K., Katsaros, P., Bozzano, M. (eds.) IMBSA 2019. LNCS, vol. 11842, pp. 32–46. Springer, Cham (2019). https://doi.org/10.1007/978-3-030-32872-6_3
8. Batteux, M., Prosvirnova, T., Rauzy, A.: Efficient Modeling of large Markov chains models with AltaRica 3.0. In: Proceedings of the 31st European Safety and Reliability Conference (ESREL). Angers, France (2021). https://hal.archives-ouvertes.fr/hal-03429225
9. Batteux, M., Prosvirnova, T., Rauzy, A., Yang, L.: Reliability assessment of phased-mission systems with Altarica 3.0. In: Proceedings of the 3rd International Conference on System Reliability and Safety (ICSRS), pp. 400–407. IEEE, Barcelona, Spain (2018). https://doi.org/10.1109/ICSRS.2018.00072
10. Cassandras, C.G., Lafortune, S.: Introduction to Discrete Event Systems. Springer, New-York, NY, USA (2008)
11. Epstein, S., Reinhart, M., Rauzy, A.: The open PSA initiative for next generation probabilistic safety assessment. In: Proceeding of 9th International Conference on Probabilistic Safety Assessment and Management 2008, PSAM 2008, vol. 1, pp. 542–550. IAPSAM, Hong-Kong, China (2008)
12. Gamma, E., Helm, R., Johnson, R., Vlissides, J.: Design Patterns - Elements of Reusable Object-Oriented Software. Addison-Wesley professional computing series, Addison-Wesley, Boston, MA 02116, USA (1994)

13. Noble, J., Taivalsaari, A., Moore, I.: Prototype-Based Programming: Concepts. Languages and Applications, Springer-Verlag, Berlin and Heidelberg, Germany (1999)
14. Prosvirnova, T., Rauzy, A.: Automated generation of minimal cut sets from Altarica 3.0 models. Int. J. Crit. Comput. Based Syst. **6**(1), 50–79 (2015). https://doi.org/10.1504/IJCCBS.2015.068852
15. Rauzy, A.: Guarded transition systems: a new states/events formalism for reliability studies. J. Risk Reliab. **222**(4), 495–505 (2008). https://doi.org/10.1243/1748006XJRR177
16. Rauzy, A.: Anatomy of an efficient fault tree assessment engine. In: Virolainen, R. (ed.) Proceedings of International Joint Conference PSAM 2011/ESREL 2012, pp. 3333–3343. Helsinki, Finland (2012)
17. Rauzy, A.: Notes on computational uncertainties in probabilistic risk/safety assessment. Entropy **20**(3), 162 (2018). https://doi.org/10.3390/e20030162
18. Zimmermann, A.: Stochastic Discrete Event Systems. Springer, Berlin, Heidelberg, Germany (2008)

Component Fault and Deficiency Tree (CFDT): Combining Functional Safety and SOTIF Analysis

Marc Zeller[✉][iD]

Siemens AG, Otto-Hahn-Ring 6, 81739 Munich, Germany
marc.zeller@siemens.com

Abstract. In order to assess AI/ML-based systems in terms of safety, is it not sufficient to assure the system in terms of possible failure but also consider functional weaknesses/insufficiencies of the used algorithms according to Safety Of The Intended Functionality (SOTIF). Therefore, we introduce the concept of the so-called *Component Fault and Deficiency Tree (CFDT)*. With this extension of the Component Fault Tree (CFT) methodology cause-effect-relationships between individual failures as well as functional insufficiencies and system hazards of the specified system can be described. Hence, it is possible to conduct safety analysis to apply for AI/ML-based systems. Thereby, we are able to show that all risks have been sufficiently mitigated and document efficiently the various mitigation schemes on different system levels.

Keywords: Safety · Machine learning · Artificial intelligence · Component fault trees

1 Introduction

In order to be able to certify safety-critical systems, we must show that all risks have been sufficiently mitigated. Nowadays, safety standards (such as IEC 61508 [5] or ISO 26262 [6],) highly recommend to use deductive and inductive safety analysis techniques like *Failure Mode and Effect Analysis (FMEA)* [4] or *Fault Tree Analysis (FTA)* [11] in order to show that all identified system hazards have been mitigated sufficiently. All these analyses show the cause-effect-relationship of individual failures and system hazards for the specified system. Thereby, a failure is defined as an event that occurs when the delivered service deviates from correct service [1].

However, systems incorporating *Artificial Intelligence (AI)/Machine Learning (ML)* pose new challenges. In order to assess AI/ML-based systems in terms of safety, is it not sufficient to assure the system in terms of possible failure but also the *Safety Of The Intended Functionality (SOTIF)* must be considered. Therefore, novel safety standards such as *ISO 21448 Road vehicles - Safety of the Intended Functionality* [3] are created. ISO 21448 defines SOTIF, as the absence of unreasonable risk due to hazards resulting from functional insufficiencies of the intended functionality. Hence, in contrast to existing safety standards, SOTIF has a different view on the system. In order to build and assess the safety of systems incorporating AI/ML hazards coming from failures as well as hazards resulting from functional insufficiencies of the intended functionality must be mitigated sufficiently. Therefore, we need to extend safety analysis techniques in order to create cause-effect-relationships for individual failures as well as functional insufficiencies and system hazards for the specified system.

With *Component Fault Trees (CFTs)* there is a model- and component-based methodology to model cause-effect-relationships for individual failures and system hazards, which supports reuse by a modular and compositional safety analysis strategy [2,7,8]. Due to the failure propagation approach CFTs are also particularly well suited to model and document failure mitigation strategies on different levels of the system. Based on the description of the cause-effect-relationships in form of a CFT both Fault Trees and FME(D)As can be generated. However, the CFT methodology currently focuses on individual random failures of the system and not on functional insufficiencies of the intended functionality.

In order to enable the assurance of AI/ML-based systems with safety-critical functionalities, we extend the CFT methodology to a so-called *Component Fault and Deficiency Tree (CFDT)* in order to describe cause-effect-relationships for individual failures as well as functional insufficiencies and system hazards for the specified system.

2 Background: Component Fault Tree (CFT)

A CFT consists of a set of CFT elements where each CFT element is defined by the tuple $CFT = (IFM, OFM, B, G, SubCFT, C)$ [8] comprising

- a set of input failure modes $IFM = \{ifm_1, \ldots, ifm_n\}$
- a set of output failure modes $OFM = \{ofm_1, \ldots, ofm_m\}$
- a set of internal failure events $B = \{b_1, \ldots, b_r\}$ (so-called basic events), which describe random HW failures of the component
- a set of Boolean gates $G = \{g_1, \ldots, g_s\}$, where each gate has exactly one output $g_i.out$ and one or more inputs $g_i.in_j$ as well as a Boolean formula (e.g. $g.out = g.in_1 \vee g.in_2$ representing an OR-gate)
- a set of sub-CFT elements SubCFT which is defined by the tuple

$$SubCFT = (IN, OUT, cft_i)$$

where $IN = \{in_1, \ldots, in_a\}$ is a set of input failure mode,
$OUT = \{out_1, \ldots, out_b\}$ a set of output failure modes,
and $cft_i \in CFT$ a mapping to a another CFT element
- a set of directed edges C with

$$C \subseteq (IFM \cup B \cup G.out \cup SubCFT.OUT) \times (OFM \cup G.IN \cup SubCFT.IN)$$

With CFTs it is possible to represent all information of a classical fault tree, including *Common Cause Failures (CCFs)*, in a modular and hierarchical way [7]. An example of a simple CFT element is depicted in Fig. 1.

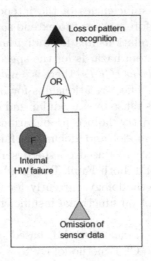

Fig. 1. Exemplary CFT description the failure propagation of a component

3   Component Fault and Deficiency Tree (CFDT)

To specify cause-effect-relationships for individual failures as well as functional insufficiencies and system hazards, we need to introduce a concept corresponding to failures. Therefore, we define the combination of weaknesses/limitations originating from the design or the specification or limitations in the implementation of the intended functionality (e.g. insufficiency of the decision algorithm) and a triggering condition (e.g. according to ISO 21448 a "specific conditions of a driving scenario that serve as an initiator for a subsequent system reaction possibly leading to a hazardous behavior") as a so-called *deficiency*. Similar to failures, deficiencies can lead to a malfunction or malfunctioning behavior within the system which may lead to a potential hazard at the system boundary (see Fig. 2). In a model for the safety analysis of a system incorporating AI/ML functionalities, both failures and deficiencies need to be represented appropriately.

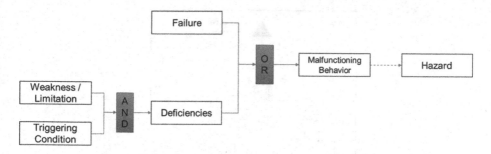

Fig. 2. Relationship between failures and deficiencies

In order to describe functional insufficiencies and system hazards of the specified system in the same model, we extend the CFT methodology as follows:

A *Component Fault and Deficiency Tree (CFDT)* is defined as a superset of a CFT ($CFDT \supset CFT$) which consists of a set of CFDT elements where each CFDT element is defined by the tuple:

$$CFDT = (IFM, OFM, B, D, M, G, SubCFDT, C')$$

While the definition of IFMs, OFMs, basic events B, and gates G, are the same as in CFTs, we extend the definition as follows:

- a set of deficiencies $D = \{d_1, \ldots, d_t\}$, which describe functional deficiencies of the component
- a set of measures $M = \{M_1, \ldots, M_u\}$, which describe mitigation measures defined either for functional deficiencies or for failures
- a set of sub-CFDT elements SubCFDT which is define by the tuple

$$SubCFDT = (IN, OUT, cfdt_i)$$

where $IN = \{in_1, \ldots, in_a\}$ is a set of input failure mode,
$OUT = \{out_1, \ldots, out_b\}$, a set of output failure modes, and
$cfdt_i \in CFDT$ a mapping to a another CFDT element
- a set of directed edges C' with

$$C' \subseteq (IFM \cup B \cup D \cup M \cup G.out \cup SubCFDT.OUT)$$
$$\times (OFM \cup G.IN \cup SubCFDT.IN)$$

An example for a CFDT element is depicted in Fig. 3 and in Fig. 4:

4   Analysis Using Component Fault and Deficiency Trees

The CFDT methodology allows to conduct different analyses:

Qualitative Analysis: By describing the cause-effect-relationships for functional deficiencies it is possible to conduct an FMEA-like analysis and to generate an overview table which shows if measures are defined for each deficiency of

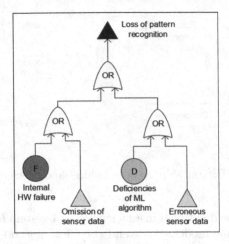

Fig. 3. Exemplary CFDT describing the failure and deficiency propagation of a component

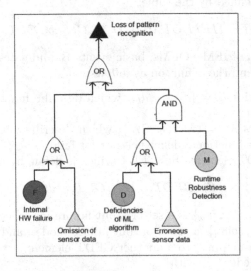

Fig. 4. Exemplary CFDT describing failure and deficiency propagation as well as the measure to mitigate the failure/deficiency

each component which would otherwise lead to a potential hazards. Moreover, it is possible to conduct an analysis similar to qualitative Fault Tree Analysis (Minimal Cut Set Analysis) to show which combinations of deficiencies (cut sets) can lead to a specific hazard.

Quantitative Analysis: Similar to the basic events in classic fault trees, also deficiencies can be annotated using probabilities which allow the quantitative Fault Tree Analysis using well known algorithms [9] to calculate the probability that a specific hazard occurs. Since for the quantification of deficiencies uncertainties need addressed, techniques such *Bayesian Networks* could be used [10]. Moreover, measures can be annotated with a *Diagnostic Coverage (DC)* value (similar to FMEDA) based on expert judgement or available field data. Hence, we can conduct an FMEDA-like analysis to determine the residual risk that a hazard will occur.

Common Cause Deficiencies Analysis: The CFDT methodology allows us to define so-called *Common Cause Deficiencies (CCDs)* analogous to CCFs. Hence, the CFDT model can also be used to determine the CCDs of a design.

Based on these analyses we can document the absence of unreasonable risk of a system incorporating AI/ML-based functions. Moreover, it can also be used to identify drawbacks of the system design.

5 Conclusions and Future Work

The presented extension the CFT methodology allows to describe cause-effect-relationships and mitigation schemes on different system levels for individual failures as well as functional insufficiencies and system hazards for the specified system. With this approach it is possible to extend exiting safety analysis techniques to apply for AI/ML-based systems incorporating functional deficiencies. Thereby, we are able to show that all risks have been sufficiently mitigated and document efficiently the various mitigation schemes on different system levels. Hence, safety analyses can be created for both classical function safety (e.g. according to IEC 61508) and SOTIF (according to ISO 21448) using one single model.

In the future, we will apply the CFDT methodology in the safety assurance of different industry projects. Moreover, we will further enhance the approach based on the feedback from the application in these projects, e.g. with respect to the sound representation of triggering events in the safety analysis model.

References

1. Avizienis, A., Laprie, J.C., Randell, B., Landwehr, C.: Basic concepts and taxonomy of dependable and secure computing. Dependable Secure Comput. IEEE Trans. 1(1), 11–33 (2004). https://doi.org/10.1109/TDSC.2004.2
2. Höfig, K., et al.: Model-based reliability and safety: reducing the complexity of safety analyses using component fault trees. In: 2018 Annual Reliability and Maintainability Symposium (RAMS) (2018)
3. International Organization for Standardization (ISO): ISO/PAS 21448 - road vehicles-safety of the intended functionality (2019)
4. International Electrotechnical Commission (IEC): IEC 60812: Analysis Techniques for System Reliability - Procedure for Failure Mode and Effects Analysis (FMEA) (1991)
5. International Electrotechnical Commission (IEC): IEC 61508: Functional safety of electrical/electronic/programmable electronic safety related systems (1998)
6. International Organization for Standardization (ISO): ISO 26262: Road vehicles - Functional safety (2011)

7. Kaiser, B., et al.: Advances in component fault trees. In: Proceedings of the 28th European Safety and Reliability Conference (ESREL) (2018)
8. Kaiser, B., Liggesmeyer, P., Mäckel, O.: A new component concept for fault trees. In: Proceedings of the 8th Australian Workshop on Safety Critical Systems and Software, pp. 37–46 (2003)
9. Ruijters, E., Stoelinga, M.: Fault tree analysis: a survey of the state-of-the-art in modeling, analysis and tools. Comput. Sci. Rev. **15–16**, 29–62 (2015). https://doi.org/10.1016/j.cosrev.2015.03.001
10. Thomas, S., Groth, K.M.: Toward a hybrid causal framework for autonomous vehicle safety analysis. Proc. Inst. Mech. Eng. J. Risk Reliab. (2021). https://doi.org/10.1177/1748006X211043310
11. Vesely, W.E., Goldberg, F.F., Roberts, N.H., Haasl, D.F.: Fault Tree Handbook. US Nuclear Regulatory Commission (1981)

Designing Mitigations of Faults
and Attacks

A Capella-Based Tool for the Early Assessment of Nano/Micro Satellites Availability

Guillaume Brau[1](✉), Eric Jenn[1], and Silvana Radu[2]

[1] Institut de Recherche Technologique Saint-Exupéry, Toulouse, France
{guillaume.brau,eric.jenn}@irt-saintexupery.com
[2] European Space Agency – European Space Research and Technology Centre, Noordwijk, The Netherlands
silvana.radu@esa.int

Abstract. This paper presents a solution to evaluate the availability of a satellite system on the basis of its physical architecture modelled using the Capella Model-Based Systems Engineering environment. In the paper, we propose a set of modelling concepts to capture the fault occurrence, error propagation, and failure occurrence processes. Focus is placed on the effect of radiations on hardware components. We propose the constructs to represent the error detection, masking and mitigation means. Finally, we illustrate the use of the tool to evaluate the availability of a simple satellite platform.

Keywords: Model-based systems engineering · Model-based safety analysis · Capella · System availability · Satellites · Cosmic radiations

1 Introduction

Since the last five years, the space domain is experiencing a strong and increasing demand for "low-cost" nano and micro satellites, sometimes deployed in very large constellations. In this extremely competitive "new space" market, cost and performance need to be improved drastically while maintaining or lowering weight and power consumption. Commercial off-the-shelf (COTS) components such as System-on-Chip (SoC) play a fundamental role in this evolution by providing high processing capabilities, low power and high flexibility. Unfortunately, those components are generally not designed to withstand the high level of radiations and high-energy particles of the space environment due to inadequate manufacturing technologies and/or small transistor sizes.

In order to compensate this high level of sensitivity to radiations, dedicated fault detection, isolation and recovery (FDIR) mechanisms are needed, and those mechanisms must be selected and implemented in the most efficient way with respect to the mission availability objectives. In this context, being able to couple the model used to support design activities and the model used to perform availability analysis in the same modelling environment would significantly facilitate the exploration of candidate solutions. In this paper, we present the ELMASAT (EarLy Model-based Availability assessment of nano/micro SATellites) tool that couples Model-Based Systems Engineering (MBSE)

© The Author(s), under exclusive license to Springer Nature Switzerland AG 2022
C. Seguin et al. (Eds.): IMBSA 2022, LNCS 13525, pp. 155–169, 2022.
https://doi.org/10.1007/978-3-031-15842-1_12

and Model-Based Safety Analysis (MBSA) within the Capella Systems Engineering environment. We also show how the tool has been used to calculate the availability of a satellite system.

The rest of this paper is organized as follows. Section 2 introduces the availability assessment viewpoint and the related analysis methods provided by the ELMASAT tool. We present an experimentation of the ELMASAT tool on a satellite case study in Sect. 3. Section 4 deals with related work and we conclude with possible directions for future work in Sect. 5.

2   ELMASAT Tool

The ELMASAT availability assessment tool is built upon the Capella MBSE environment that we briefly introduce in Sect. 2.1. The base environment is extended with several concepts related to dependability (e.g., fault, error, failure, etc.), thus providing a complete viewpoint to perform availability analysis (Sect. 2.2). Availability computation is discussed in more detail in Sect. 2.3.

2.1   System Architecture in Capella

Capella is an open-source solution for Model-Based Systems Engineering. Capella is the "companion tool" to the Arcadia systems engineering method[1]. Initially developed by Thales to support the company's internal needs, it is now freely available as an Eclipse project[2]. We choose the Capella environment because of its large dissemination and its openness. Openness is a strong requirement since we need to extend the domain model and build a new "viewpoint" exploiting this extended model. It is worth noting that several studies, including, e.g., Bitetti et al. [1], have used Capella to support part of RAMS (Reliability, Availability, Maintainability, Safety) analyses; however, availability analysis is not addressed in these studies (see Sect. 4). Hereafter, we briefly introduce the main concepts of the method used in the approach implemented in the ELMASAT tool. More information on Capella/Arcadia can be found, for instance, in [2].

The Capella modelling environment and its associated engineering method address different *perspectives* of the engineering process, including those supporting the operational analysis, system analysis, logical and physical architecture. The ELMASAT tool focuses on the physical architecture of the system. Indeed, this is at this level that the effects of radiations, such as Single-Event Upsets can be captured. This is also the level where the relation between a function and its execution architecture can be expressed.

An example of a system architecture described in Capella, coming from the satellite case study in Sect. 3, is given on Fig. 1. This diagram shows the architectural elements involved in availability assessment: physical functions (in green), mapped on behavioural physical components (in blue), themselves mapped onto node physical components (in yellow). Basically, functions specify what is to be done while physical components

---

[1] A very synthetic view of the method can be found at https://www.eclipse.org/capella/arcadia. html.

[2] Available at https://www.eclipse.org/capella.

describe how it is done (or implemented). Functions exchange items through connections between their input and output ports. Ports are represented by small squares at the edges of functions or components while connexions are lines connecting ports. In a complete model, the functional communication links would themselves be "mapped" onto physical links; this is not represented here.

Functions may be involved in one or several *functional chains*. Graphically, a functional chain represents a path crossing several functions involved in the realization of one higher-level function.

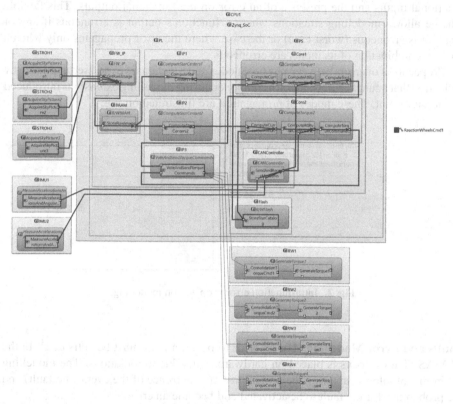

Fig. 1. A Capella model ("Reaction Wheels Command" functional chain deployed on CPU1). (Color figure online)

2.2 Building an Availability Assessment Viewpoint

Availability and Error Propagation. In the tool, availability is defined and computed with respect to one or several functional chains: a functional chain is considered "available" if a certain combination of the functions that constitute the chain is available. The availability of a function is defined with respect to its outputs: a function is available if its outputs are error-free.

Errors propagate in the system via two channels. First, errors propagate via functional exchanges between functions and, inside a function, via the functional dependencies between its inputs and its outputs. The latter case corresponds to the situation where a function processes erroneous data received from other (failed) functions. Second, errors propagate from physical nodes to functions. A typical example is the one where the processor executing some software function is faulty.

In the ELMASAT tool, propagation of errors between functions exploits the connections between the functional ports. Inside a function, propagation is modelled using logical equations expressing the causal relation between the presence of an error on some functional inputs and the presence of an error on the functional outputs. This flexible scheme allows modelling situations where a function's output is erroneous if any of its input is erroneous (worst-case) or the case where the error propagates only when a specific combination of its inputs are erroneous.

Propagation of errors between physical nodes and functions is expressed explicitly by indicating that a function depends on a component using modelling extensions introduced by the viewpoint. These modes of propagation are illustrated on Fig. 2.

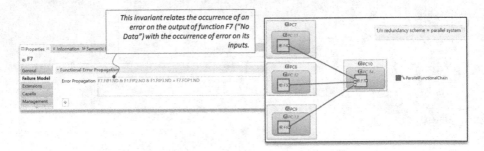

Fig. 2. Intra-function error propagation modelling.

Faults and Error Modelling. For an error to occur, a fault must be activated[3]. In the ELMASAT tool, focus is placed on hardware faults due to radiations. The modelling environment allows capturing the probability of occurrence of the event (the fault) and the probability for the fault to be activated and become an error.

Error Detection and Mitigation, Consolidation Schemes. Without any error mitigation means, an error affecting a functional chain (so the service delivered by the system) would eventually lead to a system failure and, consequently, to the unavailability of the system. The ELMASAT tool models error detection and mitigation means using specific functions (see Fig. 3). The error detection function "observes" (or "monitors") the outputs of any function, detects the occurrence of an error, and triggers a mitigation function. The mitigation function operates on the physical node to eliminate the error

---

[3] "An error is that part of the system state which is liable to lead to subsequent failure: an error affecting the service is an indication that a failure occurs or has occurred. The adjudged or hypothesized case of an error is a fault" [3].

(i.e., to "repair" the node). Since those functions are similar to those contributing to deliver the operational services, they can be deployed on any physical node, including the one that is monitored. This allows to account for the effect of a failure of the structure that implements an error detection and monitoring function.

The ELMASAT tool also supports the modelling of various redundancy schemes, including n-out-of-m in the cold and hot modes. Again, this is achieved using dedicated functions embedding the consolidation logic (see Fig. 3).

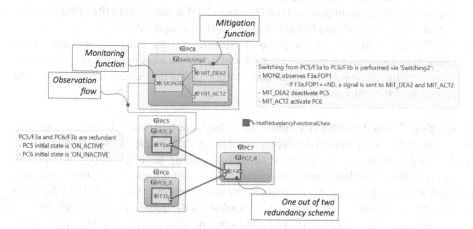

Fig. 3. Error detection and mitigation.

2.3 Availability Computation

Once the fault occurrence, error monitoring and mitigation processes have been modelled, the availability of functional chains can be computed. The ELMASAT tool implements two calculation schemes: one directly computing the availability by traversing the structure of the Capella model and accounting for the contribution of each component, and another one based on stochastic simulation. In the latter case, the relevant part of the Capella model is transformed into an AltaRica model [4] that can be first validated using interactive simulation and evaluated using stochastic simulation.

Analytical Availability Evaluation. The "analytical" evaluation of availability is performed by traversing the model and applying classical availability calculation formulae according to the following procedure.

1. The probability of failure of each hardware component is computed considering (i) the fault occurrence rate, (ii) the probability for the fault to lead to an error, and (iii) the intrinsic protection of the component.
2. The probability for a function to fail due to a hardware error is computed taking into account the failure probability of the dependent hardware component, and the

propagation probability of the error to the function considering the actual usage of the hardware component by the function. This computation is done for all hardware fault types and for all hardware components on which the functional component depends.

3. The probability for a function to fail due to an erroneous input is computed using an *error propagation formula* that expresses the relation between the presence of a failure at the output O of a function and the presence of errors at its inputs. For instance, for a two-inputs function F1, expression "F1.IP1.ND | F1.IP2.ND = F1.OP1.ND" means that "there is an error of type No Data (ND) at the output OP1 of function F1 if there is an error of type ND either at input IP1 or input IP2".

4. Finally, the availability is computed considering (i) the hardware and functional failure probabilities computed in steps 2 and 3, (ii) the mission duration and (iii) the recovery time. The recovery time takes into account the detection latency and the duration of the mitigation itself.

Simulation-Based Availability Evaluation. The simulation-based method uses an intermediate AltaRica 3 model that is processed using the AltaRica toolchain. The AltaRica model combines two components: **classes** modelling generic components such as hardware nodes, "standard" functions, consolidation and mitigation functions, etc., and **systems** instantiating the previous classes, creating the communication links between the instances, and defining the predicate – or **observer** – used to estimate availability.

For instance, Fig. 4 gives the interface and state machine of a repairable node (*RNode-Act*) whose AltaRica model is given on Fig. 5. The propagation of errors from its input to its output is described, respectively by the ne_i and ne_o variable in Fig. 5 (line 2). Another input to be considered for reparation is the mitigation command (mc_i variable at line 3). The state of the node is modelled using two variables encoding respectively its activation state (variable _state) and its error state (variable e) on lines 5, 6. The state of the node changes according to the occurrence of *events* such as an activation event (act_evt, line 12), the occurrence of a single-bit upset (sbu_evt, line 10), etc. An event occurs when a *transition* is fired, i.e., when its guard condition is asserted. The relation between the occurrence of events and the evolution of time is modelled using the delay clause (constant, Dirac, etc.). Finally, *assertions* determine the value of the output (ne_o) from the value of state variables.

Comparison of the Two Methods. Each method has its own pros and cons.

The analytical method estimates availability by traversing the structure and apply simple probability calculations, therefore it is very fast. However, this method can only be used for simple architectures in which the effect of a fault cannot propagate to the same component via multiple paths. To handle more complex situations, computation of minimal cutsets and, possibly, application of a rare event approximation would be required.

When it is applicable, the accuracy of the method depends on the magnitude of the failure rates (λ) and mission duration (T_m). For instance, the average availability of a non-repairable system ($\tilde{A} = 1 - \frac{1}{2}\lambda T_m$) is a "valid" approximation[4] of the actual value

---

[4] As per [5], this approximation is applicable if $\lambda T_m < 0.1$.

$$A = 1/T \int_0^T e^{-\lambda t} dt = \frac{1}{T_m} \left[-\frac{1}{\lambda} e^{-\lambda t} \right]_0^{T_m} = 1/(\lambda T_m)\left[1 - e^{-\lambda T_m}\right] \text{ for "small values" of } \lambda t$$

where the exponential can be approximated by a linear function.

The simulation-based method is applicable to any architecture including those involving complex behaviours. However, for stochastic simulation to provide accurate results, events of interest (e.g., failures) must be observed "sufficiently often". The AltaRica simulator provides the standard deviation of the measure to check if the number of experiments is sufficient to reach a given confidence level. When the number of experiments needs to be very large (e.g., 10^6), the duration of each simulation determines the feasibility of the approach. In particular, if the simulation mixes events with very low occurrence rates (e.g., a failure rate $\lambda = 10^{-6}$) with other events with much higher occurrence rates (e.g., a cycle time of 10 ms), each simulation may be very long to complete, and the achievable number of simulations will be insufficient to give significant results.

In practice, the analytical method may be used to evaluate early and simple architectural models in a very fast way. However, stochastic simulation is the only method of choice when it comes to evaluate the complex behaviours of FDIR mechanisms.

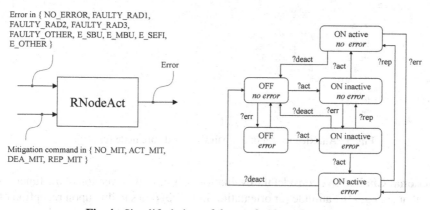

Fig. 4. Simplified view of the repairable node model.

3   Case Study

This section illustrates the use of the ELMASAT tool for the evaluation of a satellite platform availability.

```
1.   class RNodeAct extends Node;
2.   NodeFailures ne_i, ne_o (reset = OK);
3.   MitCmd mc_i (reset = NO_MIT);
4.
5.   NodeState _state (init= ON);
6.   NodeErrorState e (init= NO_ERROR);
7.
8.   event f_on_evt (delay= constant(1.0));
9.   event f_off_evt (delay= constant(1.0));
10.  event sbu_evt (delay= Dirac (0.0), expectation = 0.0);
11.  [...]
12.  event act_evt (delay= Dirac(0.0));
13.  event deact_evt (delay= Dirac(0.0));
14.  event repair_evt (delay= Dirac(0.0));
15.
16.  transition
17.     act_evt : (_state == OFF) and ( mc_i == ACT_MIT ) -> _state:= ON;
18.     deact_evt: (_state == ON) and ( mc_i == DEA_MIT ) -> { _state:= OFF; e
        := NO_ERROR; };
19.     repair_evt : (e != NO_ERROR) and (mc_i == REP_MIT) -> e := NO_ERROR; ;
20.     f_on_evt : (_state == ON) and (e == NO_ERROR) -> e := FAULTY;
21.     f_off_evt : (_state == OFF ) and (e == NO_ERROR) -> e := FAULTY;
22.     sbu_evt: (_state == ON) and (e == FAULTY) -> e := E1;
23.  [...]
24.
25.  assertion
26.  ne_o := if ( _state == OFF ) then OK
27.     else
28.        if ( ne_i == OK ) then
29.        switch {
30.           case e == NO_ERROR : OK
31.           case e == E1 : FM_SBU
32.           case e == E2 : FM_MBU
33.           case e == E3 : FM_SEFI
34.           default: OK
35.        }
36.        else
37.           ne_i;
38.  end
```

Fig. 5. AltaRica model of a repairable hardware node (excerpt).

Functional Chains. We consider the evaluation of a simplified version of the functional chain that changes the attitude (or orientation in space) of a satellite upon reception of a telecommand (Fig. 6). This functional chain includes the acquisition of the telecommand (not further modelled), the measure of the satellite attitude via the star tracker and accelerations/angular rate via the Inertial Measurement Unit (IMU), the computation of the correction to be applied, and the application of the correction using the reaction wheels. In addition, we consider the functions providing electrical power to the sensors, computations resources and actuators.

Hardware Platform. Those functions are deployed on a hardware platform composed of a set of sensors, actuators, computation resources, communications resources, and power production and distribution.

The system uses 2 Inertial Measurement Units (IMUs) providing the angular rate and linear acceleration of the satellite and 3 star tracker optical heads (STR-OHs) that acquire a sky picture from which the satellite's attitude can be computed. Redundancy is cold for the IMUs and hot for the STR-OHs. The system is also fitted with four reaction

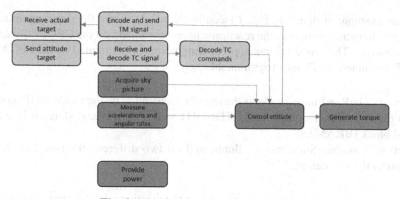

Fig. 6. Functional chains to be modelled.

wheels to control the attitude of the satellite. Redundancy is hot and three reaction wheels out of four are needed to perform the function.

The computation platform uses two processing channels operating in cold redundancy. Each board includes a Zynq 7000 SoC supervised by a Supervisor Unit (SRU). Each Zynq is composed of two Cortex A9 processing cores (PS) and a FPGA fabric (PL). In addition, each channel is fitted with multiple memories: we will only consider the Block RAM memory in the FPGA (used to store sky pictures from STR-OHs) and the NAND flash memory (used to store an on-board catalogue of the stars' positions).

Power is provided by Solar Arrays (SA) that convert solar energy into electrical energy. The SA is composed of 48 elements and at least 45 elements out of 48 are required to power the satellite[5]. The non-regulated voltage (BNR) produced by the solar array is regulated by three Conditioning modular boxes (BOMO-C, [6]). Two out of three BOMO-C are needed to perform the function. Power is then distributed via Distribution modular boxes (BOMO-S-A and S-B in cold redundancy). BOMO-Ds, connected to BOMO-S-A and BOMO-S-B in a cross-strapping scheme, perform current limitation (LCL) and power distribution to the reaction wheels. Two converter modules (CV-1 and CV-2, operating in cold redundancy) provide the secondary voltages for the CPUs and the sensors. One CV is dedicated to one CPU (no cross strapping). The inputs to the CVs are provided by the BOMOs (S-A and S-B) in a cross-strapping scheme.

Capella Model. The system is modelled using the viewpoint presented in Sect. 2.2. The model of the satellite system consists of 10 diagrams describing the various functional chains and their deployment on the physical components, thereby describing the physical architecture of the satellite. The architectural model is completed with data concerning fault occurrences, error propagations, failure modes, etc.

---

[5] To simplify the model, we consider 4 elements, with 3 elements out of 4 are required to power the satellite.

As an example of diagram, Fig. 1 (seen in Sect. 2.1) shows the deployment of the functional chain that computes the reaction wheels' command on the CPU1 ("Reaction-WheelsCmd1"). The low-level image processing part is implemented on the FPGA part of the Zynq (noted "PL", for Programmable Logic):

- Function "GetRawImage" collects the images transmitted by the FireWire IP (coming from the star tracker optical heads STR-OH1 to STR-OH3) and stores it in a local RAM block (BRAM),
- Function "ComputeStarCenters", duplicated on two different IPs (see latter), then computes the star centre.

The computation of the torque command for the reaction wheels is performed on the CPU PS part of the Zynq:

- Function "ComputeCurrentSatAttitude" finds the stars in the catalogue stored in the "Flash" memory and determines the attitude of the satellite,
- Functions "ComputeAttitudeCorrection" computes the attitude correction from both the computed current satellite attitude and data received from the IMUs through the CAN bus (accelerations and angular rate),
- Function "ComputeTorqueCommand" finally computes the torque commands for the reaction wheels (RW1 to RW4) in order to acquire the new attitude.

For safety reasons, the functional chain is redundant, i.e., the functions are deployed on two different IPs (IP1 and IP2) on the PL and two different cores (core1 and core2) on the PS. Voting between the two chains is performed by IP3 located on the FPGA ("VoteAndSendTorqueCommand").

Finally note that calculation of the reaction wheels' command can be done in a similar way via CPU2 ("ReactionWheelsCmd2"); each reaction wheel generates a torque ("GenerateTorqueX") from the commands received from the two channels (i.e., CPU1 or CPU2) via the "Consolidation" function.

The architectural description presented before is completed with failure-related information:

- Faults, fault activation rates, and protection rates against faults are attributes of a physical node component. For instance, Fig. 7 shows the "Failure Model" of the "BRAM" node physical component.
- Error propagation to functions, from the hardware on which the functions are deployed or from other functions. For instance, Fig. 8 shows the "Failure Model" of the "StoreRawImage" physical function.
- Failure modes of functions, functional chains, and the satellite system. For instance, Fig. 9 expresses that the system fails if no torque is generated to at least 2 out of 4 reaction wheels (i.e., "GenerateRWTorquesFailureMode"). Note that the failure condition is expressed using a Boolean expression.

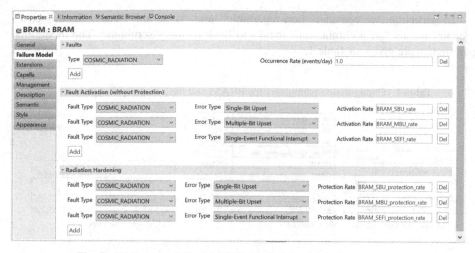

Fig. 7. "Failure model" of the "BRAM" node physical component.

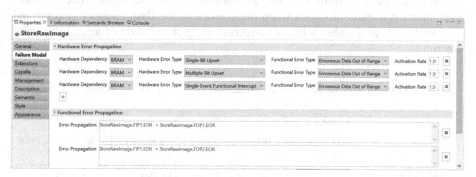

Fig. 8. "Failure model" of the "StoreRawImage" physical function.

Fig. 9. "GenerateRWTorquesFailureMode" of the "OBC1" system.

Availability Calculation. Availability is evaluated on (i) some "unitary" functional chains and (ii) the overall system.

As an example of unitary functional chain, we consider the "Reaction Wheels Command" (Fig. 1) functional chains (1&2) when faults occur on:

- BRAM and flash memories,
- CPU cores.

In particular, we consider "non-repairable" and "repairable" cases. In this case, "repair" means "error elimination" thanks to flash memory scrubbing. The modelling parameters are given on Table 1.

Table 1. Configuration parameters for BRAM and flash memory components.

BRAM_size	638976
BRAM_used_memory	63897
flash_size	256000
flash_used_memory	25600
coreUsageRate	3%

(a) Memory size and usage rates

BRAM_SEFI_rate	1,28E-02
BRAM_SEFI_protection_rate	0,61
BRAM_SBU_rate	4,48E-07
BRAM_SBU_protection_rate	0,3
BRAM_MBU_rate	4,67E-10
BRAM_MBU_protection_rate	0,29
core_SBU_rate	1,02E-02
flash_mbu_rate	6,98E-07
flash_sbu_rate	3,06E-03

(b) Failure rates (evt/day)

	Non Repairable	Repairable
flash_memory_detection_probability	0,0	1,0
flash_memory_detection_latency	0,0ms	0,0ms

(c) Recovery parameters

Results in Table 2 show that the availability of the "Reaction Wheels Command" functional chain increases when the content of the flash memory is corrected (332,499 days of availability without correction vs. 344,953 days of availability with correction).

Table 2. Availability computation of the "Reaction Wheels Command" functional chain.

	Analytical method		Stochastic simulation	
	Non Repairable case	Repairable case	Non Repairable case	Repairable case
Availability of ReactionWheelsCmd1 (days)	–	–	332,499	344,953
Availability of ReactionWheelsCmd1	0,868720915	0,916099707	0,910956164	0,945076712

The system fails if no torque is generated to 2 out of the 4 reaction wheels. This is defined by the "GenerateRWTorquesFailureMode" at the system level (Fig. 9). In order to generate the torque, it is necessary to generate a correct command and to supply power. The power supply may fail due to (a) solar panel failure or (b) a power converter failure. The modelling parameters given in Table 3 also consider the ability to "activate" CPUs redundancy, that is the ability to switch from CV-1 to CV-1 (sru_detection_probability is 1, resp. 0, means that switching is activated, resp. deactivated).

Results in Table 4 show that the availability of the system is significantly improved when redundancy is activated, allowing to switch from CV-1/CPU1 to CV-2/CPU2 in case of loss of power (260,275 days of availability without redundancy vs 286,197 days of availability with redundancy).

Table 3. Configuration parameters for solar panels and power converter boards.

solarElt1_error_rate	1,00E-03
solarElt2_error_rate	1,00E-03
solarElt3_error_rate	1,00E-03
solarElt4_error_rate	1,00E-03

(a) Solar panels failure rates (evt/day)

CV1_error_rate	1,00E-03
CV2_error_rate	1,00E-03

(b) Power converter failure rates (evt/day)

	Switching inactive	Switching active
sru_detection_probability	0,00E+00	1,00E+00
sru_detection_latency	0,00E+00	0,00E+00

(c) Switching parameters

Table 4. Availability computation of the "OBC1" system.

	Availability (days)		Availability (days)	
	Switching inactive	Switching active	Switching inactive	Switching active
Availability of OBC1 system	258,281	286,197	0,707619178	0,78410137

4   Related Work

Model-Based Safety Analysis is an emerging technology, with commercial or proprietary products built upon formal languages such as AltaRica [4]. As products based on AltaRica, notice SimfiaNeo [7] from APSYS or CECILIAS/OCAS from Dassault-Aviation which is used for the certification of jet avionic products. Such environment enables to model dysfunctional behaviour of a system to generate qualitative and quantitative safety analysis of the Electrical and Electronic Architecture. These environments also integrate a module for availability analysis based on stochastic simulation. However, the models used for dysfunctional modelling are not "synchronized" with the models used for system design.

Solutions as the COMPASS tool [8], based on the AADL language [9] and extended with the SLIM language, enable fault and FDIR modelling in relation with system architecture description. However, availability assessment is not covered. Another solution is SOPHIA [10], built on top of the SysML [11] language and Papyrus[6] environment by CEA-LIST. The SOPHIA [12] framework embeds specialized profiles and viewpoints for FTA (Fault Tree Analysis) analysis and generation using AltaRica in background, for FMEA (Failure Mode and Effects Analysis) table generation and for formal verification of properties with the NuSMV [13] language and formal solvers.

The Capella open-source environment [2], specialized for systems engineering and architectural design, offers capabilities to extend domain models and create viewpoints. Capella is the reference framework for system design at Thales, including proprietary solution for various engineering disciplines. Several viewpoints have been developed for safety analysis. The All4tech company developed the Safety Architect[7] product

---

[6] https://www.eclipse.org/papyrus/.

[7] https://www.all4tec.com/safety-architect-logiciel-amdec-fta.

enabling to capture information for safety analysis and to interoperate with the Capella and Papyrus environments. Thales Alenia Space (TAS) has also developed a reliability viewpoint for satellite industry needs [1], allowing to capture reliability data for satellite units and then to compute reliability figures of the system. However, the aforementioned Capella-based viewpoints do not allow to perform availability analysis. Furthermore, they are not precise enough to handle SoC sub-systems with decomposition details and annotations to perform safety and availability analysis.

5   Conclusion

In this paper, we have presented the ELMASAT tool that extends the Capella MBSE environment with a viewpoint to evaluate availability of a system represented by its physical architectural model. In the current version of the tool, focus is placed on hardware faults due, in particular, to radiations (Single-Event Effects).

The viewpoint captures the propagation of errors through the dependencies between the functions and their supporting hardware resources and through the functional flows. The viewpoint provides support to model and evaluate consolidation and reconfiguration schemes. Two modes of availability computations are implemented: one using an analytical formulation of availability and one based on stochastic simulation.

Even though focus is placed in the space application domain (in particular because we are interested in radiation effects), the approach and tool are domain independent and could well be used in any other industrial domain, such as automotive, where ensuring high-availability with COTS components is a major challenge.

Several extensions of the tool are possible. In the current version, values of parameters are given either "internally" in the modelling environment or "externally" using symbolic parameters valuated in an Excel sheet. A simple extension would be to retrieve those parameters from a database. More fundamentally, the tool is limited to the evaluation of availability. It could be extended to cover other RAMS analyses or, conversely, be integrated in a broader environment. This objective is to be addressed in a starting ESA project. Trade-off analysis is another aspect that could be investigated more deeply. In fact, the current version of the tool already provides support to perform simple trade-off analyses thanks to (1) the capability to use symbolic parameters in the model, (2) estimate quantities provided by other viewpoints such as mass or performance, and (3) explore multiple valuations of these parameters in an automatic manner. However, in the current approach, the architecture of the model is not a configuration parameter; so, if the user wants to investigate multiple architectures differing structurally (e.g., a 2-out-of-3 architecture vs. a dual architecture with self-checking pairs), s/he needs to build different models. An improvement would be to find a way to "parametrize" the architecture to ease the evaluation of multiple architectural choices.

Finally, as for any other model-based method, reliability and accuracy of the results strongly depend on the reliability and accuracy of the model itself. This is critical when it comes to account for low-level effects occurring in hardware components (e.g., SoCs) which complexity and limited documentation make accurate models difficult to build and assess. Therefore, providing some way to account for modelling uncertainty in the evaluation would definitively be useful.

Acknowledgements. The authors would like to thank the European Space Agency for funding this work in the context of the OSIP 2020 call under contract number 4000133652/20/NL/GLC/kk.

References

1. Bitetti, L., Ferluc, R.D., Mailland, D., Gregoris, G., Capogna, F.: Model-based approach for RAMS analyses in the space domain with Capella open-source tool. In: Papadopoulos, Y., Aslansefat, K., Katsaros, P., Bozzano, M. (eds.) IMBSA 2019. LNCS, vol. 11842, pp. 18–31. Springer, Cham (2019). https://doi.org/10.1007/978-3-030-32872-6_2
2. Voirin, J.-L.: Model-Based System and Architecture Engineering with the Arcadia Method. Elsevier, Amsterdam (2017)
3. Laprie, J.-C.: Dependability: basic concepts and terminology. In: Laprie, J.C. (ed.) Dependability: Basic Concepts and Terminology. Dependable Computing and Fault-Tolerant Systems, vol. 5, pp. 3–245. Springer, Vienna (1992). https://doi.org/10.1007/978-3-7091-9170-5_1
4. Prosvirnova, T., et al.: The AltaRica 3.0 project for model-based safety assessment. In: 4th IFAC Workshop on Dependable Control of Discrete Systems (2013)
5. Modarres, M., Kaminskiy, M., Krivtsov, V.: Reliability Engineering and Risk Analysis: A Practical Guide. CRC Press, Boca Raton (2016)
6. Sinibaldi, C., Vella, B., Bonnet, F., Spizzi, P.: Modular boxes for a modular architecture. In: 33rd Annual AIAA/USU Conference on Small Satellites (2019)
7. Machin, M., Sagaspe, L., de Bossoreille, X.: SimfiaNeo, complex systems, yet simple safety. In: 9th European Congress on Embedded Real-Time Software and Systems (2018)
8. Yushtein, Y., et al.: System-software co-engineering: dependability and safety perspective. In: 2011 IEEE Fourth International Conference on Space Mission Challenges for Information Technology (2011)
9. Feiler, P.H., Lewis, B.A., Vestal, S.: The SAE architecture analysis design language (AADL) a standard for engineering performance critical systems. In: 2006 IEEE Conference on Computer Aided Control Systems Design (2006)
10. Adedjouma, M., Yakymets, N.: A framework for model-based dependability analysis of cyber-physical systems. In: IEEE 19th International Symposium on High Assurance Systems Engineering (2019)
11. Friedenthal, S., Moore, A., Steiner, R.: A Practical Guide to SysML: The Systems Modeling Language. Elsevier, Amsterdam (2014)
12. Yakymets, N., Munoz, J., Lanusse, A.: Sophia un environnement pour l'analyse de sûreté à partir de modèles (Sophia framework for model-based safety analysis). In: 9e Congrès de Maîtrise des Risques et Sûreté de Fonctionnement (2014)
13. Cimatti, A., et al.: NuSMV 2: an OpenSource tool for symbolic model checking. In: Brinksma, E., Larsen, K.G. (eds.) CAV 2002. LNCS, vol. 2404, pp. 359–364. Springer, Heidelberg (2002). https://doi.org/10.1007/3-540-45657-0_29

Analysing the Impact of Security Attacks on Safety Using SysML and Event-B

Ehsan Poorhadi[✉], Elena Troubitsyna[✉], and György Dán

KTH – Royal Institute of Technology, Stockholm, Sweden
{poorhadi,elenatro,gyuri}@kth.se

Abstract. Safety-critical control systems increasingly rely on networking technologies, which makes these systems vulnerable to cyber attacks that can potentially jeopardise system safety. To achieve safe- and secure-by-construction development, the designers should analyse the impact of security attacks already at the modelling stage. Since SysML is often used for modelling safety-critical systems, in this paper, we propose to integrate modelling in SysML and Event-B to enable reasoning about safety-security interactions at system modelling stage. Our approach combines the benefits of graphical modelling in SysML with the mathematical rigor of Event-B to visualise and formalise the analysis of the impact of security attacks on system safety.

Keywords: Safety-security interactions · Integrated approach · Formal specification and verification · Graphical modelling

1 Introduction

Safety-critical control systems are increasingly relying on networking technologies. The resulting Networked Control Systems (NCS) inherently become the target of cyber attacks that can potentially jeopardize system safety. The interactions between safety and security are often complex, and thus, they should be analysed systematically and rigorously already in the modeling stage of system design.

SysML [9] is a graphical modeling language that is widely used for modelling safety-critical control systems. It allows the designers to describe the system architecture and the dynamic behaviour using convenient diagrammatic notation. SysML extensions addressing security have also been proposed [12]. However, while SysML facilitates a multi-view modelling of system behaviour, it should be combined with formal verification to ensure that the impact of cyber attacks on safety can be thoroughly analysed. Such an analysis should identify the conditions under which safety cannot be guaranteed and provide the input for defining appropriate security control mechanisms.

Supported by Trafikverket, Sweden.

In this paper, we focus on analysing tampering and deletion attacks. We propose an integrated approach that combines graphical modelling in SysML with formal specification and verification in Event-B [11]. Event-B is a state-based rigorous framework for correct-by-construction development of reactive systems. The framework has a powerful automated tool support – the Rodin platform [10]. Rodin provides an integrated modelling environment for specification and proof-based verification of complex systems.

In this paper, we use a subset of SysML diagrams to model the behaviour of a NCS. We define the main requirements that SysML diagrams should fulfil to enable their translation into Event-B, and an explicit analysis of safety-security interactions. Such requirements are formalised as consistency rules that should be verified to ensure correct translation into Event-B. The translation is integrated into the correct-by-construction refinement chain, i.e., at each refinement step, certain aspects of system behaviour represented in SysML are formally specified in Event-B. The resulting Event-B specification models the impact of attacks and identifies safety requirements, formalised as model invariants, which cannot be preserved. Such a specification serves as a basis for the consecutive security analysis aiming at defining security control mechanisms and prioritizing their implementation.

The rest of the paper is structured as follows. In Sect. 2 we define a generic architecture of NCS and define tampering and deletion attacks in this context. In Sect. 3, we define SysML diagrams used for modelling NCS. In Sect. 4, we briefly overview modelling in Event-B. In Sect. 5, we present our approach to translating SysML into Event-B and the reasoning about safety-security interactions, and in Sect. 6 we present the impact analysis of cyber attacks. In Sect. 7 we overview the related work and Sect. 8 concludes the paper.

2   Generic Architecture of Networked Control System

In this section, we define a generic architecture of a NCS and discuss the impact of cyber attacks on safety. The generic architecture is shown in Fig. 1. We assume, without loss of generality, that the system is responsible for maintaining some critical parameter P within a safe interval,

$$P_{min} \leq P \leq P_{max}.$$

The system behavior is cyclic. Each cycle executes a control loop that starts from the sensor measuring the parameter P and sending a message $sensor_{out}$ to the controller. The controller computes a command $cont_{out}$ and sends it to the actuator. The computation is based on a control algorithm and on the input $cont_{in}$ received from the sensor. Finally, the actuator changes its state according to the command $actuator_{in}$ that it receives from the controller. The actuator's state affects the value of the critical parameter P.

In this paper, we consider fail-safe systems, i.e., systems that can be put in a safe non-operational state if there is risk of a safety hazard. To keep the actual

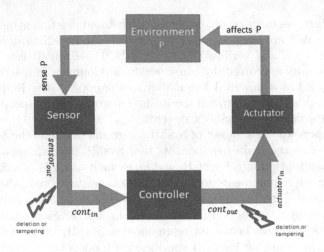

Fig. 1. Architecture of an NCS.

physical value of the critical parameter within the safe interval, we take into account an imprecision $\Delta \in \mathbb{N}$. Hence, the safety property can be defined as

$$Safety: \quad P_{min} - \Delta \leq P \leq P_{max} + \Delta \quad \vee \quad FailSafe = TRUE, \quad (1)$$

In our generic architecture of an NCS there are wireless or wired communication channels between sensor-controller and controller-actuator. These channels can be attacked. In this paper, we study Man-in-the-middle attacks resulting in tampering or deletion of messages sent over the communication channels. These attacks on the sensor-controller channel would result in the controller receiving an incorrect sensor reading or no reading at all. As a consequence, the controller could compute an incorrect, possibly hazardous control command. An attack on the controller-actuator channel would result in the direct setting of the actuator to a dangerous state. We can formalize tampering attacks as

$$sensor_{out} \neq cont_{in} \quad \vee \quad cont_{out} \neq actuator_{in}, \quad (2)$$

i.e., the sent and the received messages are different. The deletion attack can be formalized as

$$cont_{in} = null \quad \vee \quad actuator_{in} = null, \quad (3)$$

where *null* represents an empty message. The attacker can combine deletion and tampering attacks on both channels to create a powerful attack scenario that can bypass defense mechanisms and violate safety.

To systematically analyze the impact of cyberattacks on safety, in this paper we propose an approach that combines graphical modeling in SysML with

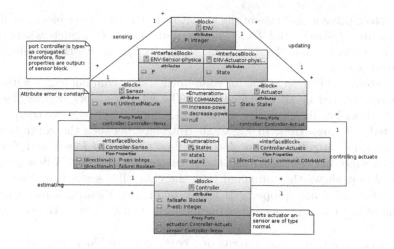

Fig. 2. A BDD for a generic NCS.

formal specification and formal verification in Event-B. In the next section, we will describe how to model an NCS in SysML in such a way that cyber attacks could be explicitly represented in the consequent translation into Event-B specifications.

3   SysML Representation of NCSs

System modeling language (SysML) [9] is a general-purpose modeling language for system engineering applications. Different aspects of system architecture and dynamic behaviour can be modelled using different subsets of nine SysML diagrams. In our work, this subset includes the block definition diagram (BDD), the state machine diagram (SMD), and the sequence diagram (SD).

To represent the system architecture, we use BDD, which allows us to model system components and their interfaces. We use the SMD to represent the internal dynamic behavior of each component. Finally, we use the SD to model interactions between the components and represent communication protocols. Next we present our approach to SysML modelling of NCS that facilitates subsequent analysis of safety-security interactions in Event-B.

Block Definition Diagram. To represent the architecture of an NCS, we create the BDD. The main modeling primitive of BDD is called a *block*. To explicitly represent cyber attacks, we require that each element of our architecture, including the communication channel, is represented as a corresponding instance of a block. Figure 2 shows the BDD for our generic NCS created according to this principle.

The blocks visualize internal constants and variables of components as typed *attributes* of blocks. For our sensor block, we define the constant value *error* to show the maximum sensor imprecision. In the actuator block, we define an attribute to represent the state of the actuator. In the controller block, we define two attributes $failsafe$ and P_{est}. The attribute $failsafe$ models whether the system is put in the failsafe state. The attribute P_{est} shows the estimation of the critical parameter P.

The interface between a pair of components that communicates with each other is represented by an *interface block*. The interface block defines the data flows, i.e., describes the messages, which are exchanged between two components as directed *flow properties*. In Fig. 2, the interface between the controller and sensor named *Controller-Sensor* has two flow properties *P-sen* and *failure*. For the interface between controller and actuator, we introduce a flow property *command* that shows the command that the controller sends to the actuator. The direction of a flow property is either *in* or *out*. Figure 2 shows that the direction of both flow properties in the interface block between the sensor and controller is *in*.

To specify the inputs and outputs of a component, a block uses *ports*, which are typed by an interface block. A port is typed either *normal* or *conjugated*. If a port is normal, it is used to send or receive the flow properties according to their directions defined in the interface block. Otherwise, the direction of the flow properties are interpreted as inverse. In Fig. 2, the sensor port of the controller is typed with the *Controller-Sensor* interface as *normal* while the controller port of the Sensor block is typed with the same interface block but as *conjugated*. It implies that the flow properties $P - sen$ and $failure$ are outputs and inputs of the sensor and controller, respectively. In this work, we use integers, Boolean, or an enumeration set as the type flow properties and attributes.

In safety-critical system, safety requirements are often defined in terms of the values of a certain physical parameter. Hence, we also introduce the blocks representing the physical environment and corresponding interface blocks to represent, for example, that the sensor estimates the value of a critical physical parameter and the actuator affects its value. In our BDD diagram shown in Fig. 2, it is represented by yellow interface blocks. While BDD allows us to define system components and identify interfaces between them, the actual dynamic interactions between the components is modeled using the SD.

Sequence Diagram. A SD is used to show the interaction between components. The diagram represents the contents and the order of messages. Moreover, the SD can depict complex interactions using interaction *fragments*.

In our modelling of an NCS, we use *loop fragments* to represent the control loop. Our lifelines represent the main components of our generic NCS: the sensor, controller, and actuator as shown in Fig. 3. The lifelines correspond to the instances of the blocks in the BDD shown in Fig. 2. Also, the parameters of the messages should comply with be the flow properties defined in the corresponding interface block. For example, the messages *Failure* and *Measurement* carry the flow properties of the *controller-sensor* interface block.

The *alt fragments* show conditional interactions. We also use the alt fragment to depict the effect the deletion and the tampering attacks on a specific message. For instance, consider the message *command* in Fig. 3, which could be the target

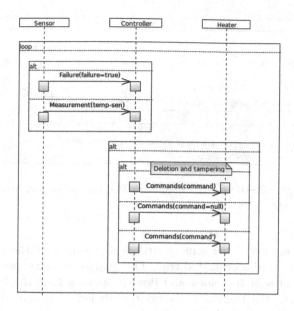

Fig. 3. An example of the SD for an NCS

of deletion or tampering attacks. To represent this, we define an alt fragment that has three alternatives. The first alternative represents the absence of attacks. The second one shows the deletion attack by defining that the parameter command is equal to *null*. Finally, the last one represents the tampering attack. Here we use prime (') to show the injected parameters.

State Machine Diagram. A State Machine Diagram (SMD) is used to represent the internal behavior of system components. It models both the component functional logic and communication protocols. We create an SMD for each block in the BDD and rely on the attributes of the block to model component behaviour. We use the fact that the component (block) can read (write) the flow properties it receives (sends) from the block ports. Figure 4 shows an example of SMD for the block actuator. We require that the transitions defined in SMD are labeled and guarded.

Labels represent the messages that the corresponding block sends or receives. We use labels $r.M$ and $s.M$ for receiving and sending message M, respectively. If a transition is labeled with a message then the message must be received or sent upon triggering the transition.

We also introduce two extra labels *env* and *start* that can be used in SMDs of the blocks *Actuator* and *ENV*, respectively. If a transition is labeled with *env*, it implies that as a result of the transition, the actuator updates its states according to the commands. If a transition is labeled with *start*, it implies that, as a result of the transition, the critical parameter block *ENV* is updated. Figure 4 shows four transitions that may be triggered when the message *Commands* is received.

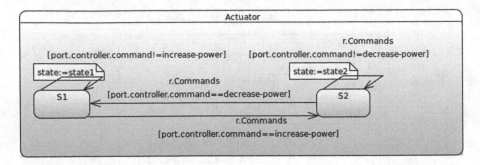

Fig. 4. An example of SMD for the actuator. The expressions in brackets show the guard of transitions.

The transitions may have some guard designating that the transition can occur only if the guard is evaluated true. The guards are the expressions defined using the attributes of the block and flow properties that the block receives. In the latter case, the transition should be labeled with a receiving message that carries the flow properties. SysML allows us to represent opaque behavior expressed in different languages. We describe the opaque behavior expressed in C to specify the guards. In Figs. 4, the guards of transitions are shown in brackets.

The effect of the transition is described using a piece of code containing the following statements: assignment, *if* and a random choice from a given set. The code could assign to the attributes of the block or the output flow properties of the block. In the latter case the transition must be labeled with a sending message that carries the flow properties. Figure 4 shows the effect of two transitions updating the state of the actuator. Note that the behavior is specified using opaque behavior based on C, but in the figure, it is depicted using a comment box.

4   Modelling and Refinement in Event-B

Event-B is a state-based formal modelling approach that promotes the correct-by-construction development paradigm and formal verification by theorem proving. In Event-B, a system model is specified using the notion of an *abstract state machine* [11]. An abstract state machine encapsulates the model state represented as a collection of variables and defines operations on the state, i.e., it describes the *behaviour* of the modelled system. Usually, a machine has an accompanying component, called *context*, which may include user-defined carrier sets, constants and their properties given as a list of model axioms. In Event-B, the model variables are strongly typed by the constraining predicates. These predicates and the other important properties that must be preserved by the model constitute model *invariants*.

The dynamic behaviour of the system is defined by a set of atomic *events*. Generally, an event has the following form:

$$e \mathrel{\widehat{=}} \textbf{any } a \textbf{ where } G_e \textbf{ then } R_e \textbf{ end},$$

where e is the event's name, a is the list of local variables, the *guard* G_e is a predicate over the local variables of the event and the state variables of the system. The body of the event is defined by the next-state relation R_e. In Event-B, R_e is defined by a *multiple* (possibly nondeterministic) assignment over the system variables. The guard defines the conditions under which the assignment can be performed, i.e., when the event is *enabled*. If several events are enabled at the same time, any of them can be chosen for execution non-deterministically.

Event-B employs a top-down refinement-based approach to system development. A development starts from an abstract system specification that non-deterministically models the most essential functional requirements. In a sequence of refinement steps, we gradually reduce non-determinism and introduce detailed design decisions. In particular, we can add new events, split events as well as replace abstract variables by their concrete counterparts, i.e., perform *data refinement*. When data refinement is performed, we should define so called *gluing invariant* as a part of the invariant of the refined machine. The gluing invariant defines the relationship between the abstract and concrete variables.

The consistency of Event-B models, i.e., verification of well-formedness and invariant preservation as well as correctness of refinement steps, is formally demonstrated by discharging the relevant proof obligations generated by the Rodin platform [10]. Rodin also provides an automated tool support for proving.

5   From SysML to Event-B: Translation Methodology

Our translation of SysML diagrams into Event-B aims at achieving two simultaneous goals. On the one hand, as the first step of translation, we check correctness of the SysML diagrams and we verify their consistency. On the other hand, we rely on formalization in Event-B to analyze the impact of cyber attacks on system safety. In this paper, due to lack of space, we only briefly outline our translation methodology and describe formal modelling of safety and security interactions in details.

Since BDD specifies the system's static structure, it defines the name-space of all elements to be used in system modelling. In our translation, BDD serves as the main mechanism to check consistency between models. For example, when we are defining the SD, we can verify that messages coincide with the interface blocks. For SMD, we check whether the block owns the attributes and flow properties that are used in SMD, and the assignments comply their types. We also check the deadlock freeness of the SMDs. To check consistency of the SMD with respect to the SD, we check whether the transition labels correspond to the messages that the block sends or receives in the SD.

CONTEXT correctness

CONSTANTS
    Measurement
    P_sen
AXIOMS
    axm1: $Measurement = \{P\_sen\}$

    axm8: ⟨theorem⟩
        $\forall fp, port \cdot fp \in Measurement \wedge port \in Interface(sensor \mapsto controller) \wedge PortOwner(port) =$
        $sensor \Rightarrow ($
        $(Direction(fp) = out \Rightarrow conjugated(port) = FALSE) \wedge (Direction(fp) = in \Rightarrow conjugated(port) =$
        $TRUE)$
        $)$
    axm9: ⟨theorem⟩
        $\forall fp, port \cdot fp \in Measurement \wedge port \in Interface(sensor \mapsto controller) \wedge PortOwner(port) =$
        $controller \Rightarrow ($
        $(Direction(fp) = out \Rightarrow conjugated(port) = TRUE) \wedge (Direction(fp) = in \Rightarrow conjugated(port) =$
        $FALSE)$
        $)$
    END

Fig. 5. An excerpt from the context in which the correctness of SD will be checked with respect to BDD. As can be seen theorems 8 and 9 show that the direction of message is consistent with the direction of flow properties that it carries.

In our translation methodology, the consistency rules are defined as a separate context of the Event-B model. Such an approach mimics defining a meta-model as a part of formal modelling. The verification conditions are formulated as context theorems. If the proof of some theorem fails then an inconsistency between the models is detected. Upon detecting an inconsistency, the designer needs to change the SysML diagrams and perform the consistency checks again. Figure 5 shows an example of the context with the defined consistency rule.

When the consistency of the SysML model has been established, we shift the focus to translating SMDs and SD, which is incorporated into the Event-B refinement process. Once the refinement process is completed, the SysML models become fully formalised in Event-B and the detailed definition of the impact of cyber attacks on safety emerges via failed proofs of certain safety invariants.

Abstract Specification. The first machine (the abstract specification) is the translation of SD that focuses on modelling sending and receiving messages. While translating SD, we specify the sets representing each type of message. The name of the parameters of messages become the elements of the sets. For instance,

$$Measurement = \{P_{sen}\}.$$

To model sending and receiving messages, we define the set *Phases*,

$$Phases = \{s_{Failure}, r_{Failure}, s_{Measurement}, r_{Measurement},$$
$$s_{Commands}, r_{Commands}, env, start\}.$$

For each message, we define the "sending-receiving" order. In addition, *Phases* has elements designating the environment involving and the start of the control cycle.

To model the order of messages according to their position in the SD, we define the guards of the events ensuring that the previous messages have been sent before sending a message down in the lifeline becomes enabled.

To model tampering and deletion attacks on a message $M(par_1, ..., par_t)$, we define two variables,

$$send_M : \{par_1, ..., par_t\} \rightarrow \mathbf{Z}, \quad receive_M : \{par_1, ..., par_t\} \rightarrow \mathbf{Z},$$

which represent the values of the parameters of the messages after sending and receiving message M. If the attacker decides to perform the deletion attack, we set function $receive_M(par_i) = null$, where *null* is an abstract constant representing an empty message. In case of the tampering attack, we choose a nondeterministic value v_i other than $send_M(par_i)$, and define $receive_M(par_i) = v_i$. Finally, in the absence of attacks, we define $receive_M = send_M$. To model sending and receiving a message, we define two events for each message correspondingly.

The final step in the SD translation is to define an event for each physical interface. This event only changes the phase of interactions. The event corresponding to the actuator-environment interface changes the phase from r_M to *env* in which M is the last message in the control loop. This event models the actuator's behaviour – changing its state according to the controller's commands.

The event corresponding to the environment-sensor interface changes the value of the *phase* from *env* to *start*. This event models the end of the environment evolution resulting in the update of the critical parameter. Figure 6 shows an excerpt from the abstract specification obtained as a result of SD translation. As can be seen, to ensure that the message *Command* will be sent after either *Measurement* or *Failure*, we add guard *grd2* to event *send-Command*. To model the attacks on the message *Command*, we add guards *grd2*, *grd3*, and *grd4* to event *receive-Command*.

Translation-Driven Refinement. Our subsequent refinement steps aim at capturing the details of SMDs modelling the behavour of system components. Our translation and the corresponding refinement process has the following order: representing the behaviour of the environment (ENV), actuator, controller, and finally, sensor.

We start the translation of the SMD with defining the set *States* containing all states as its elements. To model the current state, we define the variable $state_B \in States$, where B is the name of the block.

For each transition in the corresponding SMD, we define an event that is enabled if the current state is equal to the source of the transition. As result of triggering the event, the current state is changed to the destination state of the transition. If a transition is labeled with sending or receiving a message M ($s.M$ or $(r.M)$) then the corresponding event refines the event that models sending or receiving M. If a transition in the actuator's SMD (ENV's SMD) is labeled

INVARIANTS

inv16: $phase = r\_measurement \Rightarrow send\_measurement(P\_sen) = receive\_measurement(P\_sen)$

inv17: $(phase = r\_command \wedge deletion\_attack\_command = FALSE) \Rightarrow send\_commands(command) = receive\_commands(command)$

inv18: $(phase = r\_command \wedge deletion\_attack\_command = TRUE) \Rightarrow receive\_commands(command) = null$

EVENTS

Event send_Failure ⟨ordinary⟩ ≙

Event receive_Failure ⟨ordinary⟩ ≙

Event Physical_Interface_heater_Env ⟨⟩ ≙

Event Physical_Interface_sensor_Env ⟨⟩ ≙

Event send_Measurement ⟨ordinary⟩ ≙

  where

      grd1: $phase = start$

  then

      act1: $phase := s\_measurement$

      act2: $send\_Measurement(P\_sen) := value$

  end

Event receive_Measurement ⟨ordinary⟩ ≙

  where

      grd1: $phase = s\_measurement$

      grd2: $value = send\_measurement(P\_sen)$

  then

      act1: $phase := r\_measurement$

      act2: $receive\_measurement(P\_sen) := value$

  end

Event send_Command ⟨ordinary⟩ ≙

  where

      grd1: $value\_command \in COMMANDS$

      grd2: $phase = r\_measurement \vee phase = r\_failure$

  then

      act1: $phase := s\_command$

      act2: $send\_commands(command) := value$

  end

Event receive_Command ⟨ordinary⟩ ≙

  where

      grd1: $phase = s_{Commands}$

      grd2: $attack \in \{0, 1, 2\}$

      grd3: $attack = 1 \Rightarrow value = null$ Deletion attack

      grd4: $attack = 0 \Rightarrow value = send_{Commands}(command)$ No attacks

  then

      act1: $phase := r_{Commands}$

      act2: $receive_{Commands}(command) := value$

      act3: $attack_{Commands} := attack$

  end

Fig. 6. An excerpt of abstract specification which is the translation of SD.

with env (*start*) then the corresponding event refines the abstract event defined for the Actuator-ENV (ENV-Sensor) physical interface. To specify the events, we translate the guard of the transition into the guard of the corresponding event. The effect of the transition is translated into the actions of the corresponding event.

To translate *guards* and *behaviours*, we introduce a variable for each attribute (that is not a constant) of the relevant block. The dictionary $CtoB$ presented in Table 1 shows how guards and effects of the transitions are translated in Event-B. For translating assignments to an attribute x, we first create a parameter par_x and add the action $x := par_x$. Then for an assignment $x := e$, we add $par_x = CtoB(e)$ to the guard of the event. Note that, in order to avoid deadlock, each attribute must be assigned once per transition. If an assignment is inside of an *if statement*, we add,

$$par_{if} = TRUE \Rightarrow par_x = CtoB(e),$$

to the guard instead of $par_x = CtoB(e)$. A guard g is also translated using $CtoB$ dictionary, however, if the guard is inside of a if statement, then we apply the similar technique.

Figure 7 shows the translation of the SMD shown in Fig. 4.

MACHINE actuator_Machine
REFINES
EVENTS
Event actuator_S1_to_S2 $\langle\ \rangle$ ≙
extends receive_Command
  any
        value
        attack
  where
        grd1: $phase = s_{Commands}$
        grd2: $attack \in \{0,1,2\}$
        grd3: $attack = 1 \Rightarrow value = null$
        grd4: $attack = 0 \Rightarrow value =$
           $send_{Commands}(command)$
        grd5: $state_{actuator} = S1$ Current state
        grd6: $value = command1$
           The guard of the transition
  then
        act1: $phase := r_{Commands}$
        act2: $receive_{Commands}(command) :=$
           $value$
        act3: $attacks_{Commands} := attack$
        act4: $state_{actuator} := S2$ The entering
           state
        act5: $state := state2$ The activity of the
           transition
end

Event actuator_S1_to_S1 $\langle\ \rangle$ ≙
extends receive_Command
  any
        value
        attack
  where
        grd1: $phase = s_{Commands}$
        grd2: $attack \in \{0,1,2\}$
        grd3: $attack = 1 \Rightarrow value = null$
        grd4: $attack = 0 \Rightarrow value =$
           $send_{Commands}(command)$
        grd5: $state_{actuator} = S1$ Current state
        grd6: $value \neq command1$
           The guard of the transition
  then
        act1: $phase := r_{Commands}$
        act2: $receive_{Commands}(command) :=$
           $value$
        act3: $attacks_{Commands} := attack$
        act4: $state_{actuator} := S1$ The entering
           state
        act5: $state := state1$ The activity of the
           transition
  end

Fig. 7. Translation of actuator's SMD into Event-B. Only two out of four events are shown. Red lines are inherited from abstract event in previous machine. (Color figure online)

Table 1. SysMLtoB dictionary.

C	Event-B
&&, ||	$\wedge, \vee$
$==, <=, >=, <, >, =!$	$=, \leq, \geq, >, <, \neq$
$+, -, *, /$	$+, -, \times, \div$
if c { }	**Any** par_{if} **where** $par_{if} = TRUE \Leftrightarrow CtoB(c)$
$rand(1,n)$	**Any** par **where** $par \in 1..n$

6 Analysing the Impact of Cyber Attacks on Safety

In this section, we discuss our approach to verifying the impact of cyber attacks on safety within the SysML translation-driven refinement process. In our approach, the impact of cyber attacks on safety is analysed by checking whether the safety property 1 remains provable, i.e., if after the detailed representation of the effect of the attack on the system behaviour safety invariants remain provable then the cyber attack does not have a safety implication, and vice versa – if the invariants become violated then the cyber attack has safety implications.

Once the SMD diagram is translated into Event-B, we obtain a detailed specification of the corresponding system component and can analyse the impact of a cyber attack on its behaviour. Let $safety'$ be the first term of the disjunction defined in property 1, i.e., safety should be guaranteed after updating the physical parameters at the end of the control loop. As an example, $safety'$ can be defined either as

$$P_{min} - \Delta \leq P + x \leq P_{max} + \Delta,$$

or as

$$P_{min} - \Delta \leq P - x \leq P_{max} + \Delta,$$

for some positive x depending on the state of the actuator ($state1$ or $state2$). We define the following invariants postulating that the actuator enforces safety by preventing the critical parameter from passing the safety margin when it updates its state as follows:

$$(phase = env \wedge state = state1) \Rightarrow P_{min} - \Delta \leq P + x \leq P_{max} + \Delta,$$

$$(phase = env \wedge state = state2) \Rightarrow P_{min} - \Delta \leq P - x \leq P_{max} + \Delta.$$

The proof of the above invariants requires demonstrating that the actuator should be able to receive the correct command from the controller irrespective whether the attack is carried out or not. This implies that we should guarantee that the controller logic is correct and the attacker actions cannot put the actuator in a state that causes violation of above invariants. There requirements are modelled by the guards of the events representing sending and receiving *Commands*. Later, in the next refinement in which we translate the controller's SMD, we remove these guards.

In the next refinement steps, when the controller's SMD is translated, we change the requirements from the guard of the events to be theorems. At this point, we need to prove that the logic of the controller implies the theorems. The key invariants that conclude the theorems are,

$$phase = s_{Commands} \Rightarrow failsafe = FALSE,$$

$$phase = s_{Commands} \wedge send_{Command}(command) = increasePower \Rightarrow$$
$$P_{min} - \Delta \leq P + x \leq P_{max} + \Delta,$$

and

$$phase = s_{Commands} \wedge send_{Command}(command) = decreasePower \Rightarrow$$
$$P_{min} - \Delta \leq P - x \leq P_{max} + \Delta,$$

Proving the invariants requires that security control mechanisms detect attacks on both sensor-controller and controller-actuator channels because they lead to safety violation. In this case, the controller sets $falisafe = TRUE$, and we never reach a state of the model in which $phase = s_{Command}$. Also, depending on the details of the controller logic, we may need to introduce assumptions about the sensor's imprecision. These assumptions can be added to the guard of event in which message *Measurement* is received. In the next refinement step resulting in adding the model of the sensor, we prove the assumption about the sensor imprecision.

Finally, upon translating all SMDs, we can define the safety property 1 as an invariant of the final model and try to prove it. At this point, the prove should be discharged without introducing any further assumptions.

7   Related Work

Several previous works proposed different modelling approaches to represent the impact of security attacks on safety within Event-B framework [1,2]. The authors explored different refinement strategies as well as the use of HAZOP for requirements elicitation [3]. While our approach adopts the idea of an incremental unfolding system architecture via refinement, we rely on SysML models as an intermediate step between the informal requirements description and formal specification. We were encouraged by railway industry to integrate SysML into our modelling to help system engineers to understand both formal models and security analysis results. The work on formal modelling of cyberattacks in the railway domain is reported in our previous work [4]. In this paper, we have extended the modelling methodology proposed in [4], on the one hand, to support an integration between SysML and Event-B for generic NCS, and, on the other hand, to include modelling of deletion and tampering attacks on both channels of NCS.

The work on integrating general purpose graphical modelling and formal specification has been carried by Snook et al. [5]. Currently, there is also an UML-B plugin is available for the Rodin platform that enables an automatic translation of UML-B into Event-B specification [6]. We have adopted the similar techniques in translating state machine diagrams but focused on explicit modelling and verification of safety-security interactions.

UML-B has been used in some works to analyze the safety of NCS. For example, in [7], UML-B is used to model hybrid ERTMS level 3. However, our work includes a broader set of SysML diagrams and allows to express a richer set of properties.

Quamara et al. [8] proposed a multi-layer model-based engineering approach addressing safety-security interactions. They also rely on graphical and formal modelling but focus on identifying conflicts between safety and security requirements.

8   Conclusion

In this work, we proposed an integrated approach to modelling the impact of cyber-security attacks on safety of networked control systems. We have defined the principles of modelling networked control systems in SysML to enable an explicit reasoning about safety-security interactions. We also introduced a methodology for translating SysML BDDs, SD and SMDs into Event-B. Our methodology supports the verification of consistency of SysML diagrams as well as enables a rigorous analysis of the impact of security on safety.

Our SysML translation into Event-B has been incorporated into the correct-by-construction development process. It allowed us to explicitly analyse the impact of security attacks on the behaviour of each component as well as the overall system safety. The resultant model explicitly demonstrates which safety invariants become violated as the result of the attacks. Pro-B model checker can be used to construct the concrete attack scenarios.

The work on the integration of SysML and Event-B for modelling safety-security interactions in networked control systems has been motivated by our cooperation with railway industry. Since SysML is widely used for system modelling, we believe that the proposed integration approach can facilitate understanding of formal models and the results of modelling the security attacks by the industrial engineers.

As a future work, we are planning to investigate modelling of the other types of attacks, such as injection, reordering and delaying. It would be also interesting to work on representing the results of formal modelling in SysML, e.g. to visualise the attack scenarios. There is also an ongoing work on the automation of the proposed approach.

References

1. Troubitsyna, E., Laibinis, L., Pereverzeva, I., Kuismin, T., Ilic, D., Latvala, T.: Towards security-explicit formal modelling of safety-critical systems. In: Skavhaug, A., Guiochet, J., Bitsch, F. (eds.) SAFECOMP 2016. LNCS, vol. 9922, pp. 213–225. Springer, Cham (2016). https://doi.org/10.1007/978-3-319-45477-1_17

2. Vistbakka, I., Troubitsyna, E., Kuismin, T., Latvala, T.: Co-engineering safety and security in industrial control systems: a formal outlook. In: Romanovsky, A., Troubitsyna, E.A. (eds.) SERENE 2017. LNCS, vol. 10479, pp. 96–114. Springer, Cham (2017). https://doi.org/10.1007/978-3-319-65948-0_7

3. Troubitsyna, E., Vistbakka, I.: Deriving and formalising safety and security requirements for control systems. In: Gallina, B., Skavhaug, A., Bitsch, F. (eds.) SAFECOMP 2018. LNCS, vol. 11093, pp. 107–122. Springer, Cham (2018). https://doi.org/10.1007/978-3-319-99130-6_8

4. Poorhadi, E., Troubitysna, E., Dán, G.: Formal modelling of the impact of cyber attacks on railway safety. In: Habli, I., Sujan, M., Gerasimou, S., Schoitsch, E., Bitsch, F. (eds.) SAFECOMP 2021. LNCS, vol. 12853, pp. 117–127. Springer, Cham (2021). https://doi.org/10.1007/978-3-030-83906-2_9

5. Snook, C., Butler, M.: UML-B: formal modeling and design aided by UML. ACM Trans. Softw. Eng. Methodol **15**, 92–122 (2006). https://doi.org/10.1145/1125808.1125811

6. UML-B. https://www.uml-b.org/

7. Dghaym, D., Dalvandi, M., Poppleton, M., Snook, C.: Formalising the hybrid ERTMS level 3 specification in iUML-B and Event-B. Int. J. Softw. Tools Technol. Transf. **22**(3), 297–313 (2019). https://doi.org/10.1007/s10009-019-00548-w

8. Quamara, M., Pedroza, G., Hamid, B.: Multi-layered model-based design approach towards system safety and security co-engineering. In: 2021 ACM/IEEE International Conference on Model Driven Engineering Languages and Systems Companion (MODELS-C), pp. 274–283 (2021). https://doi.org/10.1109/MODELS-C53483.2021.00048

9. SysML. https://sysml.org/

10. The RODIN platform. http://rodin-b-sharp.sourceforge.net/

11. Abrial, J.: Extending B without changing it (for developing distributed systems). In: Proceedings of 1st Conference on the B Method, pp. 169–191, Springer, Verlag, Nantes, France, November 1996
12. Lemaire, L., Lapon, J., Decker, B., Naessens, V.: A SysML extension for security analysis of industrial control systems. In: Proceedings of the 2nd International Symposium on ICS and SCADA Cyber Security Research 2014 (ICS-CSR 2014), pp. 1–9. BCS, Swindon, GBR (2014). https://doi.org/10.14236/ewic/ics-csr2014.1

Data Based Safety Analysis

A Deep Learning Framework for Wind Turbine Repair Action Prediction Using Alarm Sequences and Long Short Term Memory Algorithms

Connor Walker[1,2], Callum Rothon[1,2], Koorosh Aslansefat[1,2(✉)],
Yiannis Papadopoulos[1,2], and Nina Dethlefs[1,2]

[1] University of Hull, Hull HU6 7RX, UK
{auracdt,k.aslansefat}@hull.ac.uk
[2] AURA CDT, Hull, UK
https://auracdt.hull.ac.uk/

Abstract. With an increasing emphasis on driving down the costs of Operations and Maintenance (O&M) in the Offshore Wind (OSW) sector, comes the requirement to explore new methodology and applications of Deep Learning (DL) to the domain. Condition-based monitoring (CBM) has been at the forefront of recent research developing alarm-based systems and data-driven decision making. This paper provides a brief insight into the research being conducted in this area, with a specific focus on alarm sequence modelling and the associated challenges faced in its implementation. The paper proposes a novel idea to predict a set of relevant repair actions from an input sequence of alarm sequences, comparing Long Short-term Memory (LSTM) and Bidirectional LSTM (biLSTM) models. Achieving training accuracy results of up to 80.23%, and test accuracy results of up to 76.01% with biLSTM gives a strong indication to the potential benefits of the proposed approach that can be furthered in future research. The paper introduces a framework that integrates the proposed approach into O&M procedures and discusses the potential benefits which include the reduction of a confusing plethora of alarms, as well as unnecessary vessel transfers to the turbines for fault diagnosis and correction.

Keywords: Condition-based monitoring (cbm) · Deep Learning (dl) · Long Short-term Memory (lstm) · Offshore Wind Farm (osw) · Repair action prediction · Supervisory Control and Data Acquisition (scada)

1 Introduction

O&M is currently the second largest sub-sector market within OSW [15] and is projected to rise to the largest sub-sector by 2050 [15]. This development leads to an increased interest into research both to drive down costs associated with O&M, as well as the safety of alarm-based systems.

C. Seguin et al. (Eds.): IMBSA 2022, LNCS 13525, pp. 189–203, 2022.
https://doi.org/10.1007/978-3-031-15842-1_14

Currently, O&M consists of three major methods: preventative, failure-based and condition-based monitoring [21]. The latter of these is the method most relevant to the success of alarm systems and alarm sequencing prediction. CBM relies on the alarm systems currently in place within turbines as well as SCADA systems [14]. SCADA has become a standard installation in larger turbines offshore in recent years, which means that the data collected is increasing rapidly, thus creating potential for new performance benchmarks within machine learning (ML) models applied in this area [18].

The alarms linked to typical SCADA systems for OSW turbines allow monitoring of almost all sub-components [10]. This is not an easy task for a number of reasons. Firstly, there is a certain risk of alarm flooding, especially since alarms may cascade during disturbances, as one symptom of the disturbance follows another. Alarm flooding refers to the relationship between alarm sequences and is defined as "10 or more enunciated alarms within a 10-minute period per operator" [11]. Where one alarm sounds, it is likely to then trigger other alarms due to the close relationships between components' behaviour and overall performance. Multiple activated alarms can often distract from the original fault, leading to more downtime on the site whilst diagnostic reports are produced [19]. Secondly, systems can generate false alarms, i.e. alarms caused by sensor failures and not as a result of process disturbances. To cascading and false alarms, one can add alarms created during maintenance. False and maintenance alarms are not only confusing for operators that oversee the health and safety of the turbine, but can also confuse automated ML algorithms, that are trained on this data, e.g. for the purposes of fault isolation or generation of repair actions [13].

Current standards across industries, including EEMUA-191 [12] and ANSI/ISA-18.2 [3], detail the design, management and procurement of alarm systems as well as the alarm management specific to process industries [5]. These standards are used as a foundation for improving alarm processing and prediction of likely repair schedules, but they don't prescribe or enforce specific techniques that address the significant problems mentioned above. To address these issues and to achieve appropriate fault isolation and ultimately repair action prediction, in this paper, we propose a novel approach utilising alarm sequences to predict repair actions accurately and efficiently. Our contributions are:

- A DL based approach to predict repair actions from a sequence of alarms. The paper experiments with both LSTM and BiLSTM algorithms for comparison of performance on this problem.
- A conceptual framework to integrate the idea of repair action prediction into OSW farm O&M procedures.
- The proposed use of reinforcement learning in a human-in-the-loop procedure to improve the accuracy of the DL model over time.

In Sect. 2, we discuss the research question. In Sect. 3, we detail our methodology and compare it to other approaches within the domain. The methodology section discusses the pre-processing of data, the design of the neural network, and experiments. Section 4 discusses results and application to industry and conclusions follow in Sect. 5.

2   Research Questions

Figure 1 shows a sample anonymised alarm sequence for a specific date. The OSW farm operators have to check these alarms and then based on experience decide or predict what should be repaired to fix the alarm. Some companies like SIEMENS provide a private and expensive software that can predict a potential required repair action(s) based on existing alarms for specific types of turbines. Based on our observation on Teesside Wind Farm, there are some specific dates that the operator faced more than 500 simultaneous alarms in a single day. This situation is challenging for human operators and, ideally, requires a technology that can assist operators by converting the large number of alarms to a small number of suggested required repair actions.

Inputs

TimeOn	TimeOnString	TimeOff	DurationSec	Turbine Name	AlarmText	
08:02:16	2016-02-22T08:02:16	22/02/2016	1094	WTG16	Alarm (1)	
08:02:16	2016-02-22T08:02:16	22/02/2016	61	WTG16	Alarm (2)	
08:02:17	2016-02-22T08:02:17	22/02/2016	64	WTG16	Alarm (3)	
08:02:18	2016-02-22T08:02:18	22/02/2016	1088	WTG16	Alarm (4)	
08:02:35	2016-02-22T08:02:35	22/02/2016	1068	WTG16	Alarm (5)	
08:03:21	2016-02-22T08:03:21	22/02/2016	1019	WTG16	Alarm (6)	
08:03:21	2016-02-22T08:03:21	22/02/2016	1020	WTG16	Alarm (7)	
08:03:22	2016-02-22T08:03:22	22/02/2016	1016	WTG16	Alarm (8)	
08:03:23	2016-02-22T08:03:23	22/02/2016	6	WTG16	Alarm (9)	Repeated Alarms
08:03:29	2016-02-22T08:03:29	22/02/2016	1008	WTG16	Alarm (9)	
08:20:17	2016-02-22T08:20:17	22/02/2016	98	WTG16	Alarm (9)	
08:20:21	2016-02-22T08:20:21	22/02/2016	352	WTG16	Alarm (10)	
08:20:23	2016-02-22T08:20:23	22/02/2016	345	WTG16	Alarm (11)	
08:20:23	2016-02-22T08:20:23	22/02/2016	74	WTG16	Alarm (12)	
08:20:30	2016-02-22T08:20:30	22/02/2016	337	WTG16	Alarm (13)	
08:21:33	2016-02-22T08:21:33	22/02/2016	0	WTG16	Alarm (14)	
08:21:43	2016-02-22T08:21:43	22/02/2016	12	WTG16	Alarm (15)	
08:26:14	2016-02-22T08:26:14	22/02/2016	8	WTG16	Alarm (16)	
08:26:23	2016-02-22T08:26:23	22/02/2016	882	WTG16	Alarm (16)	Repeated Alarms
08:26:33	2016-02-22T08:26:33	22/02/2016	2670	WTG16	Manual Stop	Alarms Caused by
08:26:34	2016-02-22T08:26:34	22/02/2016	869	WTG16	Manual Idle Stop	Manual Actions
08:40:38	2016-02-22T08:40:38	22/02/2016	1908	WTG16	Turbine in Local Operation	
08:42:13	2016-02-22T08:42:13	22/02/2016	33	WTG16	Alarm (17)	
08:42:13	2016-02-22T08:42:13	22/02/2016	34	WTG16	Alarm (18)	
08:42:14	2016-02-22T08:42:14	22/02/2016	32	WTG16	Alarm (19)	
08:42:15	2016-02-22T08:42:15	22/02/2016	9	WTG16	Alarm (20)	
08:46:17	2016-02-22T08:46:17	22/02/2016	1800	WTG01	Alarm (21)	
09:34:09	2016-02-22T09:34:09	22/02/2016	6044	WTG22	Turbine in Local Operation	
11:19:04	2016-02-22T11:19:04	22/02/2016	13043	WTG22	Turbine in Local Operation	
16:59:42	2016-02-22T16:59:42	22/02/2016	210	WTG15	Alarm (22)	
17:11:34	2016-02-22T17:11:34	22/02/2016	210	WTG27	Alarm (22)	

Fig. 1. A sample anonymised alarm sequences for a specific date

Figure 2 shows a sample of anonymised repair actions performed the same date in response to the alarms of Fig. 1. If we consider the alarm sequences observed as an input and repair actions as an output, our main research question is how a DL model can be used to predict the required repair actions given the input SCADA alarm sequences. Moreover, we ask how this model can be integrated into the operation and management processes of industry? and how it can evolve and improve itself over time.

Outputs

Turbine Name	Order Description	Order Type	Type of Work	Start Date	Start Time
WTG16	Repair Action (1)	Corrective	Repair	22/02/2016	08:00:00
WTG16	Repair Action (2)	Corrective	Repair	22/02/2016	08:30:00
WTG22	Repair Action (3)	Corrective	Repair	22/02/2016	10:00:00
WTG22	Repair Action (4)	Corrective	Repair	22/02/2016	10:30:00
WTG22	Repair Action (5)	Corrective	Repair	22/02/2016	11:00:00
WTG22	Repair Action (6)	Corrective	Repair	22/02/2016	11:30:00
WTG22	Repair Action (7)	Corrective	Repair	22/02/2016	11:30:00
WTG22	Repair Action (8)	Corrective	Repair	22/02/2016	11:45:00
WTG22	Repair Action (9)	Corrective	Repair	22/02/2016	12:30:00
WTG22		Corrective	Replacement	22/02/2016	13:30:00

Fig. 2. A sample anonymised repair actions for a specific date

3   Methodology

We address those research questions by developing DL models that perform this function based on Recurrent Neural Networks (RNN) and we show how these models can evolve and improve themselves over time using reinforcement learning. It has been shown that RNN models have great promise in Natural Language Processing (NLP) [8]. An RNN is a neural network with feedback connections. Each cell's output not only gives information to the next layer, but it also gets feedback from itself. The Long short-term memory (LSTM) network is a kind of RNN that has one input layer, one output layer, and two hidden layers. We have chosen to base our methodology on LSTM and BiLSTM models for the following advantages that they offer:

- A DL based approach to predict repair actions from a sequence of alarms. The paper experiments with both LSTM and BiLSTM algorithms for comparison of performance on this problem
- A conceptual framework to integrate the idea of repair action prediction into OSW farm O&M procedures.
- The proposed use of reinforcement learning in a human-in-the-loop procedure to improve the accuracy of the DL model over time.

The LSTM model is commonly applied in NLP, to predict the most probable response to a given sequence of inputs. In this work, inputs are the alarm sequences and responses are repair actions. LSTMs are a form of Recurrent Neural Network, that have been proven effective in time-sequence forecasting, making them well suited to this application. Word Embeddings were used to prepare the alarm and response sequences for input into the LSTM layer. Word Embeddings are a fixed-length vector representation of words [1], which provide context by situating the sequence inside a multi-dimensional semantic vector space. The embedded sequences are suitable for use as a numerical input into an LSTM layer. In this case, each alarm and response are embedded as vector.

Research by Cai et al. [5] uses an LSTM-based process to predict the next alarm in a sequence given the previous alarm, with the intention of reducing alarm nuisance and overload. We use a similar LSTM-based methodology, with the crucial difference that we predict the most probable repair response to a sequence of alarms. This has multiple benefits over the mere prediction of the next alarm in a sequence, as the operator is given advice on repair. The operator may accept or reject the suggested repair and does not have to process the alarm information in order to infer the appropriate response. This automated support allows faster response to an alarm, which allows more rapid and dynamic O&M, with reduced downtime of turbines while awaiting maintenance. Also, the likelihood of human error in the prescription of a response is reduced, provided that the system is trained to provide sufficient accuracy.

The complete methodology is shown with examples of inputs and outputs in Fig. 3. The inputs are received as a list of alarms in a time sequence, leading up to a response. These alarms then go through the pre-processing stages. Chattering alarms such as the two instances of Alarm 3 within a minute are removed, the alarms are embedded as vectors, and the alarm sequence is predicted through a Markov chain. The sequences of vectors are then input into the LSTM, with the response as the target during training. The response actions are processed to remove nuisance, mapped into vectors, and then output as recommendations. The outputs are in the form of predicted response actions with a probability, and the most likely response is taken as the prediction. Each stage of the methodology is described in more detail throughout Sect. 3.

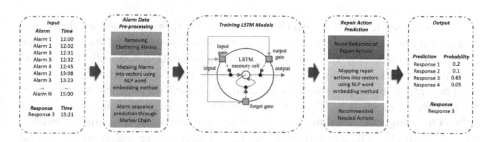

Fig. 3. Flowchart of the methodology, including examples of inputs and outputs

3.1 Data Preparation and Pre-processing

The Teesside OSW Farm was used as a case study to develop the method. This wind farm is known as Redcar Wind Farm and it is owned by EDF Energy. This OSW farm has 27, 2–3 MW turbines that can guarantee the total capacity of 62 MW. In collaboration with EDF Energy R&D London, we have received 5–years (from 2013 to 2018) of data in various forms such as alarm data, repair actions, repair plans, maintenance procedure, etc. Due to the confidentiality of the data, the results that can be shown in this section are limited and the provided data is anonymised. Figure 4 shows the class distribution of anonymised repair actions. In this figure, repair actions that had a frequency of less than 70 were filtered.

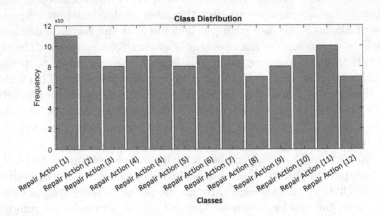

Fig. 4. Class distribution of anonymised repair actions (filtering repair actions with distribution less than 70)

The pre-processing consisted of importing data into MATLAB, and preparing them for input into the LSTM network. The input data was a set of alarms and a set of responses, with each alarm and response having a time and text. This data was normalised and used to build sequences of alarms leading up to a response in a time series.

The data types were set, with the alarm and response times set as "datetime" and alarm and response texts were set as strings. Data cleaning was performed to remove unnecessary data and to remove punctuation from the alarm and response text. The variables were then imported into MATLAB.

The data was pre-processed for each turbine, with an identical process used for turbines 1 through to 27, with turbine 10 being held back for testing. The "TimeOnString" was initialised for the alarm and response files, and a variable "mem" defined as 20, which defines the time interval over which an alarm and response can be associated. In this case, a response can be associated with an alarm that occurred up to 20 days previously, which was considered a reasonable timescale.

The training data was accumulated from the alarm and response schedules from turbines 1–27 over a period of 20 days, by iteratively passing over them and collecting alarm-response pairs. This was completed first for alarms 1–27. From this 27 timetables TT1-27 will have been generated, containing the responses and their preceding alarms. It must be noted at this time that causality has not yet been established (or more correctly, predicted), and the association is purely through the alarm occurring prior to the action.

Some further data cleaning was then performed on the timetables. Noise characters were specified and removed, and empty strings are deleted. Responses with less than 2 entries are classed as infrequent and were removed from the training dataset, as they are unlikely to contribute meaningfully to the model. This threshold was set by plotting a histogram and inspecting the data empirically.

The data was split into a training and validation set, using a holdout of 0.3, which was determined to be a suitable validation split. From the validation set, a further holdout of 0.5 was used to form the testing data, resulting in a training data set of 70% of the data, and validation and testing data sets of 15% each. The text data and the labels are then extracted from these partitioned data sets and labelled as "TextData" and "Y". A word cloud of the text training data was plotted for some initial explainability, demonstrating the distribution of keywords in the data set, showing that certain keywords were prevalent. The keywords cannot be discussed here due to the confidentiality of the dataset. The text data sets were then converted to lowercase characters, tokenised, and punctuation was erased. The benefits of pre-processing via tokenisation are outlined in [6], which demonstrates that simple tokenisation outperforms more complex pre-processing. The data was then encoded using seq2seq [17], converting the documents into sequences. Figure 5 illustrates the histogram of the document length. Based on the distribution of the document lengths, a target length of 75 was used.

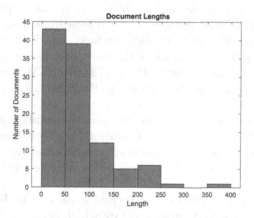

Fig. 5. Histogram of document length

3.2   Building the LSTM Network

Unlike [5], the LSTM network presented in this paper aimed to determine the most likely response (repair actions) to a sequence of alarms as opposed to the next alarm in the sequence. In this methodology, both conventional LSTM and Bi-Directional LSTM (BiLSTM) layers were trialled. When using an LSTM layer, the sequence runs from start to finish, while the BiLSTM runs start to finish and finish to start, and is generally considered to give improved accuracy of predictions, as shown in [7], and has been utilised in NLP by [4]. The structure of the LSTM model is shown in Fig. 6, both during training and during prediction.

To embed the words into vectors for input into the LSTM layer, Word2vec was used with pre-trained embeddings. Pre-trained embeddings, a form of transfer learning, are trained using wide corpuses, and give more accurate embeddings than when training from scratch. [9] recommends careful consideration of the pre-trained embeddings that are used, as the context of the training will impact how applicable the embeddings are for use in other models.

The layers of the model were defined with MATLAB variables used to set the parameters of the model which allowed for adjustment where required. The structure of the model is shown during training in Fig. 6a and during prediction in Fig. 6b.

The sequence input layer receives the sequences created in the pre-processing, and is defined as being dependent upon the input size variable, resulting in a one-dimensional input layer, corresponding to the vectorised inputs. The word embedding layer is dependent upon the embedding dimension and the number of hidden units as defined in the variables, giving an embedding layer with 300 dimensions and as many hidden units as there are unique words in the data set. The embedding layer converts the words input into vectors, allowing the LSTM/BiLSTM to process them as numerical data.

The LSTM/BiLSTM layer was defined by the hidden size, giving 300 dimensions, and the output mode defined as "last" which will output the last step of the sequence, the predicted response. This differs from more conventional use of an LSTM, which will aim to predict the next step in the sequence. In this case, the output will be a prediction of the most probable response action given an input sequence. During training, the LSTM/BiLSTM layer will receive the response action at the end of the sequence as the target, and will train based on this.

The fully connected layer is dependent upon the number of elements present in "YTrain". A softmax layer bounds the outputs between 0 and 1, and a classification layer completes the model, delivering predictions between 0 and 1 for the responses. The response with the highest probability is taken as the predicted response.

The LSTM network receives the vectorised sequences as the inputs, with the responses as the targets, and outputs a state which is passed onto the next step of the LSTM. The LSTM trains over a set number of epochs, with an Adam optimiser used. Adam was demonstrated to be more effective than Root Mean Squared Propagation (RMSProp) in many applications by [20], hence its use here. The model is validated using the 15% of data partitioned as the validation set. After the full number of epochs, a trained model is yielded, and the model can be tested and predictions generated from new data.

3.3   Training of the LSTM Network

When training the LSTM, the training parameters were considered to optimise the performance of the model. The number of epochs was set at 50, which was determined to give acceptable accuracy. The gradient threshold was set at 1, and the initial learning rate was set at 0.01. A training progress plot was enabled to give an insight into how the training was progressing. The architecture of the network during training is shown in shown Fig. 6a, with the alarm sequence documents as inputs that undergo embedding, and the vectorised response documents as the targets for training.

3.4 Testing and Prediction

The testing involved using the partitioned 15% of the data set reserved for testing, which has previously not been processed by the model. Prior to testing, the data was pre-processed in the same manner as the training and validation data, predictions were generated from the reserved data, and the accuracy was calculated based on the number of correct predictions divided by the total number of predictions.

Testing of the LSTM network was also performed with the reserved data from Turbine 10. This testing involved the input of the previously unseen data into the trained model to generate predictions. The data was pre-processed as with the data for the previous turbines, and the sequenced alarms were fed into the model, and then predicted responses and scores were produced. Based on these labels, the new reports were produced. The architecture of the trained model during testing and prediction is shown in Fig. 6b, with the alarms providing inputs into the trained model, and a response prediction being the output.

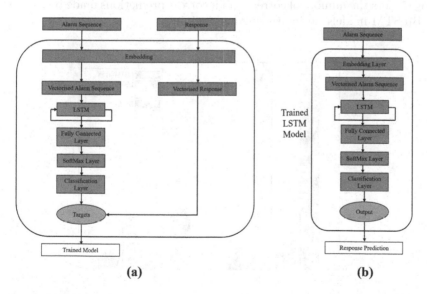

Fig. 6. a. Architecture of the model during training, b. Architecture of the trained model during testing.

4   Results and Discussion

4.1   Results

Table 1 provides the prediction accuracy of both LSTM and BiLSTM for train and test data sets.

Table 1. Prediction accuracies of LSTM vs. BiLSTM

	Training accuracy	Test accuracy
LSTM	78.65	64.70
BiLSTM	80.20	75.88

The LSTM and BiLSTM models yielded different prediction accuracies, with the BiLSTM delivering superior accuracy of 75.88%, compared to the 64.70% delivered by the LSTM. This accuracy is slightly lower than the results of 78–81.4% stated by [5], but the accuracies are comparable, and it is likely that with an improved data set and some further optimisation of the model that accuracy in the region of 90% could be achieved in future. It should be noted that the model presented by [5] predicts the next alarm in a sequence, not repair actions, so the differing aims of the papers must be considered when drawing comparisons. To give further insight into the accuracy of the models, a bar chart in Fig. 7 plots the number of correct and incorrect predictions made by the LSTM and BiLSTM models during testing and training.

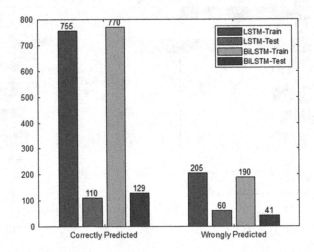

Fig. 7. Plot of the correctly and incorrectly predicted results for the LSTM and BiLSTM models during testing and training.

It is shown that the BiLSTM outperformed the one-directional LSTM narrowly during testing with more correct and less false predictions. Importantly, the BiLSTM outperformed the LSTM considerably during testing, decreasing false predictions by almost a third. Any occurrences of unnecessary or missed responses could cause issues for industry, with an unnecessary repair operation causing inconvenience and unnecessary expenditure, and a missed repair action allowing a fault to develop. Therefore, the use of a BiLSTM model is recommended in this application.

4.2 Benefits for Industry

The successful implementation of a response prediction network based on alarm sequences would have some implications for O&M planning in the OSW industry. As the proposed system considers alarms that precede a response action by up to 20 days, it is possible that a response can be predicted with fewer alarms than are currently required. While it is unlikely that an accurate response could be predicted from a single alarm, reasonably accurate predictions may be made in advance of a failure.

The prediction of a response action prior to an alarm would provide major benefits, as it would be possible to plan and undertake predictive maintenance based on early warning from alarms before a major alarm or failure occurs. The benefits of predictive maintenance would include a reduction of turbine downtime while a response is planned and implemented, and a reduction in the need for human decision-making (and therefore human error) in planning complex response. While it is unlikely that the need for a human in the process would be completely removed, supported decision-making would provide benefits for O&M planning.

It is also likely that if a response can be predicted from a shorter sequence of alarms, then it may allow issues to be rectified before they progress to a more serious, and therefore more costly issue.

4.3 Integration into Industry

In order for the OSW Industry to benefit from the use of this model, its implementation into the existing O&M alarm systems must be considered. A diagram showing the recommended integration of the repair action recommendation network is shown in Fig. 8. In the diagram, the repair action recommendation network is bounded by an orange box, with the LSTM network corresponding to the trained network shown in Fig. 6b. The addition of visualisation for explainability which is considered as a potential future development, is bounded in a green box.

The system receives alarms generated from SCADA data, which will be sequenced, and input into the LSTM network, then output response predictions to the O&M manager for approval. We are currently developing an extension of this approach to add explainability in the recommendations of the LSTM, as

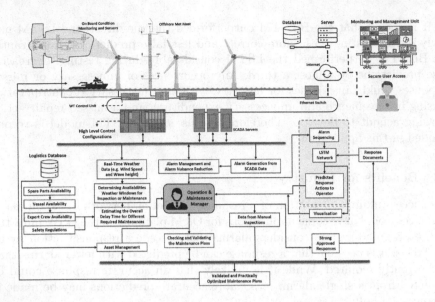

Fig. 8. System diagram of the proposed integration of the repair action recommendation network into the existing O&M alarm system.

this will allow improved understanding of the recommendations by the O&M manager.

It is unlikely that human involvement can be completely removed from the system. Therefore, it is recommended that the repair action recommendation framework is subordinate to the O&M Manager who has ultimate authority. Daily, the repair recommendation network can provide suggestions for the repair actions based on the existing alarms, and then the O&M manager reviews the outputs, choosing to accept or reject the recommendations and rating them. In a case of having low ratings, the system will change some parameters, update itself, and generate another output. The algorithm will run until the results reach a certain level of acceptance. As an example, if the O&M manager put a low rate for the recommendation, then the application asks the correct needed action and updates itself accordingly. Figure 9 illustrates the overall idea of using reinforcement learning to make the repair action recommendation more realistic.

4.4　Current Limitations

A potential limitation in the system is the varying terminology used in alarms generated from SCADA data. This may lead to misidentification of alarms, which would result in reduced accuracy of predictions. This in turn could yield incorrect predictions, or possibly false negatives, i.e. situations where the system fails to predict a response when one is required. In order to remedy this limitation, it would be necessary to either expand the training data set to include all ter-

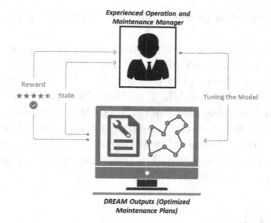

Fig. 9. A proposed procedure for using reinforcement learning-like technique and use human-in-the-loop scoring of recommendations to improve the system's performance over time.

minologies used, or to train the network for each set of terminology. As a larger data set would lead to increased training time and computational cost, it would be more realistic to train the LSTM for each set of alarms, which would differ between operators.

Another potential limitation of the system is that it depends on alarms and responses having enough occurrences to meaningfully contribute to the training. During the training of the model, any alarms with fewer than 2 occurrences were considered as too infrequent to meaningfully contribute to the training, and so were removed from the data set. This potentially leads to certain alarms being ignored, which could prevent more accurate predictions from being made, and the alarms could relate to major issues. One solution to this would be to use a larger data set, gained over a longer time period. However, this would cause increased computational cost during training, and long-term alarm data from the industry is largely unavailable.

5 Conclusions and Future Work

This paper proposed a novel approach to repair action prediction using RNNs. Both LSTM and BiLSTM models have been trained and tested to predict repair actions with the input of alarm sequences. Using 5 years of alarm sequence data by EDF Energy, we have successfully shown the potential of these networks to produce beneficial contributions to the domain by achieving test accuracy's of up to 76%. The results achieved using this DL approach have proved comparable with other research applied to relevant but different problems. With a lack of usable clean data being a major factor in achieving high prediction accuracy, it has been noted that the DL approach may have limitations in realistic applications with the current quality of data. However, one solution that has been proposed as future work is to use reinforcement learning with a human-in-the-loop procedure.

In the future, we shall use information in the data provided by EDF to distinguish between minor and major repairs. Explainability approaches will be integrated to the trained model to make its behaviour interpretable for the operators [19]. Methods like SafeML [4] will be added on top of the trained model to improve the reliability and safety of the prediction at runtime. Finally, we will experiment using DL to auto-create a temporal casual model like a dynamic fault tree that can illustrate the causality between alarm sequences. Such a model could help the system's designers and operators to gain more insights regarding the alarm sequence behaviour [2,16].

Code Availability

Regarding the research reproducibility, codes and functions supporting this paper are published online at GitHub:
https://github.com/koo-ec/OWF_Repair_Action_Recommender.
Due to the confidentiality of data provided by EDF Energy, it is not possible for the data set to be made public.

Acknowledgement. This work was supported by the Secure and Safe Multi-Robot Systems (SESAME) H2020 Project under Grant Agreement 101017258. We would like to thank EDF Energy R&D UK Centre, AURA Innovation Centre and University of Hull for their support.

References

1. Almeida, F., Xexéo, G.: Word embeddings: a survey (2019). https://doi.org/10.48550/ARXIV.1901.09069. https://arxiv.org/abs/1901.09069
2. Aslansefat, K., Gogani, M.B., Kabir, S., Shoorehdeli, M.A., Yari, M.: Performance evaluation and design for variable threshold alarm systems through semi-Markov process. ISA Trans. **97**, 282–295 (2020)
3. International Society of Automation: Management Of Alarm Systems for the Process Industries. Standard, International Society of Automation, North Carolina, United States (2016)
4. Basaldella, M., Antolli, E., Serra, G., Tasso, C.: Bidirectional LSTM recurrent neural network for keyphrase extraction. In: Serra, G., Tasso, C. (eds.) IRCDL 2018. CCIS, vol. 806, pp. 180–187. Springer, Cham (2018). https://doi.org/10.1007/978-3-319-73165-0_18
5. Cai, S., Palazoglu, A., Zhang, L., Hu, J.: Process alarm prediction using deep learning and word embedding methods. ISA Trans. **85**, 274–283 (2019)
6. Camacho-Collados, J., Pilehvar, M.T.: On the role of text preprocessing in neural network architectures: an evaluation study on text categorization and sentiment analysis. arXiv preprint arXiv:1707.01780 (2017)
7. Cui, Z., Ke, R., Pu, Z., Wang, Y.: Deep bidirectional and unidirectional LSTM recurrent neural network for network-wide traffic speed prediction. arXiv preprint arXiv:1801.02143 (2018)

8. De Mulder, W., Bethard, S., Moens, M.F.: A survey on the application of recurrent neural networks to statistical language modeling. Comput. Speech Lang. **30**(1), 61–98 (2015)

9. Ding, Z., Li, H., Shang, W., Chen, T.-H.P.: Can pre-trained code embeddings improve model performance? Revisiting the use of code embeddings in software engineering tasks. Empirical Softw. Eng. **27**(3), 1–38 (2022). https://doi.org/10.1007/s10664-022-10118-5

10. Du, M., Yi, J., Mazidi, P., Cheng, L., Guo, J.: A parameter selection method for wind turbine health management through SCADA data. Energies **10**(2), 253 (2017)

11. Beebe, D., Ferrer, S., Logerot, D.: Alarm floods and plant incidents. https://www.digitalrefining.com/article/1000558/alarm-floods-and-plant-incidents#.YkLrZefMIuV (2012). Accessed 27 Mar 2022

12. Engineering Equipment and Materials Users Association: EEMUA Publication 191 Alarm systems - a guide to design, management and procurement. Standard, Engineering Equipment and Materials Users Association, London, UK (2019)

13. Koltsidopoulos Papatzimos, A., Thies, P.R., Dawood, T.: Offshore wind turbine fault alarm prediction. Wind Energy **22**(12), 1779–1788 (2019). https://doi.org/10.1002/we.2402. https://onlinelibrary.wiley.com/doi/abs/10.1002/we.2402 wiley.com/doi/abs/10.1002/we.2402

14. Maldonado-Correa, J., Martín-Martínez, S., Artigao, E., Gómez-Lázaro, E.: Using SCADA data for wind turbine condition monitoring: a systematic literature review. Energies **13**(12), 3132 (2020). https://doi.org/10.3390/en13123132. https://www.mdpi.com/1996-1073/13/12/3132

15. Offshore Renewable Energy (ORE) Catapult: Offshore Wind Operations and Maintenance, A £9 Billion per year opportunity by 2030 for the UK to Seize. https://ore.catapult.org.uk/wp-content/uploads/2021/05/Catapult-Offshore-Wind-OM_final-050521.pdf (2021). Accessed 29 Mar 2022

16. Simeu-Abazi, Z., Lefebvre, A., Derain, J.P.: A methodology of alarm filtering using dynamic fault tree. Reliab. Eng. Syst. Saf. **96**(2), 257–266 (2011)

17. Sutskever, I., Vinyals, O., Le, Q.V.: Sequence to sequence learning with neural networks. In: Advances in neural information processing systems, pp. 3104–3112 (2014). https://papers.nips.cc/paper/5346-sequence-to-sequence-learning-with-neural-networks.pdf

18. Verhelst, J., Coudron, I., Ompusunggu, A.P.: SCADA-compatible and scaleable visualization tool for corrosion monitoring of offshore wind turbine structures. App. Sci. **12**(3), 1762 (2022). https://doi.org/10.3390/app12031762.www.mdpi.com/2076-3417/12/3/1762

19. Wei, L., Qian, Z., Pei, Y., Wang, J.: Wind turbine fault diagnosis by the approach of SCADA alarms analysis. Appl. Sci. **12**(1), 69 (2022). https://doi.org/10.3390/app12010069. www.mdpi.com/2076-3417/12/1/69

20. Zaheer, R., Shaziya, H.: A study of the optimization algorithms in deep learning. In: 2019 Third International Conference on Inventive Systems and Control (ICISC), pp. 536–539. IEEE (2019)

21. Zhou, P., Yin, P.: An opportunistic condition-based maintenance strategy for offshore wind farm based on predictive analytics. Renew. Sustain. Energy Rev. **109**, 1–9 (2019)

Tool Paper: Time Series Anomaly Detection Platform for MATLAB Simulink

Sheng Ding[✉], Skander Ayoub, and Andrey Morozov

Institute of Industrial Automation and Software Engineering, University of Stuttgart, Stuttgart, Germany
{sheng.ding,andrey.morozov}@ias.uni-stuttgart.de, skanderayoub@live.fr

Abstract. In the world of constant technological development, Cyber-Physical Systems have experienced considerable growth in complexity and diversity of application domains. Consequently, the complexity and subtlety of faults and cyberattacks have grown proportionally. Thus, traditional methods, statistical methods, and machine learning algorithms have gradually given way to new methods based on Deep Neural Networks (DNNs). However, existing researches tend to focus on specific datasets and deep learning models in an offline manner and lacks generalization.

This paper presents a new platform implemented using MATLAB's App Designer, Deep Learning Toolbox, and FIBlock. It brings together several advanced DL-based anomaly detection methods and allows the user to customize a wide range of parameters. The intended workflow comprises the following three steps: (i) Select or Upload Dataset, (ii) Configure DNN, (iii) Examine Detection Performance. In the first step, it gives users the freedom to choose between existing datasets from different Cyber-Physical System (CPS) domains or to upload their own datasets to perform studies. Several data pre-processing methods are available. We have tested our tool on three datasets. One is based on real-world scenarios and the other two are generated from Simulink models. In the second step, a DNN architecture can be selected, where Network hyperparameters and training options can be set via an easy-to-use interface. This helps to find the suitable values for each scenario. In the third step, results are displayed graphically by the tool, detailing and comparing different detection methods. For detection of static datasets (offline detection), the performance is reported to users using various statistical metrics, including precision, recall, and F1 score. If the results are satisfying, users can generate corresponding detection tools as blocks that can be connected to the system for simulation in real time (online detection).

Keywords: Error detection · Simulink · Deep learning · LSTM · Time-series data · Cyber-Physical System

1 Motivation and General Concept

The manual inspection of modern systems has become more and more challenging. The reason lies with the increase in system complexity and abundance of

C. Seguin et al. (Eds.): IMBSA 2022, LNCS 13525, pp. 204–218, 2022.
https://doi.org/10.1007/978-3-031-15842-1_15

data and layers to be monitored. More and more data need to be monitored to intercept faults or attacks in real-time or to prevent them from occurring in the future. It has then become typical to automate the maintenance and control of these systems and their components. Anomaly detection has been for a long time a subject of interest.

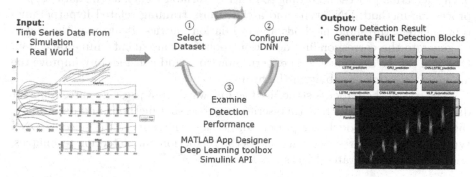

(a) Workflow for the model based anomaly detection platform.

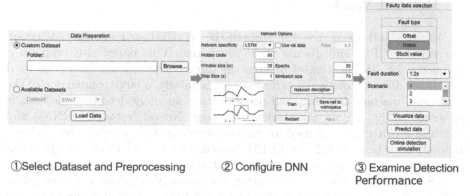

(b) Corresponding user interface for the three workflow steps.

Fig. 1. An overview of the model based anomaly detection platform.

Deep Learning (DL) based methods for anomaly detection on time series data have become of interest due to their already proven efficiency on numerous other problems in other domains. Since then, numerous improvements have emerged, claiming to outperform old techniques. According to [5], there exist different kinds of deep learning architectures that can be used for anomaly detection. The abundance of different new models and detection related techniques makes it however harder to keep track of the actual progress in the field. These models are often overly adapted to the dataset in question and their performance on new datasets can be subject to debate.

Contribution: This paper presents a platform for anomaly detection methods on univariate time-series data for CPSs. As shown in Fig. 1a, the intended workflow comprises the following three steps: (i) Select or Upload Dataset, (ii) Configure DNN, and (iii) Examine Detection Performance. The corresponding user interface for the workflow set-up are shown in Fig. 1b, and will be illustrated in the following sections. This platform allows users to evaluate the performance of the detection process according to multiple variables, such as the dataset, preprocessing method, DNN type and architecture, training related hyperparameters, different threshold methods and evaluation metrics. It also has the ability to generate the corresponding detection tools for consequent online detection. Our tool can be combined with expert knowledge and considerably improve the anomaly detection capabilityin the future.

The rest of the paper is structured as follows: Sect. 3 presents three different datasets. In Sect. 4, different time-series preprocessing methods and data preparation for the DL models are presented. Section 5 introduces the selected DNN types and architectures. Section 6 shows the prediction and detection techniques, and details the generated blocks for detection.

2   Related Work

In [13], the authors review the state-of-the-art DL-based anomaly detection methods for CPSs and discuss their limitations. This paper also proposes a taxonomy for classification of different methods. Experiments were conducted to capture different methods' performances. Similarly, a large comparison of the statistical, machine learning, and deep learning anomaly detection methods is presented in [5]. In [5,8,11], stacked Recurrent Neural Networks (RNNs) and a hybrid architecture are used for time-series prediction to ultimately achieve anomaly detection. In [12], an LSTM autoencoder is used to capture the temporal dependencies and reconstruct the features.

After computing the regression error, the anomaly detection is proceeded by setting a threshold on the prediction or reconstruction error and raising the red flag if the threshold has been exceeded. To this end, multiple thresholding methods are also possible. In [14], the error vectors are modeled to fit a multivariate Gaussian distribution whose parameters are extracted using the Maximum Likelihood Estimation (MLE) on a non-anomalous test set. The threshold is then fixed by maximizing the F_β score on an anomalous validation set. An automatic and dynamic thresholding method is introduced in [11] where each time window of the smoothed prediction errors is given an individual threshold value using its mean and standard deviation. An anomaly pruning operation is also featured to minimize false alarms. In the same paper, another way of evaluation is employed, using unweighted segments to compute true positives, false negatives et false positives.

Comparison with Other Tools: There exist tools for deep learning modeling in Matlab, e.g. Matlab app"Deep Network Designer" [6] is a user-friendly tool to build and edit deep learning networks interactively. However, when bringing it to the anomaly detection purpose, it only covers the deep learning model part and lacks the ability of time series processing, thresholding, evaluation, and comparison with other models other than deep learning. All of these steps contain different possibilities and parameters that can impact the detection results. Anomaly detection in Statistics and Machine Learning Toolbox [2] doesn't cover evaluation of deep learning models, and anomaly detection in Predictive Maintenance Toolbox [3] targets time series classification and supervised learning which requires a large number of labeled data, while we are targeting at unsupervised detection with prediction and reconstruction approach. Most related works are implemented in python, as it is the most popular language for deep learning. We observe that most research applies the proposed methods in a specific domain and on a single data set [4,7,18]. The works grouping these studies usually either compare the performance of individual methods according to a certain domain of application or compare a single method on different datasets [5,13,16]. While on a platform, more datasets along with techniques are integrated into one tool. Our goal is to provide an automatic mechanism dedicated to anomaly detection for model-based system engineering (MBSE) and safety engineers, which can be fed with data and output best detection blocks while avoiding manual implementation in code.

Benefits of the Introduced Platform: First, it is important to provide a platform for evaluating the effectiveness of multiple methods on different datasets (simulation and real-world) from several kinds of CPS. However, to the best of our knowledge, no such work has been offered yet. Second, although there exist several works for anomaly detection on public dataset implemented in python, it is important to have a native tool for model-based developers who work in Matlab/Simulink. Our tool provides the MBSE engineers the ability to generate anomaly detection blocks that could be connected to the system parts for real-time simulation. Third, the concept of the digital twin emerged and quickly become popular in system engineering. In the future, we also plan to integrate this data science tool with the MBSE of the digital twin. The goal is to combine data science and system analysis to achieve better capability. Therefore, we contribute by proposing a platform that aims to perform a detailed evaluation and performance review for time series anomaly detection.

3 Dataset

This section presents the case study dataset used for anomaly detection in our experiments. It also discusses about how the data was collected. Two synthetic dataset are generated from Simulink models. One real-world dataset is collected from a testbed.

3.1 Dataset from Simulation of Unmanned Aerial Vehicle (UAV)

This dataset is collected from a Simulink-based model adapted from [1], a support package for Parrot minidrones. Each waypoint contains information about initial position, end position, and global trajectory in the form of (x, y, z) coordinates.

For each simulation, a total of 18 features of sensors and actuators are collected, namely *accelerometer (x, y, z), gyroscope (x, y, z), altitude, motor command, Roll-Pitch-Yaw* etc. Simulation duration is equal to 60 s with a sample rate 100 Hz, meaning 6000 samples per simulation.

We inject faults using the FIBlock [9] to the x-axis of accelerometer and gyroscope sensors during simulation for faulty cases data collection. Injected faults are: Bias/Offset, stuck-at, noise, and package-drop, with each simulation containing a unique fault type. In order to mimic real-world UAV flying scenarios, faults were injected in a non-uniform manner.

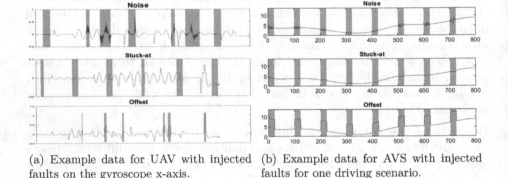

(a) Example data for UAV with injected faults on the gyroscope x-axis.

(b) Example data for AVS with injected faults for one driving scenario.

Fig. 2. Example of datasets collected from simulation with injected faults.

3.2   Dataset from Simulation of Autonomous Vehicle System (AVS)

This dataset is also generated from a Simulink model, whose design is inspired by *MOBATSim's* autonomous vehicle model [17]. A simulation consists of a normal vehicle moving along a predefined path, which is followed by another autonomous vehicle. For data collection, simulations are run considering different driving scenarios. Each simulation is run for 80 s with a sampling time equal to 0.1 s. At the end, data of **24** simulations is collected as fault free data, split equally into town and highway driving scenarios.

Same as the first data set, Faulty data is also generated using the FIBlock. The block is connected to the speed sensor of the autonomous vehicle in order to inject an *offset* with a magnitude equal to 5, *noise* of 20% from original data and *stuck-at* faults. The block was also parameterized to add faults of duration ranging from 0.6 s to 5 s with a fixed step size of 0.6 s at each iteration and spaced at a period of 9 s. Therefore, the injected fault has **eight** levels.

To summarize, **three** different faults were applied individually to each fault-free scenario, for a total of $24 * 8 * 3 + 24 = 600$ generated files. An example of faults for the same driving scenario is given in Fig. 2b. Faults have a duration of 2.4 s and are highlighted in red.

3.3 Real World Dataset: Secure Water Treatment (SWaT)

The SWaT testbed [10] is a widely used dataset in the anomaly detection domain. It is one of the few well-labeled datasets reflecting real-world data from a complex Industrial Control System (ICS). The testbed simulates a modern water treatment facility consisting of six processes. Data about both physical and cyber states was collected for 11 d, booting the system from its initial state by injecting attacks during the last 4 d of the treatment without interruptions between the phases. Attacks were injected following a certain model for a period going from minutes to hours. The attacks can happen on multiple processes simultaneously. The physical properties are defined by several sensors and actuators, whose values were reported in CSV files, indicating also for each timestamp if it involves an attack or not. Attack logs (start/end time, attack points, attack description etc.) of the 36 attacks were gathered into another file.

Figure 3 illustrates our sensor selection panel for the SWaT dataset. Each column represents a monitored sensor or actuator. Observations are represented at each row with one-second intervals and can be visually displayed. The selected column becomes highlighted in green for the case of a valid selection.

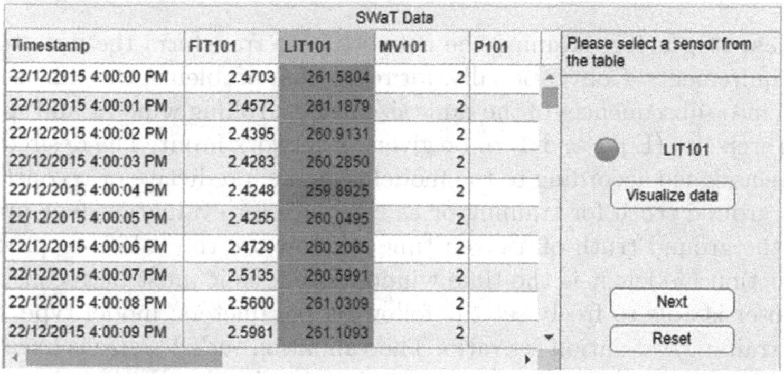

SWaT Data					
Timestamp	FIT101	LIT101	MV101	P101	Please select a sensor from the table
22/12/2015 4:00:00 PM	2.4703	261.5804	2		
22/12/2015 4:00:01 PM	2.4572	261.1879	2		
22/12/2015 4:00:02 PM	2.4395	260.9131	2		
22/12/2015 4:00:03 PM	2.4283	260.2850	2		● LIT101
22/12/2015 4:00:04 PM	2.4248	259.8925	2		
22/12/2015 4:00:05 PM	2.4255	260.0495	2		Visualize data
22/12/2015 4:00:06 PM	2.4729	260.2065	2		
22/12/2015 4:00:07 PM	2.5135	260.5991	2		
22/12/2015 4:00:08 PM	2.5600	261.0309	2		Next
22/12/2015 4:00:09 PM	2.5981	261.1093	2		Reset

Fig. 3. SWaT sensor selection panel.

4 Data Preprocessing

This section discusses different data preprocessing methods used, and the methodology adopted to prepare the data for the deep learning models.

4.1   Normalization and Standardization

There are a multitude of data preprocessing methods in ML and DL. Applying the right methods plays a major role in achieving the best possible results. Several factors come into play when choosing the right methods such as the input data format (images, sequential data, etc.), its characteristics and behavior, the DNN architecture and the desired output format.

Popular preprocessing techniques are normalization and standardization, as they allow the model to train and perform better. For the AVS and UAV datasets, according to the chosen method, a unique mean and standard deviation or minimal and maximal value of all combined simulations is computed. Only non-anomalous data is used for model training, so it will not be affected by these aspects. This way, both methods can be compared on similar ground. We also propose the user the possibility to use not preprocessed, raw data.

4.2   Data Preparation for Deep Learning Models

Following traditional deep learning workflow, the dataset must be split into a training set and a test set, respectively used during the training phase and test phase. The fault-free is employed for training and the test set is constituted of the abnormal data of each dataset. Then, the training set is randomly partitioned into a new training set T_{FF} and a validation set V_{FF}. A portion of the test set Z_A is used as an anomalous validation set V_A, which is used during the detection process.

The last step before training the network is to transform the data to fit the model requirements. Conventionally, for regression problems, the time-series are reshaped into subsequences of the same size using a rolling window and spaced by a certain step size (Eq. 1 and 3) to be given as network input. The desired output values are assigned according to the model type, i.e. predictive or reconstructive, either as ground truth for training or as reference for evaluation. For predictive models, the ground truth of a given time window are the values to predict, for reconstruction models it is the time window itself, as it must be reconstructed.

The user is able to freely set the following parameters: model type, window size and training/validation set ratio. The validation set's V_A size is fixed at 20% of the test set Z_A and the step size is fixed at 1 (Fig. 1b). With a time series of N samples, a window size w and a step size of 1, the data is partitioned into $M = N - w + 1$ new individual sequences.

5   Deep Learning Models

Now that the data is fully preprocessed and responds to the common prerequisites for the models, the networks architectures can be created. This section aims at presenting the different model architectures, highlighting their specificities, analogies and differences, as well as presenting the different hyperparameters involved in the optimization process.

5.1 Deep Learning Approaches for Anomaly Detection

Regarding anomaly detection in time-series, DL-based methods solving regression problems can be divided into two categories: **Prediction** and **Reconstruction**-based models. Let, T a univariate timeseries such as $T = (t_0, t_1, \ldots, t_n)$ with $t_i \in \mathbb{R}$, $n \in \mathbb{N}_+$, $w \in \mathbb{N}_+$ representing the window length and f the function representing the network rule.

A **predictive model** aims at predicting the k-next iterations following the given time window:

$$f\left(t_{x-w}, \ldots, t_x\right) = \left(\widehat{t}_{x+1}, \ldots, \widehat{t}_{x+k}\right) \tag{1}$$

The forecasting horizon is set to $k = 1$ in this paper, so that finally, the prediction error r used as *anomaly score* is computed as such:

$$r = \left|t_{x+1} - \widehat{t}_{x+1}\right| \tag{2}$$

A **reconstructive model's** goal is to rebuild the given input:

$$f\left(t_{x-w}, \ldots, t_x\right) = \left(\widehat{t}_{x-w}, \ldots, \widehat{t}_x\right) \tag{3}$$

The reconstruction error vector r' of a given time window is given by:

$$r' = \left|(t_{x-w}, \ldots, t_x) - (\widehat{t}_{x-w}, \ldots, \widehat{t}_x)\right| \tag{4}$$

According to the used methodology, the anomaly score is computed from the reconstruction error. This will be further explained. In all cases, the anomaly score θ is used to determine whether a timestamp is considered as anomalous if it is higher than a certain defined threshold value $\theta > \gamma$.

5.2 Hyperparameters

Before training, a certain amount of **hyperparameters** need to be defined. Traditionally, only **training** influential variables (e.g. Learning rate) and **network** influential variables (e.g. layer arrangement) are considered or listed as hyperparameters, but we consider that each preprocessing step applied to the data to be as crucial for the model performance as the other hyperparameters. We consider three types of hyperparameters:

  i **General** hyperparameters,
 ii **Training-related** hyperparameters,
iii **Network-related** hyperparameters.

These hyperparameters are are split into two categories: fixed and User-defined hyperparameters.

Fixed Hyperparameters are variables that the user is not able to change using the platform. They are listed in Table 1a. These parameters are predefined and fixed for all datasets and training scenarios.

- The *forecast horizon* is specific to the predictive model and sets the number of predicted samples for each time window.
- The *validation frequency* is set to be proportional to the size of the training set and minibatch size Z_{FF} of each dataset.
- The DNNs architectures are predefined. They are inspired by the most used architectures in the domain and are detailed in the next sections.
- Other training options and network-related hyperparameters are defined after several rounds of testing to provide consistent and robust training time and performance results across datasets.

We make the choice for the following reasons:

- To only fix basic hyperparameters to have networks that are as simple as possible to facilitate the evaluation process.
- To derivate from other studies, where the networks tend to be overly adapted to the datasets, which is not good for translation of usage.
- To provide users with the freedom to alter the hyperparameters that have the most impact on model performance.

Table 1. Hyperparameters.

Hyperparameter	Value
General	
V_A size	$0.2 * T_A$ size
Forecast horizon	1
Step size	1
Training-related	
Optimizer	Adam
Learning rate	0.001
Validation frequency	$\frac{Z_{FF}}{0.3 \cdot MinibatchSize}$
Network-related	
NNs architectures	RNN, LSTM, DNN, Hybrid
Dropout in RNNs	0.3
Dropout in Hybrids	0.25
Conv filter size in Hybrids	5

(a) Fixed hyperparameters.

Hyperparameter	Value	Initial value
General		
Preprocessing method	Standardize, rescale, raw	
$V_A/_{Faultfree}$ ratio	[0,1]	0.8
Window size	[1-Max]	35
Training-related		
#Epochs	Free of choice	35
Minibatch size	Free of choice	70
Network-related		
Network type	Prediction, reconstruction	
#Hidden units (RNN, GRU)	Free of choice	80
#Neurons	Free of choice	32
#Filters (Conv layer)	Free of choice	32

(b) User-defined hyperparameters.

User-Defined Hyperparameters: In addition to the fixed hyperparameters, we offer the user ability to freely adjust the hyperparameters listed in Tab. 1b. Compared to the fixed ones, they arguably impact the most the performance of the models. For instance, the ideal window would differ from a dataset to another, as each CPS and simulation have their own characteristics, and some model would require more epochs to adjust their rule. An overview of the network options interface can be found in Fig. 1b. For each type of network, three different network architectures are proposed. The network options panel of the UI contains a *network description* button that gives a short description of the selected network and show its structure through a pop-up window.

5.3 Predictive Models

Now given all hyperparameters, the rule in (1) can be simplified to:

$$f\left(t_{x-w}, \ldots, t_x\right) = \widehat{t}_{x+1} \tag{5}$$

The predicted timeseries has a length $M = N - w$, N being the length of the original timeseries.

Long Short-Term Memory (LSTM) Based Predictor: LSTM based models are the most commonly used model types for time-series prediction and anomaly detection. They are often structured in this manner: two stacked LSTM layers separated by a dropout layer to avoid overfitting [8].

Gated Recurrent Unit (GRU) Based Predictor: Although being less popular, some achieved satisfying performance with GRU RNNs. It is the same as the LSTM-based predictor, with GRU layers instead of LSTM layers.

Hybrid CNN-LSTM Predictor: The CNN-RNN model inspired by is used to make use of both advantages of RNNs and CNNs. Models were generated using *Matlab's R2020b Deep Learning Toolbox* [15] that does not offer 1D convolutional layers. To overcome this issue, folding/unfolding layers and flattening layers are used. The CNN part of the model is composed of a 2D convolution layer followed by a batch normalization, ReLU activation layer, another 2D convolution and ReLU layer and finally an average pooling layer. It is linked to the LSTM based model previously described using an unfolding and flattening layer.

5.4 Reconstructive Models

The task of the reconstructive models is to rebuild the given time window and follow the rule given in (3). The goal is not to achieve a perfect copy of the data $\widehat{t} = t$, but to be able to understand the main characteristics of the training set to poorly reconstruct anomalies in the test set.

Each time sample t_i is then predicted w times for $i \in [w, N - w]$. The median of the vector t_i is then calculated to compute a single value. At the end, the reconstructed timeseries has a length $M = N - 2w$.

LSTM-Based and Hybrid (CNN-LSTM) Reconstruction: These models are similar to predictive models but they perform a reconstruction task instead of the prediction.

Fully-Connected Reconstruction: Finally, our platform also proposes a basic rebuilding network composed of only fully-connected layers. The number of neurons n in the first three layers l gradually decreases so that

$$n_{l+1} = \lfloor \frac{n_l}{2} \rfloor, l = \{1, 2\} \tag{6}$$

and then rises to ultimately obtain the number of neurons of the first layer in the last layer with $n_4 = n_2$ and $n_5 = n_1$.

6   Anomaly Detection

6.1   Problem Statement

The third step in the workflow is the anomaly detection. The objective is to be able to maximize the number of anomalies detected while minimizing the number of false positives. However, this is not a simple task because in theory, there are countless types of faults or attacks that have a different impact on the data. In order to apply the best suited techniques, having some experience with the system in question is therefore highly recommended, if not mandatory.

We categorize the fault detection methods using thresholding into two groups, namely (i) supervised and (ii) unsupervised. Employing supervised thresholding techniques assumes a prior knowledge of the prediction error distribution. For the purpose of performance evaluation, we assume this distribution is known for all datasets. In contrast, unsupervised thresholding methods are not based on those assumptions and then claim to perform well on all kinds of data.

For the detection process, user can choose between the different test data according to each dataset (Fig. 1b) such as the fault type, fault duration, simulation, day etc., and to launch the Simulink model.

6.2   Supervised Thresholding

The method selected is the one presented in [14], with some modifications. Going under the assumption that the error vector values $\mathbf{r}$ are normally distributed, we use the non-anomalous validation set V_{ff} used during training to determine the mean μ and variance σ^2 employing the Maximum Likelihood Estimation (MLE). Afterwards, the previously mentioned anomalous validation set V_A is used to determine the threshold value γ by applying the probability density function (PDF) f_X on it and finding the best $\boldsymbol{F_1}$ score using the labels.

For example, Fig. 4a shows a histogram of the prediction error on V_{FF} and the fitted normal density function with a model trained on the AVS dataset. The PDF of V_A can be seen on Fig. 4b, where the faults are marked in red. Here, V_A is only composed of data containing offset faults lasting between 0.6s and 2.4s. Based on the results from Fig 4a and 4b, a general conclusion can be drawn that an appropriate threshold value could be set at $\gamma = 0.025$ to differentiate between abnormal and normal values. We also propose a variant of this method where a threshold is directly computed from the maximized $\boldsymbol{F_1}$ score on V_A. In the event that no validation data is used for training, only the second variant is available.

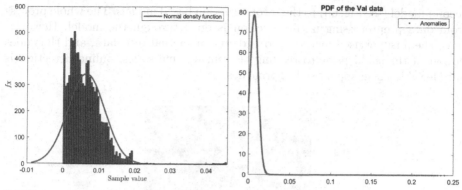

(a) Histogram of errors on V_{ff} with fitted normal density function.

(b) Probability density function of anomalous validation set V_A.

Fig. 4. Supervised thresholding.

6.3   Unsupervised Dynamic Thresholding

First, the error vector $\mathbf{r}$ is smoothed using an Exponentially-Weighted Moving Average (EWMA). The threshold γ is then selected from a range of predefined values from the set

$$\mu(\mathbf{r}) + \mathbf{z} \cdot \sigma(\mathbf{r})$$

where $\mathbf{z}$ is a range of natural numbers. The best value $z \in \mathbf{z}$ is found where

$$z_{BEST} = argmax(\mathbf{z}_{score})$$

where z_{score} is a score given to to remove false positives, an anomaly pruning method is also introduced where previously found anomalies are removed if a new, more obvious one is found, by assigning each found anomalous sequence an anomaly score and comparing it with the others.

The implementation is inspired by [11]. The z_{range}, *anomaly padding* and *window length* can also be changed on the results view on the platform to get a dynamic overview of their influence in the detection process.

6.4   Online Detection Block

As part of the third step **Examine Detection Performance**, for offline detection, results are displayed graphically by the tool, detailing and comparing the two detection methods. The performance is reported to users using various statistical metrics, including precision, recall, and F1 score. After offline detection results are checked and satisfied, users can click the online detection simulation button (depicted in Fig. 1b). Our tool will automatically generate corresponding blocks for detection.

Two kinds of Simulink models are proposed to carry out the detection. The first model (see Fig. 6a) is adapted to work with the predictive models. The second model (see Fig. 6b) to the reconstruction based models. The whole process from data preprocessing until detection is done through the model. However, since the unsupervised method proceeds on the actual test data, and thus does not set a threshold prior to reading the entire time series, online detection is only feasible using supervised approaches.

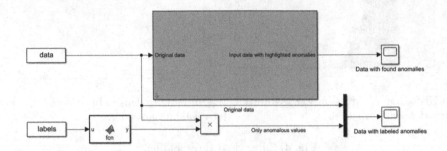

Fig. 5. Online detection with a generated detection block.

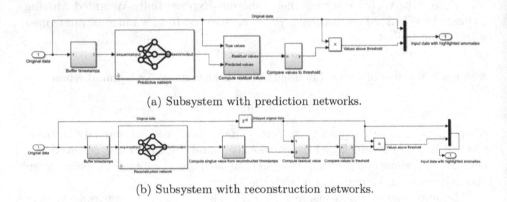

(a) Subsystem with prediction networks.

(b) Subsystem with reconstruction networks.

Fig. 6. Simulink subsystem of the detection block in Fig. 5

The advantage of online detection using the predictive model is real time anomaly flagging, while the reconstruction models will always have a delay equal to the length of the window size w. This is due to the fact that a single timestamp must be reconstructed w times to be assigned a final reconstruction value.

The mask parameters of the subsystem, in blue on Fig. 5, responsible for the steps described earlier, are the trained network and the window size. The Matlab function returns NaN values for non-anomalous timestamps and 1 for abnormal observations, then it is multiplied with the original data to only return a signal composed of the anomalous values, which will be highlighted in red on the Simulink scope. Flagged anomalies are marked in red and can be compared with the true labels on a different scope.

7   Conclusion

7.1   Results

In this paper, a platform has been presented to evaluate multiple deep learning models and techniques for anomaly detection in CPSs on univariate time series. Three datasets in total from different CPS types are made available, two of them issuing from simulation data from UAV and AVS systems and the last one contains data from real a world water treatment testbed ICS.

The user can either choose to train the model on raw data or preprocess it using standardization on rescaling. Moreover, data preparation related parameters such as window length and validation data ratio can freely be set through the interface before the data is then automatically prepared. The platform offers two different regression model types: prediction and reconstruction models. Several model related hyperparameters can be modified for each model. For the training related hyperparameters, the number of epochs and minibatch size are configurable. Two different thresholding methods are put at disposal for comparison. The first one defines a fixed threshold value from the anomalous test set and the other one is unsupervised, and its parameters can be dynamically edited on the platform. The results are displayed graphically. Finally, the detection process can also be simulated through Simulink, providing an outlook of the detection processes in the case of deployment on a real-life system on streaming data. The platform is open source and available on GitHub.[1]

7.2   Limitation and Future Work

Currently our tool has a number of limitations that we plan to overcome in the future. The three main of them are as follows. First, the current version of our tool is only used for univariate time series. We haven't taken signal dependency into account and the tool is not able to detect the contextual anomaly. Second, although big data is the reason for utilizing deep learning models, we haven't performed any case study on large dataset. Our emphasis lies on easier monitoring and intercepting faults or attacks. Third, we still have works to do to make our tool more user-friendly. This includes refining a comprehensive user guide and API reference and illustrating how to do extensions such as changing the fixed parameters (which have a small influence on the detection according to our experiments) and testing other techniques.

Acknowledgements. This publication is based on the research project SofDCar (19S21002), which is funded by the German Federal Ministry for Economic Affairs and Climate Action.

References

1. Simulink support package for parrot minidrones documentation - mathworks deutschland. https://de.mathworks.com/help/supportpkg/parrot/

---

[1] https://github.com/mbsa-tud/tsad_platform.

2. Anomaly detection (2022). https://www.mathworks.com/help/stats/anomaly-detection.html
3. Anomaly detection in industrial machinery using three-axis vibration data (2022). https://www.mathworks.com/help/predmaint/ug/anomaly-detection-using-3-axis-vibration-data.html
4. Bontemps, L., Cao, V.L., McDermott, J., Le-Khac, N.-A.: Collective anomaly detection based on long short-term memory recurrent neural networks. In: Dang, T.K., Wagner, R., Küng, J., Thoai, N., Takizawa, M., Neuhold, E. (eds.) FDSE 2016. LNCS, vol. 10018, pp. 141–152. Springer, Cham (2016). https://doi.org/10.1007/978-3-319-48057-2_9
5. Braei, M., Wagner, S.: Anomaly detection in univariate time-series: a survey on the state-of-the-art. arXiv preprint arXiv:2004.00433 (2020)
6. Build networks with deep network designer (2022). https://www.mathworks.com/help/deeplearning/ug/build-networks-with-deep-network-designer.html
7. Canizo, M., Triguero, I., Conde, A., Onieva, E.: Multi-head CNN-RNN for multi-time series anomaly detection: an industrial case study. Neurocomputing **363**, 246–260 (2019)
8. Ding, S., Morozov, A., Vock, S., Weyrich, M., Janschek, K.: Model-based error detection for industrial automation systems using LSTM networks. In: Zeller, M., Höfig, K. (eds.) Model-Based Safety and Assessment, pp. 212–226. Springer International Publishing, Cham (2020). https://doi.org/10.1007/978-3-030-58920-2_14
9. Fabarisov, T., Mamaev, I., Morozov, A., Janschek, K.: Model-based fault injection experiments for the safety analysis of exoskeleton system. In: 30th European Safety and Reliability Conference (2021)
10. Goh, J., Adepu, S., Junejo, K.N., Mathur, A.: A dataset to support research in the design of secure water treatment systems. In: Havarneanu, G., Setola, R., Nassopoulos, H., Wolthusen, S. (eds.) CRITIS 2016. LNCS, vol. 10242, pp. 88–99. Springer, Cham (2017). https://doi.org/10.1007/978-3-319-71368-7_8
11. Hundman, K., Constantinou, V., Laporte, C., Colwell, I., Söderström, T.: Detecting spacecraft anomalies using lstms and nonparametric dynamic thresholding (2018)
12. Lindemann, B., Fesenmayr, F., Jazdi, N., Weyrich, M.: Anomaly detection in discrete manufacturing using self-learning approaches. Procedia CIRP **79**, 313–318 (2019)
13. Luo, Y., Xiao, Y., Cheng, L., Peng, G., Yao, D.D.: Deep learning-based anomaly detection in cyber-physical systems: progress and opportunities. ACM Comput. Surv. (CSUR) **54**(5), 1–36 (2021)
14. Malhotra, P., Vig, L., Shroff, G., Agarwal, P.: Long Short Term Memory Networks for Anomaly Detection in Time Series (2015)
15. Matlab deep learning toolbox (2020). https://de.mathworks.com/help/deeplearning/index.html. The MathWorks, Natick, MA, USA
16. Nazarenko, A., Safdar, G.: Survey on security and privacy issues in cyber physical systems. AIMS Electron. Electr. Eng. **3**, 111–143 (2019). https://doi.org/10.3934/ElectrEng.2019.2.111
17. Saraoglu, M., Morozov, A., Janschek, K.: Mobatsim: model-based autonomous traffic simulation framework for fault-error-failure chain analysis. IFAC-PapersOnLine **52**(8), 239–244 (2019)
18. Tariq, S., et al.: Detecting anomalies in space using multivariate convolutional LSTM with mixtures of probabilistic PCA, pp. 2123–2133 (2019). https://doi.org/10.1145/3292500.3330776

Keep Your Distance: Determining Sampling and Distance Thresholds in Machine Learning Monitoring

Al-Harith Farhad[1][iD], Ioannis Sorokos[2(✉)][iD], Andreas Schmidt[2][iD],
Mohammed Naveed Akram[2(✉)][iD], Koorosh Aslansefat[3][iD],
and Daniel Schneider[2][iD]

[1] University of Mannheim, Schloss, 68131 Mannheim, Germany
`afarhad@mail.uni-mannheim.de`
[2] Fraunhofer IESE, Fraunhofer-Platz 1, 67663 Kaiserslautern, Germany
`{ioannis.sorokos,andreas.schmidt,naveed.akram,`
`daniel.schneider}@iese.fraunhofer.de`
[3] University of Hull, Cottingham Road, Hull HU6 7RX, UK
`k.aslansefat@hull.ac.uk`

Abstract. Machine Learning (ML) has provided promising results in recent years across different applications and domains. However, in many cases, qualities such as reliability or even safety need to be ensured. To this end, one important aspect is to determine whether or not ML components are deployed in situations that are appropriate for their application scope. For components whose environments are open and variable, for instance those found in autonomous vehicles, it is therefore important to monitor their operational situation in order to determine its distance from the ML components' trained scope. If that distance is deemed too great, the application may choose to consider the ML component outcome unreliable and switch to alternatives, e.g. using human operator input instead. SafeML is a model-agnostic approach for performing such monitoring, using distance measures based on statistical testing of the training and operational datasets. Limitations in setting SafeML up properly include the lack of a systematic approach for determining, for a given application, how many operational samples are needed to yield reliable distance information as well as to determine an appropriate distance threshold. In this work, we address these limitations by providing a practical approach and demonstrate its use in a well known traffic sign recognition problem, and on an example using the CARLA open-source automotive simulator.

Keywords: Machine Learning · Monitoring · Safety · Uncertainty

1 Introduction

The continuous expansion of the application fields of *Machine Learning* (ML) into safety-critical domains, such as autonomous vehicles, entails an increasing

C. Seguin et al. (Eds.): IMBSA 2022, LNCS 13525, pp. 219–234, 2022.
https://doi.org/10.1007/978-3-031-15842-1_16

need for suitable safety assurance approaches. One key aspect in this regard is getting a grasp on the confidence associated with the output of an ML component. While some ML models provide a probabilistic output that can be interpreted as a level of confidence, such output alone is not sufficient to establish overall trust. Significant progress has been made towards addressing this question, with approaches that introduce more sophisticated evaluation of a given model's outputs. Model-specific approaches base their evaluation on understanding of the internals of the given ML model, e.g. [23] focus on the second-to-last layer of a given deep neural network. On the other hand, model-agnostic approaches treat models as black-boxes, basing their evaluation on properties that can be examined externally, e.g. in [16], surrogate models are constructed during training to later provide uncertainty estimates of the ML model in question. An additional concern for evaluating ML models, is that the evaluation must also satisfy the application requirements, in particular with regards to performance. For instance, the authors of [25] propose auxiliary networks for evaluation, but the computational capacity needed to estimate them hinders their roll-out into real-time systems. On a general note, A safety argument for a system with ML components will typically be very specific for a given application and its context and comprise of a diverse range of measures and assumptions, many of which we would expect to include both development-time approaches and runtime approaches, with ours falling under the latter category.

SafeML, proposed in [2] and improved in [1], is a runtime approach for evaluating ML model outputs. In brief, SafeML compares training and operational data of the ML model in question and determines whether they are statistically 'too distant' to yield a trustworthy answer. The work in [1] further demonstrates a bootstrap-based p-value estimation extension to improve confidence in measurements. However, the existing literature does not explain how to address specific challenges for practical application of SafeML.

Our contribution is to identify these limitations and propose an approach that enables a systematic application of SafeML and overcomes these limitations. In the remainder of Sect. 1, we provide a more detailed description of previous work on SafeML. We then discuss what its practical limitations are, provide the motivation behind our approach, and then further detail our contributions.

1.1 SafeML

SafeML is a collection of measures that estimate the statistical distance between training and operational datasets based on the *Empirical Cumulative Distribution Function* (ECDF). In [2], the estimated distance has been shown to negatively correlate with a corresponding ML model's accuracy. In the same paper, a plausible workflow of applying SafeML for monitoring ML was also proposed. The workflow allows an ML task to be divided into two phases, an offline/training phase and an online/application phase. In the training phase, it is assumed that we have a trusted dataset and there is no uncertainty associated with its labels. An ML model, such as a deep neural network or a support vector machine, can be trained using the trusted data for classification or regression tasks.

After its validation, in the online/application phase, the same trained model and a buffer are provided to gather a sufficient number of samples from inputs. The number of buffered samples should be large enough that the distance determination can be relied upon, but the existing approach does not provide further guidance on how this number should be specified. When a large enough number of samples is obtained, the ECDF of each feature and each class is calculated based on the trained classifier decisions. The ECDF-based statistical distance measures are used to evaluate the differences between the trusted dataset and the buffered data. To ensure that the statistical measures are valid, a bootstrap-based p-value evaluation method is added to the measurements, as in [1]. The user of the method must then specify a minimal distance threshold (and optionally additional ones) for the distance measures. The proposed workflow suggests that if the outcome is slightly above the minimal threshold, additional data can be requested. On the other hand, if the outcome is significantly above the threshold value (or a specified additional threshold), alternative actions can be taken, e.g. operator intervention. If the outcome is below the minimal threshold (or a specified additional threshold), the decision of the Machine Learning algorithm can be trusted and the statistical distance measures can be stored to be reported.

As SafeML is model-agnostic, it can be flexibly deployed in numerous applications. In [1,2], Aslansefat et al. already presented experimental applications of SafeML for security attack detection [27], and *German Traffic Sign Recognition Benchmark* (GTSRB) examples [29]. For security intrusion detection, SafeML measures were used to compare the statistical distances against the accuracy of classifier. In the GTSRB example, the model was trained, and the incorrectly classified set of images was compared against randomly selected input images from the training set.

1.2   Motivation

As mentioned in Sect. 1.1, applying SafeML requires the specification of the number of runtime samples that needed to be acquired, and at least the minimal distance threshold for acceptance/rejection. Both parameters must be defined during development time, as they need to be known by the time the ML model is in operation. Existing work on SafeML does not investigate nor provide guidance for establishing these parameters, leaving it up to the user to find reasonable values.

However, this is not a trivial matter, as identifying appropriate thresholds has application-related implications. As will be highlighted further in Sect. 3, an inadequate number of runtime samples may result in low statistical power of the SafeML-based evaluation, whereas collecting too many samples can be inefficient and limit application performance. Addressing these limitations is the focus of this publication.

Statistical power is the probability of a correctly rejected null-hypothesis test, i.e., the probability of a true positive, given a large enough population [7]. Conversely, by presetting a required level of statistical power, the population size needed to correctly distinguish two distributions can be calculated through power analysis. Similarly, distance thresholds that are too low can lead to flooding the host application with false positive alarms, whereas distance thresholds that are too high can lead to potentially critical conditions being overlooked. Concretely, we establish the following research questions:

RQ1: Dissimilarity-Accuracy Correlation. Can we confirm that data points seen during operation that are dissimilar to training data impact the model's performance in terms of accuracy?

RQ2: Sample Size Dependency. Can we determine whether the sample size affects the accuracy of the SafeML distance estimation?

1.3   Paper Contribution and Outline

The contribution of this paper is three-fold. First, we use power analysis to specify sampling requirements for SafeML monitoring at runtime. Second, we systematically determine appropriate SafeML distance thresholds. Finally, we apply the above method in the context of an example automotive simulation.

The remainder of the paper is structured as follows: In Sect. 2, we discuss background and related work, including approaches both similar to and different from SafeML. In Sect. 3, we describe our approach for systematically applying SafeML and determining relevant thresholds, as well as our experimental setup. In Sect. 4, we discuss our experimental results, before recapping our key points and discussing future work in Sect. 5.

2   Background and Related Work

To briefly recap, in [1, 2] the authors propose statistical distance measures to compare the distributions of the training and operational datasets; the measures are based on established two-sample statistical testing methods, including the Kolmogorov-Smirnov, Anderson-Darling, Cramer von Mises [8], and Wasserstein methods [24]. The statistical distance measures used by SafeML capture the dissimilarity between two different distributions, but the approach itself does not propose an explicit threshold at which those distributions are not equivalent, nor a means for determining one systematically.

Setting meaningful thresholds is a reoccurring problem in ML and data-driven applications. A method based on the 3-sigma rule was shown to provide suitable threshold criteria in Hidden Markov Models under the assumption of normal distribution [6]. Our approach is similar in the sense that we used the same principle, but we did not assume that our datasets are normally distributed. Therefore, instead of a 3-sigma rule, we opted for a gradual increase of the threshold based on the sigma value. We will elaborate on this further in Sect. 3.

A prerequisite for the transition of AI applications to safety- and security-critical systems is the existence of guarantees and guidelines to assure underlying system dependability. A method was proposed in [25] to assure a model's operation within the intended context in a model-agnostic manner, with an additional autoencoder-based network being used to detect semantic novelty.

However, the innate problem of using neural networks, including autoencoders, is their black-box nature with respect to explainability, which inhibits the establishment of dependability guarantees. Hence, the use of a more explainable statistical method could serve as a solution to this issue. This includes our proposed approach, as the ECDF-based distance to the training set could provide additional insight into the model's decision.

In [23], the authors propose a commonality metric that, inspects the second-to-last layer of a *Deep Neural Network* (DNN). The proposed metric expresses the ratio between the activation of the neurons in the last layer during training (across all training instances) versus their activation during operation, for the given operational input. The approach shares common ideas with SafeML, but diverges in terms of being model-specific, as the metric directly samples the last layer's neurons. In contrast, SafeML does not consider model internals and makes no assumption on the distribution of the training and operational data.

Efforts have been made to ensure a dependable and consistent behavior in AI-based applications. These have taken various forms, from providing generative models, whose outputs can be interpreted as confidence in the predictions, to the aforementioned novelty detection. Design-time safety measures are introduced in [28], where the robustness of neural networks could be certified through a novel abstract domain, before deployment. Similarly, a feature-guided safety testing method for neural networks is proposed in [30] to evaluate the robustness of neural networks by feeding them through adversarial examples. Markov decision processes have also been proposed to be paired with neural networks to verify their robustness through statistical model checking [12].

Uncertainty wrappers are another notable concept [13–16]. This mathematical concept distinguishes ML uncertainty into three layers I) model performance, II) input quality, and III) scope compliance, and provides a set of useful functions for evaluating the existing uncertainties in each step. The uncertainty wrapper can be compared to SafeML in the third layer (scope compliance). Both of them are model-agnostic.

Safeguard AI [17] proposes calculating the likelihood of *out-of-distribution* (OOD) inputs and adding it to the loss function of the ML/DL model. This approach also uses a *Generative Adversarial Network* (GAN) to produce boundary data in order to create a more accurate OOD. In comparison to SafeML, the approach is model-specific and cannot be evaluated at runtime.

Another common theme across approaches for safeguarding ML models is the investigation of all conceivable input perturbations to produce robust, safe, and abstract interpretable solutions and certifications for ML/DL models [9, 10, 18–20, 26]. These approaches are also model-specific and do not provide runtime solutions. Similar to previous approaches, *DeepImportance* is a model-specific solution that presents a new *Importance-Driven Criteria* (IDC) as a layer-wise function to be assessed during the test procedure and provides a systematic framework for ML testing [11]. Regarding the reliability evaluation of ML models, only a small number of solutions have been provided so far. One of these is ReAsDL, which divides the input space into tiny cells and evaluates the

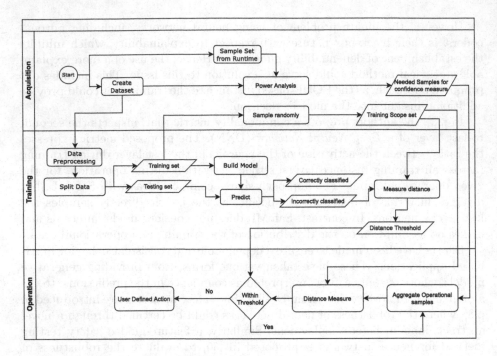

Fig. 1. Process flowchart

ML/DL reliability based on the cells' robustness and operational profile probability [31,32]. This solution is model-agnostic and focuses on classification tasks similar to SafeML. The NN-Dependability-kit suggests a new set of dependability measures to assess the impact of uncertainty reduction in the ML/DL life cycle. The authors also included a formal reasoning engine to ensure that the ML/DL dependability is guaranteed. The approach can be used for runtime purposes [3].

3 Methodology

In this section, we present our refined approach for applying SafeML, in the form of a proposed workflow, and address the question of how to determine the sampling and distance thresholds. To validate our approach, we applied SafeML to ML monitoring during simulation and, also used it against an existing dataset, the GTSRB. In the next section, we will describe the experimental design for our empirical evaluation of the proposed approach.

3.1 Process Workflow

The process workflow for determining the needed number of samples as well as the distance threshold is divided into three stages, as shown in Fig. 1.

– **Acquisition:** In this stage, two datasets are involved, a training dataset and a testing dataset. In our empirical experiments (see Sect. 3.2), these datasets are generated from the simulation, but they should generally be derived during development. At this point, power analysis is used to find the number of samples to determine the difference between the operational dataset and the training set. This factor can be calibrated for the application at hand, as it determines an additional number of samples beyond the minimum needed to achieve the determined test power. The effect size for the power analysis is established between the training set and the testing set, using Cohen's d coefficient [4].

– **Training:** The training dataset is processed and split into a training set and a testing set. A sub-sample of the smaller training set is uniformly sampled to represent the *Training Scope Set* (TSS) in the calculation of statistical distances, which maintain its features in order to reduce computational complexity during runtime. A model is then built from the smaller training set and used to predict the outputs of the testing set. The result is further distinguished into correctly and incorrectly classified outputs, where SafeML measures evaluate the statistical distance between the incorrectly classified outputs and the TSS. The resulting distances are finally used as the initial distance threshold. This initial distance threshold is then increased gradually by a factor of the standard deviation until a user-defined safety performance level is met.

– **Operation:** Once the trained model is in operation, the value obtained in the 'Acquisition' stage is used to aggregate operational data points into an operational set. SafeML measures evaluate the statistical distance between this operational set and the TSS. If the value falls within the defined threshold, the model continues its operation normally, otherwise, a signal is sent to run a user-defined action.

3.2   Experiment Setup

We performed experiments on the German Traffic Sign Recognition Benchmark (GTSRB) [29] and on a synthetic example dataset in the CARLA simulator[1] [5] to evaluate our approach. CARLA is an automotive simulator used for the development, training, and validation of autonomous driving systems. The dataset generated from CARLA was used to evaluate the confidence level of SafeML predictions and the autopilot decisions of the simulated vehicle. The GTSRB dataset is a collection of traffic sign images, along with their labels used for benchmarking the ML algorithms. It was first used in 2011. The dataset is a good representation of the safety-critical application of ML-components. Hence, it was also considered in this work for the evaluation of the presented approach.

The CARLA setup allows us to identify a systematic method for estimating the minimum number of required samples and the distance acceptance threshold though a fixed-point iteration, as well as to determine their implication on the

---

[1] https://carla.org.

model's prediction and how they correlate to the model's performance. It also offers multiple maps called Towns, with different sizes and properties, which allows for the experiment to be repeated. A simple model was built from a dataset sampled from CARLA, using a vehicle autopilot with varying driver profiles (shown in Table 1). This corresponds to the 'Acquisition' step in section Sect. 3.1. Three types of driving profiles were considered: safe, moderate, and dangerous. We should note that the profiles (and the model) were not designed with the aim to provide an accurate risk behavior estimation, but rather as a source of plausible ground truth for evaluating SafeML. A collection of classifiers were trained as the subject ML models for the CARLA dataset with results shown in Table 2. The models' inputs are the three location coordinates and the outputs are ordinally-encoded speed levels at the given coordinates (0: slow, 1: moderate, 2: fast).

As the dataset for GTSRB is already available, the creation of the dataset was assumed to be complete from the 'Acquisition' phase. Then a network was built to classify the GTSRB dataset. We built a simple convolutional neural network, as such networks are known for their superior performance on image applications. We then applied the above mentioned approach. This allows obtaining the minimum number of required samples and the distance acceptance threshold for this application.

Table 1. Properties of driver profiles

Property/driving profile	Safe	Moderate	Dangerous
Max speed	30% below limit	At limit	30% above limit
Traffic signs	Abide by all	Ignore 50%	Ignore 100%
Automatic lane-change	No	Yes	Yes
Distance to other cars	5 m	3 m	0 m

Table 2. Performance of trained models on the simulated CARLA dataset

Model	Class	Recall	Precision	F1-Score
kNN	0	0.89	0.95	0.92
	1	0.96	0.90	0.93
	2	0.96	0.95	0.96
Random Forest	0	0.83	0.52	0.64
	1	0.81	0.88	0.84
	2	0.72	0.92	0.81
LSTM	0	0.92	0.99	0.96
	1	0.99	0.91	0.95
	2	1.00	1.00	1.00

We trained a CNN network. The network was able to achieve an accuracy of around 99.73%. We remind readers that SafeML is model-agnostic, and other ML models could also have been used. This high accuracy resulted in very few incorrect samples for testing SafeML. Thus, one of the minority classes was excluded in order to be considered as an out-of-scope class, reducing accuracy to 97.5%. This added greater disparity to enable validation of SafeML.

In [2], SafeML distance measures have been shown to negatively correlate with the accuracy of the model. From this fact, and according to the first research question established in Sect. 1.2, we hypothesize that misclassified points would have a higher distance than correctly classified data points due to their dissimilarity to the training set.

Furthermore, from principles of statistical analysis, it is established that, if an insufficient number of samples is used during hypothesis testing, there is a risk of the statistical tests not achieving sufficient power. According to our second research question in Sect. 1.2, our corresponding hypothesis is that the number of samples correlates with confidence of dissimilarity (the magnitude of the distance).

The experiment concluded by following the 'Operation' step of the process workflow explained in Sect. 3.1. In the CARLA example, the same experiment was reproduced in different environment setups to ensure consistency of the results. In GTSRB, this was performed on the test set, which can be replaced by runtime dataset, at runtime.

Table 3. Mean and standard deviation of the statistical distances of the entire test set (CVM: Cramer von Mises, AD: Anderson-Darling, KS: Kolmogorov-Smirnov, WS: Wasserstein)

	Prediction	CVM	AD	KS	WS
kNN	Correct	1569.71, 617.60	8.577, 3.03	0.0193, 0.0043	3.192e−05, 1.153e−05
	Incorrect	5743.45, 2085.75	35.35, 11.12	0.083, 0.0139	1.430e−04, 5.264e−05
Random Forest	Correct	3780.74, 227.29	18.59, 0.97	0.0341, 0.0007	1.238e−04, 1.875e−05
	Incorrect	10478.63, 1147.64	56.73, 4.78	0.1068, 0.0161	4.368-04, 6.654e−05
LSTM	Correct	2744.89, 895.56	13.63, 3.26	0.0578, 0.0034	4.356e−05, 2.276-05
	Incorrect	7892.06, 1033.94	43.24, 3.23	0.1772, 0.0871	2.134e−04, 1.033e−04

4   Results

4.1   Preliminary Findings

Before continuing with the workflow of the simulation, an analysis of the trained model was used to test the hypotheses predefined in Sect. 3.2, namely:

RQ1: Dissimilarity-Accuracy Correlation was tested by calculating the statistical distance between the correctly classified data points and the TSS, as well the incorrectly classified data points and the training scope. Table 3 shows the mean and standard deviation of each of the statistical distance measures used. It shows that the incorrectly classified points are highly dissimilar to the TSS (higher distance), supporting the corresponding hypothesis.

RQ2: Sample Size Dependence: Due to the model's accuracy of 95%, the number of correctly classified data points was significantly larger than that of incorrectly classified points when the distances in Table 3 were calculated. To account for the number of samples, the distances were calculated over a varying number of randomly sampled points of each group. As shown in Fig. 2, the distance of incorrectly classified points is always larger than the distance of correctly classified points and increases with increasing number of samples. This can be attributed to several factors, such as: (a) increased distinction between the distributions and (b) a shift of the average value of the distances when the number of available samples increases, which removes skewness in the distribution.

4.2   Experiment Results

Following the process workflow presented in Sect. 3.1, each stage produced its corresponding values after being executed on the "Town 1" standard map from CARLA. In the 'Acquisition' stage, power analysis was used on each of the driver profiles. The highest number of samples returned was 91. Multiplying this by an additional factor of 1.3 yielded a final number of samples of 120, which aligned with our sampling batches; the operational samples were collected in batches over 4 s with a simulation resolution of 30 frames per second. The performance of the trained model is shown in Table 2, where the kNN model was used in the evaluation of the results due to its simplicity and high reported performance. The resulting threshold values for SafeML are shown in Table 4.

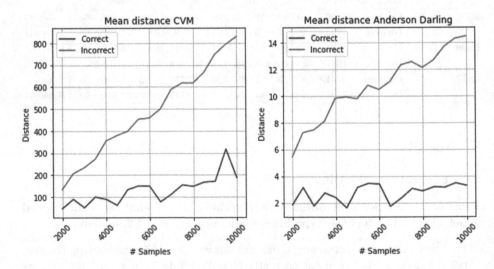

Fig. 2. Statistical distance over varying sampling sizes

Table 4. Threshold parameters used for Town 1 (CVM: Cramer von Mises, AD: Anderson-Darling, KS: Kolmogorov-Smirnov, WS: Wasserstein)

Prediction	CVM	AD	KS	WS
Mean	387.83	9.64	0.087	1.38e−4
Standard deviation	171.57	3.61	0.02	6.22e−5

The acceptable performance of the ML-model is a design decision obtained from the application requirements specified. In our example, let us consider the correctness over a batch. Since each batch contains multiple frames, let us assume a batch is considered correctly classified if its overall accuracy is 0.8 (96 correct points out of 120). Consequently, a batch is assumed to be incorrectly classified if its overall accuracy is 0 (focusing on worst-case scenarios), with all of its members being misclassified. This high limit was chosen to represent an extreme scenario that minimizes the number of false alarms.

The performance of each of the distance measures in SafeML was evaluated on different driver profiles as shown in Figs. 3 and 4, where the true positive rate (batches with 0 accuracy that were above the threshold) and the false positive rate (batches with 0.8 accuracy that were above the threshold) were plotted over a varying increase in the threshold in increments of 0.1 of the standard deviation.

Figure 3 shows the standard deviation factor by which the threshold should be increased to yield reliable identification by SafeML. The plot compares incorrect

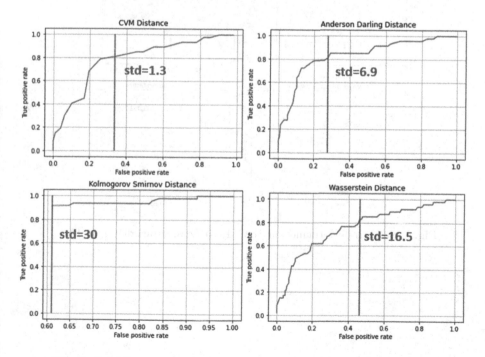

Fig. 3. SafeML performance on Town 1 with moderate driver profiles

(i.e., false positive rate) versus correct SafeML alarms (true positive rate), set to a threshold of 0.8 (as mentioned previously, this threshold can be determined based on application-level requirements). Through this method, a suitable factor for the distance measures was found, with the exception of Kolmogorov Smirnov, where a similar percentage of false positive rates was achieved for the distance measures.

The same process was repeated for the dangerous driver profile shown in Fig. 4, where similar plot curves were observed, and the threshold points could be established following similar steps as for the moderate profile. However, the performance ratio between true and false positive rate is exceptionally bad. The experiment was repeated on "Town 2" and "Town 4" with similar results.

Repeating the process workflow on the GTSRB shows quite a similar trend, where the correct classification and the incorrect classification are completely separable by setting a suitable distance threshold, as shown in Fig. 5. The number of samples (with each sample being an image) required can be seen on the x-axis. In this case, the majority of the incorrect classifications represent an out-of-scope class. The distance was calculated using features derived from the last layer of the CNN instead of from the raw pixels. More detailed results can be found in the git repo.

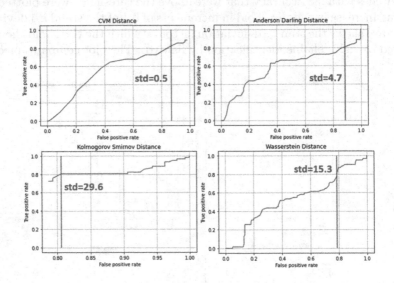

Fig. 4. SafeML performance on Town 1 with dangerous driver profiles

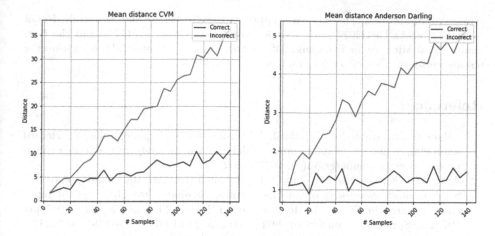

Fig. 5. Statistical distance over varying sampling sizes for GTSRB

5   Conclusion and Future Work

In this paper, we addressed the challenge of determining sampling and distance thresholds for SafeML, a model-agnostic, assessment tool for scope compliance. Our approach incorporates power sampling during the development stage of the subject ML model in order to determine the number of samples necessary to achieve sufficient statistical power while applying the SafeML distance evaluation during the runtime stage. Furthermore, we proposed means of identifying appropriate distance thresholds, based on the observed performance of the ML model during development-time simulation. We validated our approach experimentally, using a scenario developed in the CARLA automotive simulator as well as the publicly available GTSRB dataset.

Apart from the SafeML applications discussed earlier in Sect. 2, at the time of writing, additional examples are being researched, such as using SafeML for cancer detection via x-ray imaging as well as for pedestrian detection, financial investment, and predictive maintenance.

Regarding future work, we are considering further directions to improve SafeML, including investigating the effect of outlier data' and the effect of dataset characteristics (see [22]), using dimensionality reduction, accounting for uncertainty in the dataset labels (see [21]), and expanding the scope towards graph, quantum, and time-series datasets.

Code Availability

Regarding the reproducibility of our research, codes and functions supporting this paper have been published online at: https://tinyurl.com/4a76z2xs.

Acknowledgements. This work was supported by the Secure and Safe Multi-Robot Systems (SESAME) H2020 project under grant agreement 101017258 and the German Federal Ministry for Economic Affairs and Climate Action (BMWK) within the research project "FabOS" under grant no. 01MK20010A.

References

1. Aslansefat, K., Kabir, S., Abdullatif, A., Vasudevan, V., Papadopoulos, Y.: Toward improving confidence in autonomous vehicle software: a study on traffic sign recognition systems. Computer **54**(8), 66–76 (2021)
2. Aslansefat, K., Sorokos, I., Whiting, D., Tavakoli Kolagari, R., Papadopoulos, Y.: SafeML: safety monitoring of machine learning classifiers through statistical difference measures. In: Zeller, M., Höfig, K. (eds.) IMBSA 2020. LNCS, vol. 12297, pp. 197–211. Springer, Cham (2020). https://doi.org/10.1007/978-3-030-58920-2_13
3. Cheng, C.H., Huang, C.H., Nührenberg, G.: nn-dependability-kit: engineering neural networks for safety-critical autonomous driving systems. In: International Conference on Computer-Aided Design (ICCAD), pp. 1–6. IEEE (2019)
4. Cohen, J.: A power primer. Psychol. Bull. **112**(1), 155 (1992)
5. Dosovitskiy, A., Ros, G., Codevilla, F., Lopez, A., Koltun, V.: CARLA: an open urban driving simulator. In: 1st Annual Conference on Robot Learning (2017)
6. Duan, J., Zeng, J., Zhang, D.: A method for determination on HMM distance threshold. In: 2009 Sixth International Conference on Fuzzy Systems and Knowledge Discovery, vol. 1, pp. 387–391 (2009). https://doi.org/10.1109/FSKD.2009.732
7. Ellis, P.D.: The Essential Guide to Effect Sizes: Statistical Power, Meta-Analysis, and the Interpretation of Research Results. Cambridge University Press, Cambridge (2010). https://doi.org/10.1017/CBO9780511761676
8. Evans, D.L., Drew, J.H., Leemis, L.M.: The distribution of the Kolmogorov–Smirnov, Cramer–von Mises, and Anderson–Darling test statistics for exponential populations with estimated parameters. In: Glen, A.G., Leemis, L.M. (eds.) Computational Probability Applications. ISORMS, vol. 247, pp. 165–190. Springer, Cham (2017). https://doi.org/10.1007/978-3-319-43317-2_13
9. Fischer, M., Balunovic, M., Drachsler-Cohen, D., Gehr, T., Zhang, C., Vechev, M.: Dl2: training and querying neural networks with logic. In: International Conference on Machine Learning, pp. 1931–1941. PMLR (2019)
10. Gehr, T., Mirman, M., Drachsler-Cohen, D., Tsankov, P., Chaudhuri, S., Vechev, M.: Ai2: safety and robustness certification of neural networks with abstract interpretation. In: Symposium on Security and Privacy (SP). IEEE (2018)
11. Gerasimou, S., Eniser, H.F., Sen, A., Cakan, A.: Importance-driven deep learning system testing. In: 42nd International Conference on Software Engineering (ICSE). IEEE (2020)
12. Gros, T.P., Hermanns, H., Hoffmann, J., Klauck, M., Steinmetz, M.: Deep statistical model checking. In: Gotsman, A., Sokolova, A. (eds.) FORTE 2020. LNCS, vol. 12136, pp. 96–114. Springer, Cham (2020). https://doi.org/10.1007/978-3-030-50086-3_6
13. Jöckel, L., Kläs, M.: Increasing trust in data-driven model validation. In: Romanovsky, A., Troubitsyna, E., Bitsch, F. (eds.) SAFECOMP 2019. LNCS, vol. 11698, pp. 155–164. Springer, Cham (2019). https://doi.org/10.1007/978-3-030-26601-1_11

14. Jöckel, L., Kläs, M., Martínez-Fernández, S.: Safe traffic sign recognition through data augmentation for autonomous vehicles software. In: 2019 IEEE 19th International Conference on Software Quality, Reliability and Security Companion (QRS-C), pp. 540–541. IEEE (2019)
15. Kläs, M., Jöckel, L.: A framework for building uncertainty wrappers for AI/ML-based data-driven components. In: Casimiro, A., Ortmeier, F., Schoitsch, E., Bitsch, F., Ferreira, P. (eds.) SAFECOMP 2020. LNCS, vol. 12235, pp. 315–327. Springer, Cham (2020). https://doi.org/10.1007/978-3-030-55583-2_23
16. Kläs, M., Sembach, L.: Uncertainty wrappers for data-driven models. In: Romanovsky, A., Troubitsyna, E., Gashi, I., Schoitsch, E., Bitsch, F. (eds.) SAFECOMP 2019. LNCS, vol. 11699, pp. 358–364. Springer, Cham (2019). https://doi.org/10.1007/978-3-030-26250-1_29
17. Lee, K., Lee, H., Lee, K., Shin, J.: Training confidence-calibrated classifiers for detecting out-of-distribution samples. In: International Conference on Learning Representations (2018)
18. Mirman, M., Gehr, T., Vechev, M.: Differentiable abstract interpretation for provably robust neural networks. In: International Conference on Machine Learning. PMLR (2018)
19. Mirman, M., Singh, G., Vechev, M.: A provable defense for deep residual networks. arXiv preprint arXiv:1903.12519 (2019)
20. Müller, M.N., Makarchuk, G., Singh, G., Püschel, M., Vechev, M.: PRIMA: precise and general neural network certification via multi-neuron convex relaxations. arXiv preprint arXiv:2103.03638 (2021)
21. Northcutt, C.G., Jiang, L., Chuang, I.L.: Confident learning: estimating uncertainty in dataset labels. J. Artif. Intell. Res. (JAIR) 70, 1373–1411 (2021)
22. Oreski, D., Oreski, S., Klicek, B.: Effects of dataset characteristics on the performance of feature selection techniques. Appl. Soft Comput. 52, 109–119 (2017)
23. Paterson, C., Calinescu, R., Picardi, C.: Detection and mitigation of rare subclasses in deep neural network classifiers. In: 2021 IEEE International Conference on Artificial Intelligence Testing (AITest), Los Alamitos, CA, USA, pp. 9–16. IEEE Computer Society, August 2021. https://doi.org/10.1109/AITEST52744.2021.00012. https://doi.ieeecomputersociety.org/10.1109/AITEST52744.2021.00012
24. Ramdas, A., Trillos, N.G., Cuturi, M.: On Wasserstein two-sample testing and related families of nonparametric tests. Entropy 19(2), 47 (2017)
25. Rausch, A., Sedeh, A.M., Zhang, M.: Autoencoder-based semantic novelty detection: towards dependable AI-based systems. Appl. Sci. 11(21) (2021). https://doi.org/10.3390/app11219881
26. Ruoss, A., Baader, M., Balunović, M., Vechev, M.: Efficient certification of spatial robustness. arXiv preprint arXiv:2009.09318 (2020)
27. Sharafaldin, I., Lashkari, A.H., Ghorbani, A.A.: Toward generating a new intrusion detection dataset and intrusion traffic characterization. ICISSp 1, 108–116 (2018)
28. Singh, G., Gehr, T., Püschel, M., Vechev, M.: An abstract domain for certifying neural networks. Proc. ACM Program. Lang. 3, 1–30 (2019). https://doi.org/10.1145/3290354
29. Stallkamp, J., Schlipsing, M., Salmen, J., Igel, C.: Man vs. computer: benchmarking machine learning algorithms for traffic sign recognition. Neural Netw. 32, 323–332 (2012). https://doi.org/10.1016/j.neunet.2012.02.016. http://www.sciencedirect.com/science/article/pii/S0893608012000457

30. Wicker, M., Huang, X., Kwiatkowska, M.: Feature-guided black-box safety testing of deep neural networks. In: Beyer, D., Huisman, M. (eds.) TACAS 2018. LNCS, vol. 10805, pp. 408–426. Springer, Cham (2018). https://doi.org/10.1007/978-3-319-89960-2_22
31. Zhao, X., et al.: Assessing the reliability of deep learning classifiers through robustness evaluation and operational profiles. arXiv:2106.01258 (2021)
32. Zhao, X., Huang, W., Schewe, S., Dong, Y., Huang, X.: Detecting operational adversarial examples for reliable deep learning. arXiv:2104.06015 (2021)

Dynamic Risk Assessment

Engineering Dynamic Risk and Capability Models to Improve Cooperation Efficiency Between Human Workers and Autonomous Mobile Robots in Shared Spaces

Jan Reich[1], Pascal Gerber[1(✉)], Nishanth Laxman[1], Daniel Schneider[1], Takehito Ogata[2], Satoshi Otsuka[3], and Tasuku Ishigooka[3]

[1] Fraunhofer Institute for Experimental Software Engineering IESE, Kaiserslautern, Germany
{jan.reich,pascal.gerber,nishanth.laxman, daniel.schneider}@iese.fraunhofer.de
[2] European Research and Development Centre, Hitachi Europe GmbH, Munich, Germany
takehito.ogata@hitachi-eu.com
[3] Research and Development Group, Hitachi Ltd., Hitachi, Ibaraki, Japan
{satoshi.otsuka.hk,tasuku.ishigoka.kc}@hitachi.com

Abstract. Coexistence or even cooperation of autonomous mobile robots (AMR) and humans is a key ingredient for future visions of production, warehousing and smart logistic. Before these visions can become reality one of the fundamental challenges to be tackled is safety assurance. Existing safety concepts have significant drawbacks, they either physically separate operation spaces completely or stop the AMR if its planned trajectory overlaps with a risk area constructed around a human worker based on a worst-case assumption. In the best case, this leads to only less-than-optimal performance, in the worst case an application idea might prove to be completely unfeasible. A general solution is to replace static worst-case assumptions with dynamic safety reasoning capabilities. This paper introduces a corresponding solution concept based on dynamic risk and capability models which enables safety assurance and at the same time allows for continuous optimization of performance properties.

Keywords: Dynamic risk management · Situational awareness · Automated guided vehicles · Runtime safety monitor · Dynamic risk assessment · Model-based safety engineering · Cyber-physical system

1 Introduction

Autonomous systems such as autonomous mobile robots (AMR) have an enormous potential to improve further economic efficiency in application domains such as production or smart logistics. There are, however, numerous scenarios

C. Seguin et al. (Eds.): IMBSA 2022, LNCS 13525, pp. 237–251, 2022.
https://doi.org/10.1007/978-3-031-15842-1_17

in which a spatial co-existence or even cooperation of autonomous systems and human workers is required. Safety thus needs to be assured, whereas existing safety concepts either physically separate operation spaces completely or stop the AMR if its planned trajectory overlaps with a risk area constructed around a human worker based on a worst-case assumption. This leads to unnecessary AMR stops, which impacts the overall performance or even the general feasibility of AMR applications.

A general solution is to replace static worst-case assumptions with dynamic safety reasoning capabilities. Systems are empowered to monitor relevant properties of themselves and their context, extrapolate to a certain extent into the future, and reason about the implications that can be deduced from this information concerning the current risk. Worst-case assumptions are thus replaced by actual knowledge about the current situation augmented by future predictions for specific properties. Relevant context comprises the physical environment, including human workers and co-existing or cooperating systems. The context information is either attained directly by the system's sensors or by communication with third parties, such as infrastructure/edge/cloud devices cooperating systems or even humans. Reliance on such situational awareness and reasoning mechanisms necessitates that the safety of those mechanisms can be argued convincingly. While this is a challenge in itself, we believe in the general feasibility and that the benefits will, in many cases, significantly outweigh the additional effort and complexity.

In this work, we specifically focus on an industrial AMR application and use context information in terms of specific situation features, such as dynamic variations of human worker behavior, to dynamically assess the risk of the operational situation. At the same time, we dynamically assess the AMR's safety-related capabilities, which are also subject to change due to internal failures, sensor limitations, and fluctuations in physical context properties. Finally, we use the attained knowledge about both aspects, the current risk, and the current capabilities, to dynamically scale safety areas around humans and AMRs, as they have been conceived in previous work on *Symbiotic Safety Systems* [3].

The main contributions presented in this paper are (1) the definition of an abstract behavior causality ontology to express and analyze critical behavior deviations for human workers and AMR, (2) the integration of the models in a dynamic safety monitoring architecture and (3) an exemplary evaluation of the expected efficiency boost potential when using the resulting dynamic safety monitors in passing and overtaking scenarios. The paper is structured as follows: Sect. 2 puts the challenge of safe human-robot cooperation into a smart logistics context, reviews different possible safety concepts and related work for behavior and capability prediction. Section 3 subsequently introduces a method to engineer situation-aware risk and capability models based on a behavior causality ontology. In addition, it outlines the integration of the risk and capability monitor into the *Symbiotic Safety System* architecture. Section 4 evaluates the expected efficiency benefit of using the dynamic models in passing and overtaking scenarios between AMR and human workers compared to using worst-case movement assumptions. Finally, Sect. 5 concludes the paper and lays out future work directions.

2 Safe Human-Robot Cooperation

2.1 Safe Human-Robot Cooperation in Smart Logistics

The **main task of a logistics warehouse** is to efficiently carry in, store the goods appropriately, and carry out on-demand to be dispatched to a customer. First, goods must be carried in from trucks into a sorting area, where they are unpacked, inspected, and sorted to be transferred to an optimal storage place. Then, upon the dispatch request, the goods are picked up in the storage area, moved into the packaging area, prepared for dispatch, and carried out into trucks again. In *smart* **logistics warehouses**, these tasks are not only performed by human workers and human-operated machines like forklifts, but automation concepts are used to relieve humans from tedious work and make warehouse operations more efficient (Fig. 1). Although autonomous mobile robots (AMR) or autonomous forklifts (AFL) can be beneficially used for the efficient transport of goods, human workers can much better inspect and label the quality of goods. Thus, the optimal operation of a logistics warehouse requires the cooperation of humans and autonomous machines in shared spaces. However, this efficiency boost can only be realized if the residual collision risk between robots and humans is acceptably low.

Different safety concepts exist to address this challenge with varying consequences on assurance effort and resulting efficiency. The most straightforward idea is **assigning distinct static work areas for human workers and AMRs**, e.g., by physical barriers like fences or traditional safety functions like light curtains. As AMRs pick up goods directly at the location where humans inspect them, physical separation is not optimal. A **more efficient safety concept is to make the distinct movement areas dynamic**, i.e., to dynamically construct a so-called risk area around human actors, which represents the short-term movement space and constantly moves along with an actor during operation (Fig. 1 right). The AMR is designed in a way that overlaps between its intended trajectory and the risk area of a nearby human and will immediately lead to a safe stop until the overlap ceases to exist. Since there are several influences like malfunctions or functional inefficiencies that may cause an AMR to deviate from its intended trajectory, a so-called *capability area* is dynamically constructed around an AMR, accounting for the impact of those influences. Thus, capability and risk areas built for a short-term time horizon are dynamically checked, and exclusive possession right is granted to human actors during overlap. The efficiency of this dynamic safety concept is dependent on the adequacy of predicted risk and capability areas to match real actor movement as adequately as possible, in particular, that it is not wrongly determined as smaller than reality. As such, the adequate determination of risk and capability area extents is decisive for safety and efficiency.

One **common approach to solve this problem is to use worst-case assumptions** regarding the operational situation, i.e., the risk area extents are selected based on human worker behavior leading to the most critical situation conceivable. An example for an assumed maximum radial approximation speeds

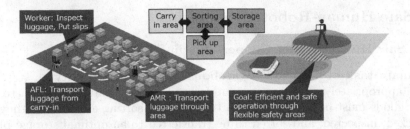

Fig. 1. Left: Smart logistics warehouse - tasks in sorting area. Right: Illustration of safety challenge with spatial overlap between human worker and AMR action ranges.

of humans towards machines in factory contexts is given in ISO 13855 with 1,6 m/s [1]. Although this approach leads to provable safety if the assumption is valid, it inevitably leads to an efficiency loss since worst-case situations rarely occur, and the AMR will often stop unnecessarily.

To run operations more efficiently without arriving at a higher collision risk, we have to **eliminate conservative AMR behavior in *low-risk* situations**. Detecting situation features indicating a high likelihood of uncritical behavior of human workers enables AMRs to be less conservative. Compared to searching the most critical situations within the operational domain, the consideration of specific low-risk situations adds more complexity to engineering an adequate situation detection mechanism and its safety assurance. Thus, the efficiency potential comes with the cost of increased assurance effort. However, by choosing the worst-case assumption as a baseline and detecting situation features indicating *lower risk* to inform risk area extent decrease, we relieve ourselves from having to deliver a completeness argument for the situation analysis. Instead, new features can be gradually added to detect low risk and improve efficiency.

Problem Statement. The efficiency of dynamic safety concepts relying on worst-case assumptions can be improved by dynamically detecting low-risk situations and adapting the AMR behavior accordingly based on modified risk and capability area extents. To that end, model-based methods for risk-driven situation analysis and integrating the resulting risk and capability models into runtime monitors are required.

2.2   Related Work

For dynamic safety assurance of AMR in cyber-physical systems, conceptual approaches to model and predict the relationship between situation features and behaviors at runtime were proposed.

Uncontrollable Actors. Behavior prediction in the context of risk-sensitive motion planning, e.g., [2], or trajectory verification, e.g., [5]: In both approach classes, external actor trajectories are predicted to check Spatio-temporal overlap with an ego trajectory. However, predicting high-accuracy trajectories requires very fine-granular/continuous input feature resolution so that a high-integrity perception of those features is hardly assurable. In addition, changes in risk are typically initiated by events on the tactical level, so a causal risk relationship on a more abstract (=non-trajectory) level would be favorable to increase assurability of feature perception, i.e., to use coarse-grained state distinction rather than continuous input feature detection. Initial approaches have been proposed to raise the abstraction level of dynamic risk monitors [4,8]. The source of risk relationships in these approaches are hazard and risk assessment activities carried out during design time safety engineering. Here, the risk model is not related to a trajectory but captures the abstract relationship between situation features on the tactical level and the presence of behaviors leading to the presence or absence of hazardous events. The respective approaches claim their assurability by not having to specify safety criteria in the spatio-temporal situation space but in a less complex tactical situation space.

Controllable Actors. In contrast to non-controllable actors, the determination of the extent of an AMR's movement space (i.e., its capability area) is a simpler problem, like the AMR's design and intended system behavior is known. Dynamic capability assessment approaches focus on modeling the relationship between events causing deviating system behavior from intention. These models serve as input for dynamic monitoring of system operation and its quality guarantees. Ability and skill graphs are models that represent what the system must do (skill) and how well (ability) to fulfilling its functional specification. These models can be used to synthesize runtime monitors enabling a dynamic assessment of capability availability through self-awareness [7]. Conditional Safety Certificates (ConSerts) [9] are Boolean success trees relating functional safety-related events with safety guarantees based on predefined and precertified safety concept variants. ConSerts represent dynamic, variable, and modular safety concepts, where safety guarantees can be inferred at runtime based on the state of runtime evidence.

Apart from the concrete techniques for risk and capability prediction, more generic model-based frameworks for modeling and safety analysis of cyber-physical systems exist, too. *SafeConcert* [6] provides a metamodel for the safety analysis of socio-technical systems consisting of technical elements, humans and even organizations. Although SafeConcert has a large overlap with the ontology in this paper, the most important difference is that the risk area prediction in this paper treats the human as an element of the operational situation whose controllability is predicted by means of behavior prediction. In *SafeConcert*, the human is treated as part of the system and consequentially can have "failure modes" that are addressed by safety concepts. In addition, SafeConcert is a pure design-time modeling and analysis approach to building a safe system, while the purpose in this paper is the engineering of runtime safety monitors.

In summary, for the problem of modeling the relationship between situation features and critical human worker behaviors on the one hand and situation features and critical AMR behaviors on the other hand, several approaches exist. However, to the best of the authors' knowledge, no model-based approach exists that combines both concepts in a holistic framework with the aim of engineering

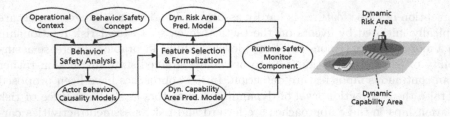

Fig. 2. Methodological steps for engineering distributed runtime safety monitors.

dynamic safety monitors. This paper intends to fill this research gap with the following contributions:

1. A holistic modeling concept combining risk and capability models to account for behavioral variability of uncontrollable and controllable actors.
2. A behavior causality ontology applicable to *both* humans and machines providing systematic guidance for situation feature identification during behavior safety analysis with the aim to synthesize runtime safety monitors.
3. An exemplary evaluation of the expected benefit of using the approach in passing and overtake scenarios in contrast to using worst-case assumptions.

3 Situation-Aware Behavior Safety Analysis

3.1 Method Overview

This section describes the methodological big picture to engineer dynamic risk and capability models, which realize a behavior safety concept and are finally processed by a distributed runtime safety monitoring component (Fig. 2).

The **behavior safety concept** defines a behavior specification satisfying the safety goal "Perform safe stop, when predicted dynamic risk and capability areas overlap". In this paper, we use a dynamic behavior safety concept, which predicts movement areas around uncontrollable actors like human workers (*risk area*) and controllable actors like AMR (*capability area*).

Both areas can be perceived as convex hulls of the possible actor behaviors for a given time horizon in the current situation. We are interested in distinguishing critical from uncritical behaviors instead of trajectories, because risk varies more significantly through unsafe behaviors than for the unsafe trajectory planning for a given safe behavior. Thus, we deem an abstraction suitable to account for this aspect. To formally realize it, we model risk and capability areas with geometric shapes with just enough parameters to express the presence or absence of critical behavior intents. The selected type of shapes, e.g. ellipses, circles or triangles, may differ for different actor types depending on the behavioral degrees of freedom. In Fig. 2 on the right, distinguishing critical lateral from uncritical longitudinal behaviors can be modeled with the semi-axis length parameters of an ellipsis to vary longitudinal and lateral extents independently.

With such simplified models, safety can be achieved if the model extents are predicted accurately and if a risk and capability area overlap triggers a safe AMR stop. However, unsafe situations can emerge if either of both areas are predicted smaller than they actually are. The *behavior safety analysis* step aims at systematically analyzing causal influence factors capable of indicating the likelihood of actor behavior options in a given situation. The resulting artifact of this analysis and modeling is the actor behavior causality model, which captures causal relationships between situation features and their influence on the actor behaviors to be distinguished regarding their risk potential. The operational context is systematically analyzed for situation factors by means of an abstract behavior causality ontology, which models the different steps of a generic cognitive decision-making process. Since autonomous systems try to imitate defined human behaviors, this cognitive process can be interpreted to guide the causal analysis of both human and machine behaviors. The difference lies in the interpretation scheme and in the types of risk-relevant situation features. For instance, the capability area of a controlled actor such as an AMR is mainly affected by the component failures or environmental factors affecting sensor performance. In contrast, the risk area of an uncontrolled actor such as a human worker is mainly affected by features indicating situational awareness or controllability of potentially unsafe situations.

The result of the behavior safety analysis is a set of models linking behavior-influencing situation features to different risk and capability area sizes for different actor types. However, the features need to be prioritized to achieve an optimal cost-benefit ratio. As such, the *feature selection* aims at finding the set of features that provide the maximum efficiency benefit for a particular technical architecture of the warehouse system given the cost constraints of adding a feature. While a particular feature may have, in general, a high-efficiency potential, it could still be excluded from usage. For instance, if there is no sensor available yet for reliable or cost-effective measurement of a feature or if measuring helpful features would violate human privacy rights, this can lead to the decision not to use a particular feature. Since future developments may change this, having realization-independent behavior causality models enables step-wise inclusion of features into realization and, therefore, a step-wise improvement of efficiency in line with technological innovation for feature sensors.

The models engineered during behavior safety analysis are qualitative and as such, they are not formally inferrable yet. Thus, in order to turn the prediction models processable by a runtime safety monitor, a *modeling formalism* with automated inference support is required. Different modeling formalisms exist in literature, ranging from simple Boolean logic models to more sophisticated model types with supporting temporal dependencies and probabilistic uncertainty propagation. In this paper, we use Boolean logic to express causal relationships between situation features and area parameters. Based on the model and inference algorithm, a runtime safety monitor component deployed to an AMR dynamically determines the state of situation features. Furthermore, it infers both risk and capability area extent parameters. To do that, infrastruc-

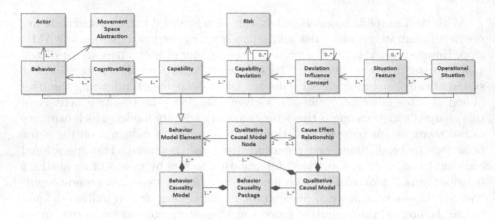

Fig. 3. Behavior causality ontology as a blueprint for situation analysis.

ture or human worker sensing devices can extend the perception capabilities of the AMR's sensors as will be shown in Sect. 3.3.

3.2 Behavior Causality Model Engineering

In order to engineer situation-specific risk and capability models used in a safety-critical function, two requirements need to be met: First, we need to express how situation features lead to variations in assumed actor movement, and second, we need to argue about the risk associated with the presence or absence of situation features. The latter is needed, because behavior intents can be affected in multiple ways by the same situation feature, leading to different risks in different scenarios. The *behavior causality ontology* (Fig. 3) aims at fulfilling the requirements by providing elements to express the complete causal chain of behavior emergence for different actors with a particular focus on capability-impairing situation features.

The conceptual backbone of the ontology is a decomposition of *behaviors* into *cognitive steps*, which enable actors to enact a behavioral decision based on *capabilities* for situation perception, reasoning and plan execution. The general idea is that there is a sequence of cognitive steps an actor follows to safely and efficiently accomplish a specific behavior or sequence of behaviors (=working task). Popular cognition models usable for both humans and machines are Sense-Plan-Act or, more fine-grained, Sense-Understand-Decide-Act. *Risk* can be associated with the likelihood and consequences of a particularly required capability being impaired or not present, represented by the *capability deviation*. A capability deviation is influenced by the presence or absence of *situation features* in an *operational situation*. Situation features can be grouped, as they contribute to similar abstract *deviation influence concepts*, which have similar effects on a particular capability deviation. For instance, the deviation influence concept "occlusion" affects the capability "Localize other actors" and occlusion can be caused by a variety of different situation features such as unobservable corners, blocking

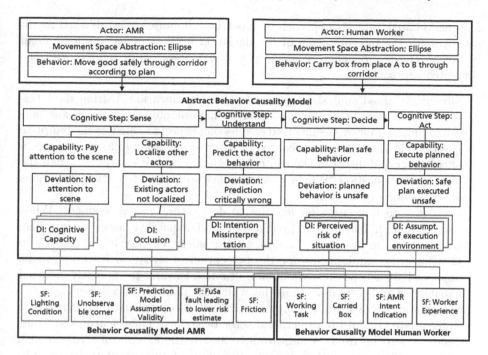

Fig. 4. Exemplary behavior causality model instances for AMR and human worker.

objects, or lighting conditions (Fig. 4). These *behavior model elements* are composed in a *behavior causality model*. The behavior causality model thus captures the semantic meaning of capabilities required to render behavior and the impact of situation features on the presence or absence of these capabilities. In contrast, the *qualitative causal model* represents a generic graph with nodes and relationships, which model *cause-effect relationships* between behavior model elements. Qualitative causal models, as well as behavior causality models, are composed in a *behavior causality package*.

Figure 4 shows an exemplary instantiation of the behavior causality ontology for human workers and AMRs in the logistics warehouse context. For both actor types, ellipses are used to envelop the movement space around planned behaviors representing working tasks. The abstract behavior causality model in the middle of Fig. 4 is the exemplary result of a behavior safety analysis performed on capabilities required for both actors to execute their behaviors safely. For the identification of situation features (SF in Fig. 4) potentially affecting the presence of a capability, engineers have to interpret the abstract deviation influence (DI) concepts in the context of actor behavior in a situation. Concretely, the engineer systematically goes through each capability of the actor cognitive model and analyzes situation influences. For AMRs, these influences can be analyzed in common safety analysis activities, which are already carried out during functional and operational safety assurance today. For human workers, we followed a scenario-based analysis approach in this study, because no established methods exist for the interpretation of the deviation influence concepts for human behavior. The key benefits of engineering behavior causality models with the presented approach are:

- More constrained analysis scope for feature identification: During the interpretation of deviation influence concepts in concrete scenarios, it was perceived much easier by the involved engineering experts to answer the template question "Which <situation features> lead to <deviation influence concept> affecting <capability> in the context of <behavior> of <actor>?" than the more generic question "Which <situation features> lead to critical deviations of <behavior> of <actor>?"
- Possibility to link situation features to design-time risk assessment: When using situation features to predict risk and capability areas at runtime, they should be traceable to design-time safety engineering processes so that integrity requirements for the perception of situation features can be expressed. This is possible via linking situation features to explicitly modeled capabilities and their deviations, for which the risk can be assessed.
- Systematic generation of a comprehensive collection of situation features that differentiate critical from uncritical actor behaviors. These features are thus candidates to be used as indicators to switch the extents of dynamic risk and capability areas within dynamic behavior safety concept realizations to improve operation efficiency (see Sect. 4).

3.3   Dynamic Safety Monitoring Architecture Integration

Having means to model the influence of situation features on risk and capability areas as described in the previous subsections, Fig. 5 shows the integration of the prediction component into the *Symbiotic Safety System* architecture. The *Symbiotic Safety System* realizes *Dynamic Collision Avoidance* on the warehouse level based on information provided by various sources as part of the *Field Digitization*. The core component is the determination of risk and capability area overlap and the assignment of an exclusive area on overlap, i.e. the AMR is instructed to safely stop, if an area is exclusively assigned to a HW. In previous work, [3], the extents of risk and capability areas were statically defined based on worst-case assumptions. The *dynamic risk and capability area prediction* introduced in this paper is highlighted in orange in Fig. 5 and feeds the dynamic area extents into the *exclusive area assignment* component. *Safety Control* on the one hand supervises safe stopping based on information about current positions of AMR and HWs and on the other hand indicates safety-relevant information to HWs. This can either happen through the audio-visual signaling capabilities of the AMR or directly be sent to HMI glasses worn by the HW, if available. The aim is to actively improve the HW's controllability by improving situational awareness. The situation features, which are needed for the *dynamic risk and capability area prediction* can be reliably detected by a combination of AMR-local sensors (e.g. for fault diagnosis or localization), HW-local sensors like the

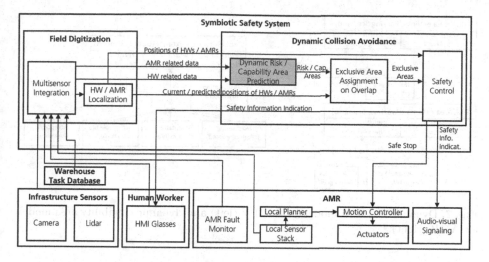

Fig. 5. Integration of *Dynamic Risk/Capability Area Prediction* (indicated in orange) into symbiotic safety system architecture.

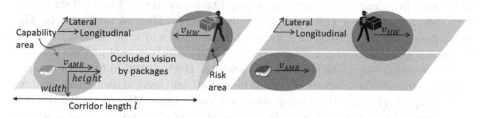

Fig. 6. Passing (left) and overtake (right) scenarios evaluated in the case study.

HMI glasses (e.g. for HW view direction), infrastructure sensors (e.g. for localization) and the warehouse task database (e.g. for deriving assumptions from the working task like the higher expectation of view obstruction, when the HW currently carries a box).

4 Expected Efficiency Benefit Evaluation

This section exemplarily evaluates the expected benefit of using dynamic risk area prediction models in passing and overtaking scenarios compared to using fixed area extents based on worst-case assumptions. The efficiency metric used in the evaluation is the time an AMR needs to pass safely through a corridor.

4.1 Passing Scenario

In the passing scenario, AMR and human worker (HW) move with speeds v_{AMR} and v_{HW} in opposite directions along a corridor with length l (Fig. 6 left).

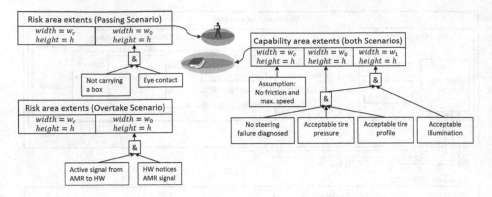

Fig. 7. Dynamic risk area model for the HW (left) and dynamic capability area model for AMR (right).

By making use of the behavior safety analysis method described in Sect. 3, Boolean behavior causality models have been derived for the scenario for dynamically detecting varying risk area and capability area extents (Fig. 7). Two modes with different assumed width extents are modeled for the risk area models. The worst-case risk area extent is always selected with width w_c unless the risk-decreasing situation features "not carrying a box" and "eye contact" are present, where we assume w_0 to be the risk area's width. Both situation features in combination indicate the absence of occlusion and a basic level of awareness, leading to the hypothesis that the human worker notices the AMR and will take this into account for behaving safely. This turns the situation into a non-worst case situation and represents the efficiency potential. For the AMR's capability area extents, three modes with varying assumed capability area widths have been modeled accordingly, where w_c represents the worst-case, and w_0 and w_1 represent the area widths resulting from different situation feature combinations.

In workshops with our industry partners from Hitachi, we ensured that selected situation features were reliably detectable at runtime with state-of-the-art sensors and algorithms assumed to be available in smart logistics warehouses. These include HMI devices worn by human workers to indicate eye gaze and present working tasks, as well as AMR-local and infrastructure sensors to determine tire, illumination and failure conditions.

As an evaluation benchmark, we compute the average AMR's corridor passing time t_{WC}^0 (Eq. 1) by assuming the constant presence of HW risk area width w_c, where the AMR needs to stop and can only continue to move after the HW has stepped out of his capability area. For this computation, assumptions are required for the likelihood of a HW being present in the corridor simultaneously to the AMR $P(HW)$, speeds of AMR v_{AMR} and HW v_{HW}, the length of the AMR d_{AMR} and the corridor length l.

$$t_{WC}^0 = P(\overline{HW}) \left(\frac{l}{v_{AMR}} \right) + P(HW) \left(\frac{l}{v_{AMR}} + \frac{d_{AMR}}{v_{HW}} \right) \tag{1}$$

By assuming $P(HW) = 0.7, v_{HW} = 1.6\,\frac{m}{s}, v_{AMR} = 5.0\,\frac{m}{s}, d_{AMR} = 0.85\,\text{m}, l = 42\,\text{m}$, the benchmark average AMR corridor passing time is $t^0_{WC} = 8.77\,\text{s}$.

In our best-case scenario, the absence of carrying boxes and the presence of eye contact are taken into account to adapt the risk area extent to w_0 leading to no required stop for the AMR, i.e., driving with maximum v_{AMR} along the full corridor length. In addition to the parameters of Eq. 1, further assumptions about for the likelihood that an occlusion is present $P(OC)$ and the conditional probability that eye-contact is present given no occlusion $P(EC|\overline{OC})$ are required for the average passing time t^0_{DYN}, given by Eq. 2.

$$t^0_{DYN} = \left[P(\overline{HW}) + P(HW)P(EC|\overline{OC})P(\overline{OC})\right] \left(\frac{l}{v_{AMR}}\right) \tag{2}$$

$$+ P(HW)\left[(P(\overline{EC}|\overline{OC})P(\overline{OC}) + P(OC)\right] \left(\frac{l}{v_{AMR}} + \frac{d_{AMR}}{v_{HW}}\right)$$

By assuming similar parameter values for $P(HW), v_{HW}, v_{AMR}, d_{AMR}, l$ and additionally $P(OC) = 0.5, P(EC|\overline{OC}) = 0.8$, the average AMR corridor passing time with dynamic risk area models is $t^0_{DYN} = 8.62\,\text{s}$.

4.2   Overtake Scenario

In the overtake scenario (Fig. 6 right), AMR and HW are moving in the same longitudinal direction. With the worst-case assumed risk area around the HW, the AMR cannot overtake the HW with v_{AMR}. Instead, the AMR will constantly drive behind the HW with a maximum speed v_{HW} until the end of the corridor. Hereby, the first term describes the time required by the AMR to reach an arbitrary location s on the corridor, with its regular speed v_{AMR}. From location s on, it must reduce its speed to that of the HW, ensuring a sufficient distance to the HW over the remaining distance of the corridor. By using the same variables like in Eq. 1, the average passing time of an AMR t^1_{WC} is given by Eq. 3.

$$t^1_{WC} = P(HW)\frac{1}{l} \int_0^l \frac{s}{v_{AMR}} + \frac{l-s}{v_{HW}} ds + P(\overline{HW})\frac{l}{v_{AMR}} \tag{3}$$

By assuming parameter values for $P(HW), v_{HW}, v_{AMR}, l$ like in Eq. 1, the average AMR corridor passing time with worst-case assumptions is $t^1_{WC} = 14.65\,\text{s}$.

To improve the efficiency in the overtaking scenario, a different set of situation features have been selected for the dynamic risk area model based on the method described in Sect. 3 (see Fig. 7 left bottom). Based on the analysis, a reduction of the risk area width from worst-case mode w_c to best-case mode w_0 is hypothesized to be safe, if it can be assumed that the HW is aware of the AMR arriving from the back. This is achieved by issuing an active audio-visual signal to the HW and detecting the HW's turn-around reaction as an indicator of awareness. The result of extending Eq. 3 with an additional parameter $P(AW)$ indicating the likelihood of HW awareness of AMR (=successful turn-around after active AMR signaling) leads to the average AMR corridor passing time with dynamic risk area models t^1_{DYN} (Eq. 4).

$$t^1_{DYN} = P(HW)\frac{1}{l}\int_0^l P(\overline{AW}|HW)\left(\frac{s}{v_{AMR}} + \frac{l-s}{v_{HW}}\right) ds \qquad (4)$$
$$+ P(AW|HW)P(HW)\frac{l}{v_{AMR}} + P(\overline{HW})\frac{l}{v_{AMR}}$$

By assuming similar parameter values for $P(HW), v_{HW}, v_{AMR}, l$ and additionally $P(AW|HW) = 0.5$, the average AMR corridor passing time with dynamic risk area models is $t^1_{DYN} = 11.52\,s$.

5 Conclusion

In this paper, we aimed to answer the research question of how to systematically engineer risk and capability models that can be used within the *Symbiotic Safety System* to optimize efficiency while still guaranteeing safety dynamically. To that end, we introduced a holistic modeling approach combining risk and capability models to account for behavioral variability of uncontrollable (human workers) and controllable actors (AMR) during dynamic safety monitoring. The modeling approach is accompanied by a method for situation-aware behavior safety analysis providing systematic guidance for risk-relevant situation feature identification during behavior safety analysis. We exemplarily applied the engineering approach for a concrete industrial AMR use case and thus evaluated the feasibility and applicability of the engineering approach. The key benefits of engineering behavior causality models with the presented approach are:

- More constrained analysis scope and thus guidance for domain experts to identify risk-relevant situation features more easily
- Possibility to link situation features to design-time risk assessment and therefore having formal traceability to design-time safety engineering activities required for arguing safety standard compliance for the dynamic safety monitoring mechanisms
- Systematic generation of a comprehensive collection of situation features that differentiate critical from uncritical actor behaviors. These features are candidates to be used as indicators to switch the extents of dynamic risk and capability areas within dynamic behavior safety concept realizations to improve operational efficiency.

Further, we evaluated the dynamic safety approach in the context of passing and overtake scenarios inside a logistics warehouse and obtained evidence regarding its expected benefit in contrast to static safety concepts based on worst-case assumptions. The expected runtime benefit evaluation demonstrated that, given the used parameter assumptions, the dynamic safety monitoring approach presented in this paper can provide a relative efficiency improvement compared to worst-case parameters of $(t^0_{WC} - t^0_{DYN})/t^0_{WC} \approx 2\%$ in passing scenarios and of $(t^1_{WC} - t^1_{DYN})/t^1_{WC} \approx 21\%$ in overtaking scenarios. Thus, we conclude that using a dynamic monitoring approach has more efficiency boost potential in overtaking scenarios than for passing scenarios. However, the evaluation results can only be a rough estimate of the true efficiency potential, as the parameter assumptions were selected based on expert knowledge. In reality, these assumptions will likely vary in different instances of smart logistic warehouses and have to be continuously validated based on data both during design-time and operation time. Accounting for this vital aspect, i.e., to identify, validate and monitor conditional probabilistic assumptions of the dynamic risk and capability area models and a more accurate quantification of efficiency improvement, is planned to be the subject of future work. A concrete starting point is to support uncertainties by extending the Boolean models used in this paper to probabilistic inference models like Bayesian networks. Further, cooperative scenarios involving different systems of different manufacturers imply additional challenges to be tackled, i.e., the safety-related properties and capabilities of the cooperation partners are typically not fully known through distribution, and safety-related information is not shared to the extent that would be desirable. We used the ConSert approach [9] to address this issue within this project, but details could not be included in this paper due to space restrictions and are thus planned to be the subject of another publication.

References

1. ISO 13855:2010, Safety of machinery—Positioning of safeguards with respect to the approach speeds of parts of the human body
2. Eggert, J.: Risk estimation for driving support and behavior planning in intelligent vehicles. AT - Automatisierungstechnik **66**(2), 119–131 (2018)
3. Ishigooka, T., Yamada, H., Otsuka, S., Kanekawa, N., Takahashi, J.: Symbiotic safety: safe and efficient human-machine collaboration by utilizing rules. In: Design, Automation and Test in Europe (DATE) Conference 2022, pp. 280–281. IEEE (2022)
4. Khastgir, S., Sivencrona, H., Dhadyalla, G., Billing, P., Birrell, S., Jennings, P.: Introducing ASIL inspired dynamic tactical safety decision framework for automated vehicles. In: 2017 IEEE 20th International Conference on Intelligent Transportation Systems (ITSC), Yokohama, Japan, pp. 1–6 (2017)
5. Mehmed, A., Steiner, W., Antlanger, M., Punnekkat, S.: System architecture and application-specific verification method for fault-tolerant automated driving systems. In: IEEE Intelligent Vehicles Symposium (IV), Paris, France (2019)
6. Montecchi, L., Gallina, B.: SafeConcert: a metamodel for a concerted safety modeling of socio-technical systems. In: Bozzano, M., Papadopoulos, Y. (eds.) IMBSA 2017. LNCS, vol. 10437, pp. 129–144. Springer, Cham (2017). https://doi.org/10.1007/978-3-319-64119-5_9
7. Nolte, M., Bagschik, G., Jatzkowski, I., Stolte, T., Reschka, A., Maurer, M.: Towards a skill- and ability-based development process for self-aware automated road vehicles. In: 2017 IEEE 20th International Conference on Intelligent Transportation Systems (ITSC), Yokohama, Japan, pp. 1–6 (2017)
8. Reich, J., Trapp, M.: SINADRA: towards a framework for assurable situation-aware dynamic risk assessment of autonomous vehicles. In: 2020 16th European Dependable Computing Conference (EDCC), pp. 47–50. IEEE (2020)
9. Schneider, D., Trapp, M.: Conditional safety certification of open adaptive systems. ACM Trans. Auton. Adapt. Syst. **8**(2), 1–20 (2013)

SafeDrones: Real-Time Reliability Evaluation of UAVs Using Executable Digital Dependable Identities

Koorosh Aslansefat[1]([✉]), Panagiota Nikolaou[2], Martin Walker[1],
Mohammed Naveed Akram[3], Ioannis Sorokos[3], Jan Reich[3], Panayiotis Kolios[2],
Maria K. Michael[2], Theocharis Theocharides[2], Georgios Ellinas[2],
Daniel Schneider[3], and Yiannis Papadopoulos[1]

[1] University of Hull, Hull, UK
k.aslansefat@hull.ac.uk
[2] KIOS Research and Innovation Center of Excellence and Department of Electrical
and Computer Engineering, University of Cyprus, Nicosia, Cyprus
[3] Fraunhofer Institute for Experimental Software Engineering (IESE),
Kaiserslautern, Germany

Abstract. The use of Unmanned Arial Vehicles (UAVs) offers many
advantages across a variety of applications. However, safety assurance
is a key barrier to widespread usage, especially given the unpredictable
operational and environmental factors experienced by UAVs, which are
hard to capture solely at design-time. This paper proposes a new reliability modeling approach called SafeDrones to help address this issue by
enabling runtime reliability and risk assessment of UAVs. It is a prototype instantiation of the Executable Digital Dependable Identity (EDDI)
concept, which aims to create a model-based solution for real-time, data-
driven dependability assurance for multi-robot systems. By providing
real-time reliability estimates, SafeDrones allows UAVs to update their
missions accordingly in an adaptive manner.

Keywords: Unmanned Aerial Vehicles (UAVs) · Fault Tree Analysis
(FTA) · Markov model · Real-time reliability and risk assessment ·
Executable Digital Dependable Identity (EDDI)

1 Introduction

There are many potential applications for Unmanned Aerial Vehicles (UAVs),
including logistics, emergency response, filming, traffic monitoring, search and
rescue, rail surveillance, and infrastructure inspection [9]. However, one of the
major barriers to widespread deployment and acceptance of UAVs is that of
safety, particularly for operations in urban areas where UAV failure brings a
higher risk of harm. For instance, during testing for Amazon's planned fast drone-
based delivery service, their drones crashed five times over a four-month period
in 2021 [28]. Therefore, safety and reliability must be key objectives during both

C. Seguin et al. (Eds.): IMBSA 2022, LNCS 13525, pp. 252–266, 2022.
https://doi.org/10.1007/978-3-031-15842-1_18

the design and operation of UAVs to help minimise risk and improve likelihood of mission success [23].

Reliability can be defined generally as the probability of a system functioning correctly over a given period of time [29]. There is a long history of reliability engineering techniques intended to help analyse, understand, and prevent failures. Among the most popular are Fault Tree Analysis (FTA) [31] and Failure Modes and Effects Analysis (FMEA). Such techniques were originally manually applied but over time have evolved and now form integral parts of comprehensive, tool-supported methodologies, encompassed under Model-Based Safety Analysis [27]. Using such approaches during the design of a UAV, it is possible to determine the ways in which it can fail and the likelihood of those failures.

Even so, UAVs must often operate independently in dynamic, unpredictable environments with varying mission goals, all of which are difficult to capture in a design-time analysis model. By combining design-time knowledge with safety monitoring applied at runtime, we can perform dynamic reliability evaluation and obtain a clearer picture of UAV reliability during operation.

This paper proposes a new model-based approach to improve reliability and safety of UAVs called SafeDrones. SafeDrones builds upon static design-time knowledge in the form of fault trees by combining them with dynamic Markov-based models and real-time monitoring to perform continuous reliability evaluation at runtime. The result is a modular safety monitor known as an Executable Dependable Digital Identity (EDDI), which can then be used to inform operational decision making.

The rest of the paper is organized as follows: in Sect. 2, a brief background on relevant techniques is provided. Section 3 introduces SafeDrones and explains its proposed methodology. An experimental implementation is described in Sect. 4 and results discussed in Sect. 5, to illustrate the capabilities and limitations of the idea. Finally, conclusions and future research directions are presented.

2 Background

2.1 Fault Tree Analysis

Fault Tree Analysis (FTA) is a widely used, top-down reasoning approach for reliability analysis. It begins with a given system failure (the top event) and progressively explores possible combinations of causes until individual component failures have been reached. It is capable of both qualitative (logical) and quantitative (probabilistic) analysis, but requires the use of extensions to model dynamic relationships between causes and components and thus model dynamic failure behaviour [5]. Markov chains are often used to perform the quantitative analysis of dynamic fault trees but this can result in significant complexity due to the state-space explosion problem [1,10].

Although these limitations make fault trees less common for runtime applications, fault trees have also been used at runtime, particularly for diagnosis purposes. For example, by connecting sensor readings as inputs to "complex basic events" (CBE) in the fault tree, the failure model can be updated in real-time to provide potential diagnoses of problems, predictions of future failures, and reliability evaluation [16]. Such an approach is extended and used in SafeDrones.

There has also been some work on the use of FTA for UAVs specifically. Reliability improvement of UAVs through FTA and FMEA in design review procedures has been studied in [13]. [19] proposes a procedure for reliability improvement in a cost-effective way based on FTA. It also reduced the uncertainty in failure data via Dempster-Shafer theory. In [20], the Michigan UAV is evaluated through qualitative failure analysis. However, these papers address only the design-time evaluation of UAVs, while in SafeDrones, both design-time and runtime evaluation are assessed.

2.2 Reliability Modelling Using Semi-Markov Processes (SMP)

Given the limitations of FTA when applied to highly dynamic systems, particularly adaptive, unmanned systems like UAVs, they are often combined with other techniques such as Markov Processes and Petri-Nets. Markov Processes are a well-known tool for reliability evaluation, particularly when it comes to dynamic behaviours such as repair, priority, and sequences. A Semi-Markov Process (SMP) is a special type of Markov process that has the ability to work with non-exponential failure distributions [29]. SMP can be defined using the following set: $(p, P, F(t))$. p is the initial probability distribution vector, P is the conditional transition probabilities matrix, and $F(t)$ describes the matrix of distribution functions of sojourn times in i^{th} state, when j^{th} state is next.

Let X_i, $\forall i = 0, 1, 2, \ldots$ be random variables. The time-homogeneous SMP X is determined by a vector of initial state probabilities $p(0)$ and the matrix of conditional transition probability $P(t) = \lceil P_{ij}(t) \rceil$ is computed by Eq. (1). In this equation, $P_{ij}(t)$ satisfies the Kolmogorov-Feller equation [29].

$$P_{ij}(t) = P\{X(t) = j | X(0) = i\} = \delta_{ij}[1 - G_i(t)] + \sum_{k \in S} \int_0^t P_{kj}(t - x) dQ_{ik}(x) \quad (1)$$

where $\delta_{ij} = 1$ if $i = j$ and $\delta_{ij} = 0$ otherwise, G_i is the distribution of the sojourn time in state i described by Eq. (2) [11], and $Q_{ij}(t)$ describes the kernel matrix by Eq. (2).

$$G_i(t) = P\{S_i \leq t \mid X_0 = i\} = \sum_{j=1}^{i} Q_{ij}(t) \quad (2)$$

where $S_i, i = 0, 1, 2, \ldots$ is the state of the system at time t and $Q_{ij}(t)$ is $P\{X_1 = j, S_i \leq t \mid X_0 = i\}$. The solution of Eq. (1) can be found by applying the Laplace Stieltjes Transformation (LST) in matrix form by Eq. (3) [6]. Note that $\tilde{p}(t)$ represents the probability vector in time domain and $\tilde{p}(s)$ represents the probability vector in LST domain.

$$\tilde{p}(s) = \lceil 1 - \tilde{q}(s) \rceil^{-1} \tilde{g}(s)) \quad (3)$$

Having solved Eq. (3) with taking the inverse LST of $\tilde{p}(s)$, the unconditional state probabilities in time domain are determined as $P(t) = P(0)P(t)$. Finally, the reliability of a system can be computed through summation of probability of operational state in the SMP. To calculate the MTTF, the transition matrix should have the following canonical form where there are r absorbing states (forming R) and t transient states (forming Q).

$$P = \begin{bmatrix} Q & R \\ 0 & I \end{bmatrix} \tag{4}$$

For the fundamental P matrix, consider $N = (I - Q)^{-1}$ and let t_i be the average number of steps before reaching the absorbing state, given that the chain starts in state s_i, and let t be the column vector whose i^{th} entry is t_i. The column vector of t can be written as follows:

$$t = \begin{bmatrix} t(NA_1) & t(NA_2) & \dots & t(NA_n) \end{bmatrix}^T = NC \tag{5}$$

where C is a column vector whose elements are one. Having calculated t, each of its elements represents the mean time to failure (MTTF) of the corresponding state.

In the area of reliability evaluation of UAV using Markov processes, there are a few existing research works. For example, Guo J. et al. [15] focused on the balancing issue of the propulsion system in multi-rotor UAVs and proposed a solution based on Markov chains. Aslansefat, K. et al. [7] proposed a set of Markov models for different possible configurations in the propulsion system of multi-rotor UAVs, taking into account not just the balancing issue but also the controllability aspects which make the model more dynamic.

In this paper, the Markov models proposed by [7] are used for the propulsion system and as a CBE (discussed in Sect. 3). As one of the contributions in this paper, the Markov models are also extended to use 'Motor status' as a symptom and be able to re-calculate the reliability and MTTF during the mission. For instance, if the real-time monitoring and diagnosis unit in the robot detects a motor failure in motor status based on the available sensors that the robot has, the proposed approach will select the equivalent state in the SMP that represents the motor failure and re-calculate the probability of failure and MTTF from that state to the failure state.

2.3   Reliability Modeling Using Arrhenius Equation

The lifetime reliability of a processing unit has a strong correlation with its temperature [21]. Moreover, a processor's temperature depends on the UAV's performance and utilization. To capture this interaction between reliability and temperature, the Arrhenius equation has been used. The Arrhenius equation is used to compute the MTTF acceleration factor (AF) depending on the processor's actual and reference temperatures.

$$AF = e^{\frac{Ea}{k}\left(\frac{1}{T_r} - \frac{1}{T_a}\right)} \tag{6}$$

where Ea is the activation energy in electron-volts, k is Boltzmann's constant (8.617E−05), T_r is the reference temperature and T_a is the actual temperature.

The acceleration factor (AF) is then used by the MTTF model to evaluate the effects of temperature on the MTTF. The final MTTF of the processor is calculated using the following equation:

$$MTTF = \frac{MTTF_{ref}}{AF} \tag{7}$$

where $MTTF_{ref}$ is the reference MTTF, estimated at the reference temperature. $MTTF_{ref}$ is usually given by the system's designers.

2.4   The Executable Digital Dependable Identity (EDDI)

Despite existing standards and guidelines, there is a great deal of variation in how assurance of dependability attributes is realized and claimed for concrete systems. This makes it difficult for third parties like certification authorities to analyze and evaluate the assurance approach in general, and especially when the systems are to be open, adaptive, or autonomous, like platooning cars [17].

To overcome this issue, Digital Dependability Identities (DDI) were created [2,26]. A DDI is a structured, modular, and hierarchical model of a system's dependability properties. An assurance case is at the heart of the DDI, arguing for the assurance of the appropriate dependability attributes and connecting all models and artefacts (e.g. requirements, assumptions, architectural models, dependability analyses, evidences) essential for the argumentation. A DDI is created and updated throughout the design process, issued when the component or system is launched, and then maintained during the component or system's lifespan. DDIs are utilized for the hierarchical integration of systems to "systems of systems" in the field, as well as the integration of components to systems during development.

An Executable Digital Dependability Identity (EDDI) is an extension of the DDI concept that is intended to be executable at runtime. It leverages the design-time dependability models stored in the DDI and augments them with event monitoring and diagnostic capabilities to provide real-time feedback on reliability, security, and safety issues, thereby supporting safe operation and dynamic dependability management. Importantly, EDDIs are intended to act cooperatively when applied within a distributed multi-robot or multi-agent system, enabling on-the-fly reconfiguration, communication, and adaptation. The idea is to support dynamic adaptive system assurance and dependability management through event monitoring, run-time diagnostics, risk prediction, and recovery planning.

Like DDIs, EDDIs are based on the Open Dependability Exchange metamodel [12]. An EDDI generally consists of some higher-level ODE-based system models for diagnostics, capability (e.g. success trees) and risk prediction (e.g. fault trees, Bayesian networks) and lower-level models for event monitoring and reliability estimation (e.g. Markov models, Bayesian networks). Once connected to sensor data and other pertinent system information, the EDDI can use these models to perform calculations to provide feedback and recommendations to the host system.

3   Methodology

SafeDrones is an approach for real-time reliability and risk evaluation of multi-robot (multi-UAV) systems. The main goal of this work is to develop an early prototype instantiation of the EDDI concept for runtime reliability estimation for UAVs. It makes use of fault trees as the overall model with CBEs to support dynamic evaluation. A fault tree consisting of 9 main failure categories and 28 basic events is proposed for a generic UAV in the appendix. However, to simplify the explanation of the methodology, a smaller fault tree of the UAV is provided in Fig. 1.

The contribution and capabilities of the SafeDrones approach are as follows: 1) SafeDrones expands the idea of FTA with CBEs to not only consider SMPs but also other evaluation functions like the Arrhenius Equation; 2) it proposes the idea of having symptom events for each CBE; 3) it is also able to handle reliability evaluation of reconfigurable systems by using pre-defined models in one CBE (e.g. consider a hexacopter capable of reconfiguring its propulsion system on-the-fly from PNPNPN configuration to PPNNPN configuration, where P and N represent clockwise and anticlockwise rotation of the propellers respectively), and 4) finally, SafeDrones provides Python functions which can be executed on each UAV and provide real-time reliability and MTTF evaluation. This paper primarily explores the first and fourth capabilities.

The tree provided in Fig. 1 has three CBEs for battery failure, propulsion system failure and processor failure. The processor failure has a symptom of actual temperature (T_a is the symptom) and based on the Arrhenius Equation (see Sect. 2.3), the reliability and the MTTF values of this basic event can be updated during the mission. The idea can be implemented for any component in the robot where its reliability can change based on temperature variation. The middle CBE is for the battery failure. This model is provided by [18] and considers battery degradation as well as failure. In this paper, we have used the battery model with four degradation levels and the battery level status B_S is included as a symptom. So, based on the battery level status, the initial probability vector in the SMP will be updated and then the probability of failure (unreliability of the battery) will be updated accordingly.

The third CBE is a propulsion system failure. The CBE is chosen to show the capabilities of SafeDrones for handling system reconfiguration. The first configuration is for a quad-copter that has two propellers rotating clockwise (P) and two propellers rotating anticlockwise (N) forming PNPN configuration. The second and the third configurations considered for hexa-copters with two different PNPNPN and PPNNPN configurations. The detailed construction and simplification of these models has been discussed in our previous research [7].

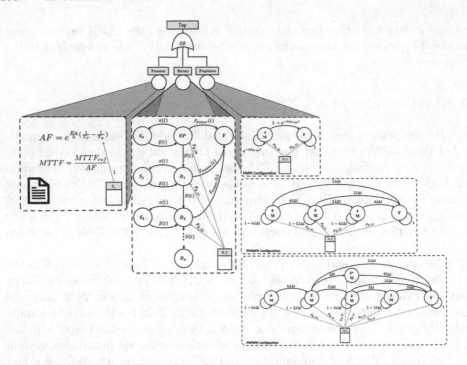

Fig. 1. Small FTA of a UAV considering complex basic events with failure symptoms and three different types of propulsion system reconfiguration

Figure 2 further illustrates the idea of merging real-time monitoring and diagnosis with FTA. In a traditional FTA, the tree consists of a top layer, a number of intermediate layers, and a basic events layer. However, in our proposed approach there is a new layer called the symptoms layer. In the symptoms layer, the safety expert(s) should identify the potentially observable events in the system and define the relation between symptoms and basic events. For instance, in Fig. 1, the symptoms are temperature, battery status, and motor status along with motor configuration. In Fig. 1, it is assumed the temperature symptom only affects the processor and has no effect on the others. In this proposed reliability modeling approach, it is recommended to use CBEs to link with the symptoms. A CBE can take many forms, e.g. a multi-state Markov chain where the symptom affects its current state, a Bayesian Network where a symptom can form a belief, or some other reliability function where a symptom can be a parameter on it, etc. The link between symptoms and basic events can be both deterministic and probabilities values.

As discussed in Sect. 2.4, the EDDI concept uses real-time evaluation of dependability attributes like reliability as function(s) to update the mission accordingly as part of a dependability-driven decision making system. This could lead to a variety of responses, such as reconfiguration during the mission (e.g. switching a hexacopter to quadcopter mode in the event of possible motor faults), changes to mission parameters (e.g. emergency landing or return to base sooner),

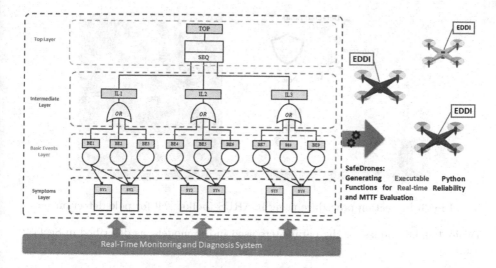

Fig. 2. Overall view on merging real-time monitoring and diagnosis system with Fault Tree Analysis

or even requests for predictive maintenance of affected parts. In SafeDrones, all the calculations are implemented in Python (available in the GitHub repository) for runtime execution. The results could also be used by technologies like ConSerts [25] to generate conditional guarantee outcomes and provide the final decision accordingly. Moreover, based on the idea provided by [14], it is possible to investigate the use of monitoring data to obtain safety model repair recommendations.

4 Experimental Implementation

To evaluate the reliability models presented in Sect. 3 we use the ICARUS toolkit [24], which uses vision-based UAV monitoring platforms to automate the inspection of medium voltage power distribution networks. As Fig. 3 shows, the UAV gathers data and provides a real-time data processing to identify poles and record their accurate positions. An off-the-shelf four-rotor UAV (DJI Matrice 300 RTK) equipped with different sensors, including temperature sensors, is used. On the top of the UAV, an NVIDIA Jetson Xavier NX embedded platform was mounted to run the deep learning and navigation algorithms, allowing the UAV to perform inspection procedures autonomously. Additionally, the UAV is equipped with the SafeDrones tool, which monitors parameters such as processor temperature, battery level and execution time to estimate UAV reliability. Furthermore, SafeDrones can recommend actions like mission abort and emergency landing if the estimated reliability falls below a predetermined threshold.

For our analysis we monitor processor temperature and battery level every 1 s to estimate the probability of failure for the UAV using the models described earlier. All the other input parameters are shown in Table 1. When the estimated

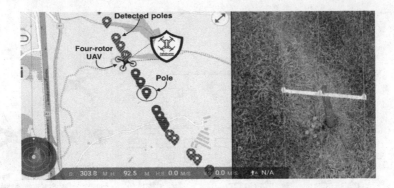

Fig. 3. Inspection procedure using ICARUS toolkit [24] for pole detection

Table 1. Input values for the parameters used in the models, as described in Sects. 2 and 3

Parameters	Description	Values
Motor parameters		
MC	Motor configuration	PNPN (P: positive clockwise direction, N: negative anti-clockwise direction)
Motor λ	Motor failure rate	0.001
Battery parameters		
Battery λ	Battery failure rate	0.0001
D	Battery degradation rate	0.0064
α	Battery usage rate	0.008
β	Battery inactivity rate	0.007
Processor parameters		
u	Utilization	1
$MTTF_{ref}$	Reference MTTF	1000 h
E_a	Boltzmann constant	8.617E−05
k	Activation energy	0.3 electron-volts
T_r	Reference temperature	29 °C

probability of failure exceeds a specific threshold (we use 0.9 as a threshold for this analysis), an emergency action is taken. In this case, the action is to perform a safe emergency landing and continue the mission with another UAV. Note that the threshold can vary, depending on the mission and the time needed to safely land the UAV. The total execution time for the fault-free inspection mission to detect all the poles is 750 s.

To demonstrate the proposed concept, we use two scenarios:

1. Fault-free scenario. In this scenario, all the components work properly without experiencing any faulty conditions.

2. Faulty scenario. In this scenario, the battery stops working properly at a specific time X causing a sharp drop in the battery level and at time Y, where $Y > X$, the processor starts overheating due to unexplained circumstances. For this analysis, X equals to 250 s and Y equals to 400 s.

5   Experimental Results

This section reports the reliability analysis results for the two scenarios described in Sect. 4.

5.1   Reliability Analysis of the Fault-Free Scenario

We first evaluate the probability of failure of the different components (battery and processor) and the total UAV for the fault-free scenario. It is assumed that the mission is about 800h. Figures 4(a) and (b) show the battery level and processor temperature respectively (collected from UAV's telemetry logs), while Figs. 4(c) and (d) show the failure probability and MTTF for each component as well as the overall UAV. As Fig. 4(c) shows, the lower the battery level, the higher probability of failure. The sharp increase here when the battery level goes below 75% is because our model discretizes the battery level into four states (25% each), resulting in a jump when each discrete state is reached. Additionally, Fig. 4(c) shows that the processor's probability of failure is also related to the UAV's cumulative processing time. The exact correlation between reliability and processor temperature is shown in Fig. 4 (i), which illustrates how the processor's MTTF changes according to the current temperature. As is clearly shown, when the processor's temperature increases, the MTTF also decreases. Finally, as can be observed in Fig. 4(c), the overall UAV failure probability does not exceed the 0.90 threshold for emergency action, indicating that the inspection mission was completed successfully. Note that the threshold value should be determined by a team of safety experts.

5.2   Reliability Analysis of the Faulty Scenario

In the first scenario, the overall probability of failure was satisfactory throughout and the UAV managed to complete the mission safely. However, it is also possible for faults to develop in any component, and so in the second scenario we investigate how the probability of failure can be changed by simulating a faulty battery and the processor overheating. Here the battery stops working properly at the 250th second. At this point the battery level drops sharply from 80% to 40% as Fig. 4(e) shows. The processor's temperature also suddenly increases at the 400th second. Figures 4(g) and (h) depict the impact of these simulated faults on the probability of failure and MTTF respectively. As Fig. 4(g) shows the failure probability threshold of the UAV is exceeded at the 500th second. This leads to an emergency landing of the UAV even if the mission was not completed. In a multi-UAV scenario, another UAV can be dynamically tasked to continue and complete the mission in this case.

The results highlight the benefits of both the proposed SafeDrones approach and the overall EDDI concept in helping to avoid dangerous accidents caused by failures. By combining safety analysis models and reliability functions executable at runtime, we can obtain a more comprehensive overview of UAV dependability during real-time operation, one that takes into account multiple subsystems and sensors as well as predefined thresholds and corresponding mitigating actions. Such an approach is particularly valuable for autonomous platforms where there is no human operator to monitor safety directly.

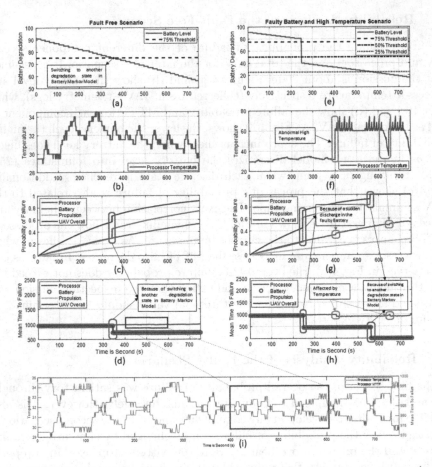

Fig. 4. Fault-Free Scenario: (a) Battery degradation (battery level in percentage), (b) Processor Temperature (c) Probability of failure (d) Mean Time to failure – Faulty Battery Scenario: (e) Battery degradation (battery level in percentage), (f) Processor Temperature (g) Probability of failure (h) Mean Time to failure – (i) Processor's MTTF and temperature for the Fault Free Scenario.

6   Conclusion and Future Work

To help address the problems of UAV reliability and risk assessment, particularly at runtime where operational and environmental factors are hard to predict, the SafeDrones reliability modeling approach has been proposed. It employs a combination of FTA with CBEs to support real-time reliability evaluation as a prototype of the EDDI concept. As part of this, it introduces a novel symptoms layer to integrate with runtime monitoring data. To illustrate SafeDrones, we applied it to a power network inspection use case to show how real-time reliability evaluation can be used to anticipate imminent failures and prevent accidents by recommending appropriate responses.

In this paper, we have focused on a single UAV. However, many UAV applications involve multiple UAVs. As part of our future work, we plan to extend SafeDrones to multiple UAVs to further explore the full EDDI concept and assess and preserve overall mission dependability in real-time. This demands modeling and dynamic evaluation of mission risk variability [22] and distributed dependability concept variability [25], which can be realized e.g. by allowing dynamic task redistribution to the remaining UAVs if one or more UAVs have increased probability of failure.

Furthermore, we plan to investigate other aspects of dependability by evaluating the reliability of machine learning components many UAVs have, e.g. for objec detection. For this, we intend to make use of SafeML [4,8]. By using SafeML, we can obtain a more complete picture of real-time UAV dependability which can then be used to update the mission accordingly and improve mission completion. In the paper, it was assumed that the monitoring system is perfect, however, it would be possible to incorporate false positive, false negative and uncertainties as future work [3].

Finally, it is important to investigate how security issues will affect UAV operation [30]. For this, we plan to consider a jamming attack scenario that will affect the communication with the GPS.

Code Availability

To improve the research reproducibility, code, functions, demo notebooks, and other materials supporting this paper are published online at GitHub:
https://github.com/koo-ec/SafeDrones.

Acknowledgement. This work was supported by the Secure and Safe Multi-Robot Systems (SESAME) H2020 Project under Grant Agreement 101017258, the European Union's Horizon 2020 grant agreement No 739551 (KIOS CoE) and from the Government of the Republic of Cyprus through the Cyprus Deputy Ministry of Research, Innovation and Digital Policy.

A   Appendix

A.1   Proposed Fault Tree of a Generic UAV

Figure 5 illustrates the proposed Fault Tree of a generic UAV consist of nine failure categories including: I) Communication system failure, II) navigation system failure, III) Computer system failure, IV) Environment detection systems, V) Propulsion system, VI) Energy system, VII) Obstacle avoidance system, VIII) Security system, and IX) Landing system.

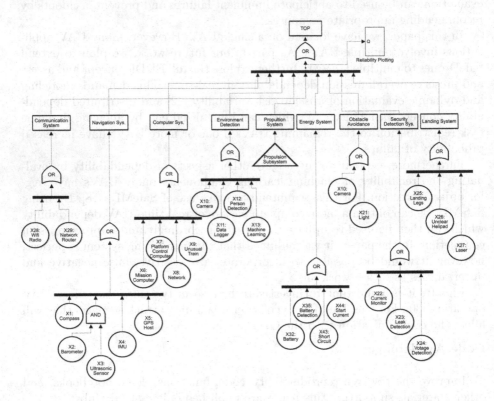

Fig. 5. Proposed fault tree of a generic UAV

References

1. Adler, R., Forster, M., Trapp, M.: Determining configuration probabilities of safety-critical adaptive systems. In: 21st International Conference on Advanced Information Networking and Applications Workshops (AINAW 2007), vol. 2, pp. 548–555. IEEE (2007)
2. Armengaud, E., et al.: DDI: a novel technology and innovation model for dependable, collaborative and autonomous systems. In: 2021 Design, Automation & Test in Europe Conference & Exhibition (DATE), pp. 1626–1631. IEEE (2021)

3. Aslansefat, K., Gogani, M.B., Kabir, S., Shoorehdeli, M.A., Yari, M.: Performance evaluation and design for variable threshold alarm systems through semi-Markov process. ISA Trans. **97**, 282–295 (2020)
4. Aslansefat, K., Kabir, S., Abdullatif, A., Vasudevan, V., Papadopoulos, Y.: Toward improving confidence in autonomous vehicle software: a study on traffic sign recognition systems. Computer **54**(8), 66–76 (2021)
5. Aslansefat, K., Kabir, S., Gheraibia, Y., Papadopoulos, Y.: Dynamic fault tree analysis: state-of-the-art in modeling, analysis, and tools. In: Reliability Management and Engineering: Challenges and Future Trends, chap. 4, pp. 73–111. CRC Press- Taylor & Francis (2020)
6. Aslansefat, K., Latif-Shabgahi, G.R.: A hierarchical approach for dynamic fault trees solution through semi-Markov process. IEEE Trans. Reliab. **69**(3), 986–1003 (2019)
7. Aslansefat, K., Marques, F., Mendonça, R., Barata, J.: A Markov process-based approach for reliability evaluation of the propulsion system in multi-rotor drones. In: Camarinha-Matos, L.M., Almeida, R., Oliveira, J. (eds.) DoCEIS 2019. IAICT, vol. 553, pp. 91–98. Springer, Cham (2019). https://doi.org/10.1007/978-3-030-17771-3_8
8. Aslansefat, K., Sorokos, I., Whiting, D., Tavakoli Kolagari, R., Papadopoulos, Y.: SafeML: safety monitoring of machine learning classifiers through statistical difference measures. In: Zeller, M., Höfig, K. (eds.) IMBSA 2020. LNCS, vol. 12297, pp. 197–211. Springer, Cham (2020). https://doi.org/10.1007/978-3-030-58920-2_13
9. Belcastro, C.M., Newman, R.L., Evans, J., Klyde, D.H., Barr, L.C., Ancel, E.: Hazards identification and analysis for unmanned aircraft system operations. In: 17th AIAA Aviation Technology, Integration, and Operations Conference, p. 3269 (2017)
10. Bouissou, M., Bon, J.L.: A new formalism that combines advantages of fault-trees and Markov models: Boolean logic driven Markov processes. Reliab. Eng. Syst. Saf. **82**(2), 149–163 (2003)
11. Cochran, J.: Wiley Encyclopedia of Operations Research and Management Science. Wiley, Hoboken (2010)
12. DEIS Consortium: Open dependability exchange metamodel. https://github.com/Digital-Dependability-Identities/ODE. Accessed 28 Apr 2022
13. Franco, B.J.D.O.M., Góes, L.C.S.: Failure analysis methods in unmanned aerial vehicle (UAV) applications. In: Proceedings of COBEM 2007 19th International Congress of Mechanical Engineering (2007)
14. Gheraibia, Y., Kabir, S., Aslansefat, K., Sorokos, I., Papadopoulos, Y.: Safety+ AI: a novel approach to update safety models using artificial intelligence. IEEE Access **7**, 135855–135869 (2019)
15. Guo, J., Elsayed, E.A.: Reliability of balanced multi-level unmanned aerial vehicles. Comput. Oper. Res. **106**, 1–13 (2019)
16. Kabir, S., Aslansefat, K., Sorokos, I., Papadopoulos, Y., Gheraibia, Y.: A conceptual framework to incorporate complex basic events in HiP-HOPS. In: Papadopoulos, Y., Aslansefat, K., Katsaros, P., Bozzano, M. (eds.) IMBSA 2019. LNCS, vol. 11842, pp. 109–124. Springer, Cham (2019). https://doi.org/10.1007/978-3-030-32872-6_8
17. Kabir, S., et al.: A runtime safety analysis concept for open adaptive systems. In: Papadopoulos, Y., Aslansefat, K., Katsaros, P., Bozzano, M. (eds.) IMBSA 2019. LNCS, vol. 11842, pp. 332–346. Springer, Cham (2019). https://doi.org/10.1007/978-3-030-32872-6_22

18. Kim, D.S., Ghosh, R., Trivedi, K.S.: A hierarchical model for reliability analysis of sensor networks. In: 2010 IEEE 16th Pacific Rim International Symposium on Dependable Computing, pp. 247–248 (2010)
19. Murtha, J.F.: Evidence theory and fault tree analysis to cost-effectively improve reliability in small UAV design. Virginia Polytechnic Institute and State University (2009)
20. Olson, I., Atkins, E.M.: Qualitative failure analysis for a small quadrotor unmanned aircraft system. In: AIAA Guidance, Navigation, and Control (GNC) Conference, p. 4761 (2013)
21. Ottavi, M., et al.: Dependable multicore architectures at nanoscale: The view from Europe. IEEE Design Test **32**(2), 17–28 (2014)
22. Reich, J., Trapp, M.: SINADRA: towards a framework for assurable situation-aware dynamic risk assessment of autonomous vehicles. In: 16th European Dependable Computing Conference, EDCC 2020, Munich, Germany, 7–10 September 2020, pp. 47–50. IEEE (2020). https://doi.org/10.1109/EDCC51268.2020.00017
23. Sadeghzadeh, I., Mehta, A., Zhang, Y.: Fault/damage tolerant control of a quadrotor helicopter UAV using model reference adaptive control and gain-scheduled PID. In: AIAA Guidance, Navigation, and Control Conference, p. 6716 (2011)
24. Savva, A., et al.: ICARUS: automatic autonomous power infrastructure inspection with UAVs. In: 2021 International Conference on Unmanned Aircraft Systems (ICUAS), pp. 918–926. IEEE (2021)
25. Schneider, D., Trapp, M.: Conditional safety certification of open adaptive systems. ACM Trans. Auton. Adapt. Syst. **8**(2), 1–20 (2013). https://doi.org/10.1145/2491465.2491467
26. Schneider, D., Trapp, M., Papadopoulos, Y., Armengaud, E., Zeller, M., Höfig, K.: WAP: digital dependability identities. In: 2015 IEEE 26th International Symposium on Software Reliability Engineering (ISSRE), pp. 324–329. IEEE (2015)
27. Sharvia, S., Kabir, S., Walker, M., Papadopoulos, Y.: Model-based dependability analysis: state-of-the-art, challenges, and future outlook. In: Software Quality Assurance, pp. 251–278. Elsevier (2016)
28. Soper, S., Day, M.: Amazon drone crashes hit Jeff Bezos' delivery dreams. https://www.bloomberg.com/news/features/2022-04-10/amazon-drone-crashes-delays-put-bezos-s-delivery-dream-at-risk. Accessed 10 Apr 2022
29. Trivedi, K.S., Bobbio, A.: Reliability and Availability Engineering: Modeling, Analysis, and Applications. Cambridge University Press, Cambridge (2017)
30. Valianti, P., Papaioannou, S., Kolios, P., Ellinas, G.: Multi-agent coordinated close-in jamming for disabling a rogue drone. IEEE Trans. Mob. Comput. (2021)
31. Vesely, W., Dugan, J., Fragola, J., Minarick, Railsback, J.: Fault tree handbook with aerospace applications. Technical report, NASA office of safety and mission assurance, Washington, DC (2002)

Author Index

Printed in the United States
by Baker & Taylor Publisher Services